Dog Heroes of September 11th

Dog Heroes of September 11th

A Tribute to America's Search and Rescue Dogs

Tenth-Anniversary Edition

By Nona Kilgore Bauer

Kennel Club Books®
A Division of BowTie, Inc.

Tenth-anniversary edition:

Lead Editor: Amy Deputato
Editor: Jennifer Calvert
Art Director: Cindy Kassebaum
Production Supervisor: Jessica Jaensch
Assistant Production Manager: Tracy Vogtman
Book Project Specialist: Karen Julian

Vice President, Chief Content Officer: June Kikuchi
Vice President, Kennel Club Books: Andrew DePrisco
BowTie Press: Jennifer Calvert, Amy Deputato, Karen Julian, Jarelle S. Stein

First edition:

Editor-in-Chief: Andrew DePrisco
Senior Editor: Amy Deputato
Associate Editor/Editor of Photography: Jonathan Nigro
Design: Bill Jonas
Layout: Sherise Buhagiar
Production: Joanne Muzyka
Index: Matthew Strubel

Kennel Club Books®
A Division of BowTie, Inc.
40 Broad Street
Freehold, NJ 07728 · USA
www.kennelclubbooks.com

Library of Congress Cataloging-in-Publication Data

Bauer, Nona Kilgore.
  Dog heroes of September 11th : a tribute to America's search and rescue dogs / by Nona Kilgore Bauer. – 10th anniversary ed.
       p. cm.
  Includes index.
  ISBN 978-1-59378-998-5
 1. Search dogs–United States. 2. Rescue dogs–United States. 3. September 11 Terrorist Attacks, 2001. I. Title.
  SF428.73B38 2011
  636.7'0886–dc22
                                   2010053772

Printed and bound in China
17 16 15 14 13 12 11   3 4 5 6 7 8 9 10

Dedication

To all of the heroic canines who served their country following the September 11, 2001, terrorist attacks and who continue to serve whenever and wherever they are needed.

Contents

Foreword
to the Tenth-Anniversary Edition

As with every other American who lived through September 11, 2001, those attacks changed my life. After the pervasive sadness and the smoke faded, we New Yorkers knew that we would one day be stronger for having survived those most heinous acts of terrorism. I am so proud of every rescuer who gave so bravely and selflessly in the hours and days and weeks after the attacks. Ground Zero justifiably became known as "Ground Hero." Many Americans forget that hundreds of those heroes were of the four-pawed variety. This beautiful book rightly pays tribute to the search and rescue dogs that worked tirelessly at the World Trade Center and Pentagon sites, as well as the cadaver dogs that searched for remains at the Fresh Kills landfill in Staten Island and the Shanksville, Pennsylvania, crash site. No American could be unmoved by the stories and images of these dogs and their handlers, who through their valiant efforts did their part to restore our great nation and to bring closure to thousands of grieving families. Their journeys, as told in these pages, reinforce our resolve to persevere, rebuild and keep our nation safe and strong. We are ever grateful to the dedicated volunteers and their superbly trained dogs who continue to serve America in our most desperate times of need. I am pleased to see that this new edition of *Dog Heroes of September 11th* continues to salute the work of these dogs and their handlers as we mark the tenth anniversary of the attacks. We will never forget what occurred on that darkest day in American history, as we all humbly and dutifully respond to the call to keep alive the memories of the victims and heroes of 9/11.

Rudolph Giuliani

Foreword
to the First Edition

by Wilma Melville
Founder and Executive Director, National Disaster Search Dog Foundation

What makes a good search dog? Is it self-confidence? Agility? Good training?

Disaster search requires very specific skills from both dog and handler in maneuvering about a rubble pile. At the World Trade Center, for example, the pile was a mountain of debris as high as seven or eight storeys made of twisted steel, wobbly uneven surfaces that kept shifting and hot spots (gaps in the rubble where fires were still burning). This was an environment full of "land mines," so to speak.

Disaster search dogs train on rubble every week. Their training emphasizes agility, and the pads of their feet are toughened for the task ahead. The dogs need to be able to respond to verbal and nonverbal direction-control signals and be able to traverse the rubble quite a distance away from their handlers.

A disaster site is a treacherous environment: noisy, chaotic, dust-filled and dark. But that is what disaster search means—having the skills and ability to perform at a high level in the worst settings imaginable. Dogs don't have these skills naturally—we train them to perform these unique tasks.

Dogs certified by the Federal Emergency Management Agency (FEMA) learn through training and much practice. This leads to self-assurance so that, by using the natural padding of their feet, the dogs can confidently cross rubble rather than scramble, dig in or cause additional shifting movement in the rubble.

FEMA certification is the hallmark of a canine whose training is specific for disaster response. The completely unnatural environment of a disaster site requires canine skills particular to that setting. FEMA certification is a national standard which, when met, means that the canine/handler search team is capable of going anywhere in the nation and performing at the highest level.

The Urban Search and Rescue (USAR) Program was developed by FEMA in 1989, and it was designed to provide assistance to local agencies

in the event of a catastrophic disaster. Twenty-eight urban search and rescue task forces are located across the country. These groups include highly trained firefighters. When a task force goes out the door, four canine search teams go as part of this well-trained group.

There are two levels of FEMA certification for search and rescue canine/handler teams. According to FEMA standards, basic certifications require that the search animal perform to specific standards under the direct supervision and guidance of the handler. The FEMA Type II (basic) level requires an elements test in five different skills: bark alert, direction control, obedience, obstacle course and a search and find on two victims.

According to FEMA standards, advanced certification requires the search animal to perform to those standards outside the direct supervision and guidance of the handler and to successfully search more difficult rescue-simulation courses. The FEMA Type I (advanced) test requires three large search areas with a total of six victims, with each area designed to test a variety of skills of both handler and canine. This is a team and must function as one. In order to keep standards high and teams alert, canine/handler teams must be recertified at least every two years in order to participate in search and rescue operations.

Twenty-one USAR task force (TF) teams worked on the World Trade Center site, and five teams responded to the Pentagon. These teams worked from September 11 through October 7, 2001. At the World Trade Center, the following teams were present: New Jersey TF1; California TF1, TF3, TF4, TF6, TF7 and TF8; Florida TF1 and TF2; Massachusetts TF1; Utah TF1; Colorado TF1; Arizona TF1; Washington TF1; Indiana TF1; Ohio TF1; Pennsylvania TF1; Texas TF1; Missouri TF1; Nebraska TF1 and Nevada TF1. For the Pentagon, the following teams were present: Maryland TF1; New Mexico TF1; Tennessee TF1; and Virginia TF1 and TF2.

This book captures the dedication and unique character of these brave canines, who along with their human handlers were called to serve this country in a time of unparalleled tragedy in American history. They did so without hesitation and performed courageously. It is important to note that not one canine was seriously injured or died during the September 11 deployment.

I am honored to know many of the dogs and handlers in this book personally—I am proud to call them friends and am glad to see their work recognized within these pages.

Preface
to the Tenth-Anniversary Edition

In recognition of the tenth anniversary of the September 11, 2001, terrorist attacks on the World Trade Center in New York City and the Pentagon in Washington, DC, Kennel Club Books again salutes and remembers the contribution of the canines who served during the months following that tragedy. For most of America, the passage of time has done little to erase the tragic memories of those horrific days, weeks and months. Ten years later, many handlers from the search and rescue teams and the canine therapy teams are still reluctant to revisit their memories of 9/11. They speak with lingering sadness, yet proudly, about their experiences, remembering the victims' families, the devastated rescue workers and the extraordinary canines who helped to bring closure to the families and friends who lost their loved ones. Although many of those canines have passed on, and others have retired from active duty, their service will not—cannot—be forgotten. For those who found closure because of them, and for their human search partners, the dogs will live forever in their hearts.

Yet the dedication and resolve of the SAR handlers—most of them still working, and now with new four-legged search partners—never wavers. While the face of tragedy may have changed during the ensuing years, the handlers and their dogs have continued to search for victims in the United States and on foreign soil whenever catastrophe threatens human life.

To that end, the National Disaster Search Dog Foundation (SDF) continues to train and expand FEMA-certified disaster search and rescue canine teams ready to deploy at a moment's notice. The SDF's role in that effort is immensely valuable and cannot be underestimated. Additionally, our many state and regional search and rescue groups and individuals also continue to maintain readiness to serve during earthquakes, floods, hurricanes and other disasters.

The terrorist attacks of 9/11 also altered the role of America's military in foreign lands. With the expansion of our military presence in Iraq and Afghanistan, new types of canine specialists now serve to protect our military forces there and in other Middle Eastern countries. Trained to alert and defend, to sniff out and indicate drugs, bombs and other explosives, they have become invaluable tools in America's arsenal of weaponry. With their superior senses of smell and hearing and their endurance, speed, courage and intelligence, military working dogs (MWDs) have saved countless lives, and their record of success in protecting our troops and finding hidden explosives has earned them a special place in the hearts of the servicepeople with whom they partner.

Thus, in addition to memorializing the contributions of the disaster search and rescue, cadaver and therapy canines of 9/11, this book also recognizes and honors the thousands of

MWDs that have served and that continue to protect our military forces and thus the American people. We are honored to profile in these pages the Labrador Retrievers that are trained at K2 Solutions in North Carolina to detect the improvised explosive devices (IEDs) that daily threaten the lives of the US Marines serving in Afghanistan. It was a privilege to work with the K2 staff, and I am deeply humbled by their trust in allowing me to share the experiences of some of the dedicated trainers who work with these amazing dogs.

In compiling this anniversary edition, I again rode a roller coaster of emotions as I wrote about the remarkable canines that search, sniff, seek, dig, comfort and do whatever is asked of them for nothing more than a biscuit or a water bottle. It is my privilege to present their stories so that America can know how blessed this country is to have these noble, humble best friends.

Preface
to the First Edition

Two thousand seven hundred and forty people perished in the attacks on the World Trade Center, including passengers from Flights 11 and 175, public-safety workers and the hijackers. Another 189 people were killed at the Pentagon, and the Pennsylvania crash claimed 44 lives.

As the above events unfolded, New York City officials and state and federal agencies initiated the largest call-up of emergency services in the history of the United States. Within hours of the attacks, FEMA task forces and state and local emergency teams from all corners of the nation deployed to the East Coast to assist in the rescue and recovery effort at the crash sites. Approximately 11,000 firefighters and emergency medical personnel responded; twenty-six of the twenty-eight FEMA task forces were deployed, ninety-six teams in all.

In this book you will meet many of the specialized canine search and rescue (SAR) teams who responded to that call. Of the estimated 250 to 300 K-9 teams who worked after 9/11, I was successful in contacting 65 search and rescue teams who were deployed to the World Trade Center and the Pentagon. You will also hear from twelve cadaver-dog handlers who worked at the Fresh Kills landfill on Staten Island, the site where the debris from the WTC was hauled, sorted and searched for human remains. They shared with me their extraordinary experiences during this, their most important mission. Some spoke at great length, with eloquence and candor, the recounting almost a catharsis. Other handlers offered brief descriptions of their experience, understandably demurring at the prospect of revisiting the emotions from that tragic time. It was apparent that the partnership between these handlers and their canines is deep and visceral. And never was it more profound than during their tour of duty after 9/11.

Without exception, the 9/11 handlers praised their dogs' ability to rise above the death and devastation and work like true professionals, well beyond their expectations. Describing their canines as eager, excited and happy to go to work or "play the game" should not be interpreted to diminish the gravity of 9/11. Dogs do not perceive such devastation as a tragedy; they are incapable of such distinctions. The disaster sites were simply more places to do their job and get their reward.

The 9/11 canines are profiled alphabetically and according to the disaster site to which they were deployed. The dogs are identified by breed and certification or search specialty, e.g., FEMA-certified Type I (advanced) or Type II (basic), cadaver search, wilderness live find or other search discipline. The canine graduates from the National Disaster Search Dog Foundation are noted as SDF. The handlers are identified by their task force or search group.

To help you better understand the SAR dog's unique physical and mental skills, their training and certification process and the organizations that support them, I also have included information on the Federal Emergency Management Agency (FEMA), the National Disaster Search Dog Foundation (SDF), the Suffolk County SPCA of Long Island and the Veterinary Medical Assistance Team (VMAT).

I have tried to stay as true as possible to the stories the handlers shared with me. One of the words I heard most often from the canine handlers

TIMELINE FOR SEPTEMBER 11, 2001

8:46 A.M. EDT
Hijacked American Airlines Flight 11 crashes into the World Trade Center's North Tower, New York City.

9:03 A.M. EDT
A second hijacked airliner, United Airlines Flight 175, hits the South Tower at the World Trade Center.

9:38 A.M. EDT
Hijacked American Airlines Flight 77 strikes the Pentagon in Washington, DC.

9:58 A.M. EDT
The South Tower collapses.

10:03 A.M. EDT
Hijacked United Airlines Flight 93 crashes in a field in Shanksville, Pennsylvania.

10:28 A.M. EDT
The North Tower collapses.

Photo: Andrea Booher/FEMA News

In a photo taken on September 14, 2001, President Bush spends some time with the USAR teams at the World Trade Center site.

was *closure*, a word sometimes overdone, but in this case surely most appropriate. Following a tragedy of the magnitude of September 11, the victims' families were desperately in need of closure, and these remarkable dogs helped make that possible.

Another phrase used often by the handlers referred to the unexpected "dual role" played by the canines during their deployment. The dogs seemed to sense that this was a time of special needs and offered wagging tails and furry hugs—no questions asked. They became instant therapists, comforting rescue workers and relatives of victims who were suffering so tremendously

from the loss of family and friends. Those few moments spent with the dogs renewed the workers' spirits and strengthened their resolve. In retrospect, one probably should not be surprised by such behavior. Stories of dogs' devotion have been recounted for centuries in literature and artwork, but never was it more necessary or apparent than after 9/11.

It is my sincere hope that the world will recognize and honor these extraordinary canines, not only for their contributions during the 9/11 crisis but also for every search and rescue mission where human life depends upon their courage, skill and dedication...and their love.

Acknowledgments

I cannot begin to express my gratitude to the many people who contributed to this anniversary edition of *Dog Heroes of September 11th*. I was once again privileged to work with amazing "dog people" who dedicate their lives to helping their communities and their country. Also, as with the first edition, it was impossible to reach every handler or every person involved in the training and handling of the canines that search, console and protect. I salute them and commend their efforts equally along with those featured in the book.

My deepest appreciation goes to the 9/11 handlers who shared memorials of their search partners; I am reminded once again how bravely you served after the terrorist attacks. To SDF founder Wilma Melville and the SDF staff for their tireless efforts to train and expand the certified search and rescue teams that stand at the ready when disaster strikes here and on foreign soil—you are the gift that keeps on giving. To Janet Reineck, my go-to person at SDF—you handled my many questions and requests with such grace and patience. To K2 Solutions founder Lane Kjellsen and K2 canine director Rodger Moore—thank you for your patience and your trust, but more importantly, for your patriotism and dedication to our military. To K2 photographer and videographer Mark Williams—your amazing photos are worth far more than the proverbial thousand words. To K2 trainers Bob George, Bruce Koonce, Erin Kendrigan, Glen Curtis, Gary Cook and Amy Hunt— what an awesome crew you are! Our country and

Border Collie Cowboy keeps an eye on the "flock" of rescue workers and K-9s at Ground Zero.

our Marines are safer thanks to your expertise and your love for the working Labrador. Thanks to Sue George, my very patient navigator at the K2 camp; to Susan Greenbaum, therapy dog co-ordinator, for reaching out to the 9/11 canine therapy teams; to the therapy dog handlers who agreed to share their stories; to the folks at Horse Creek Wildlife Sanctuary for their charity and compassion for our four-legged animal friends; to Karen LeFrak, Rick Friedberg and Rudolph Giuliani; to BowTie senior editor Amy Deputato for her patience, skill and tenacity in handling my vision for this edition of *Dog Heroes*; and finally to my editor and dear friend Andrew DePrisco for providing yet another writing "mission" to keep the 9/11 flame alive.

I am incredibly blessed to know and have worked with all of you. In the words of our canine Marine Corps, I salute you—Semper Fi-do!

ACKNOWLEDGMENTS FOR THE FIRST EDITION:

Where do I start? So many friends and professionals helped this book become a reality. What a privilege it was to be a part of this tribute to the brave dogs and handlers who, according to them, "just did their jobs." To these canine teams and to all those who are not included in these pages, a thousand thank yous—and even that is not enough.

My love and thanks to my family and step-family—my husband, children and grandchildren—who were sorely neglected during this project; to Andrew DePrisco, my editor, good friend and personal cheering section, who always keeps me motivated and smiling—I could never have done this without you; to associate editor Jonathan Nigro for jumping in and hanging on—I was your "baptism by fire"; and to John Goossen, former newspaper publisher and my best dog-buddy, for your keen eye and objectivity. Bless you all for putting up with me!

Thank you also to National Disaster Search Dog Foundation founder Wilma Melville, for your foresight and dedication to the world of search and rescue—your gift to the USAR world is beyond measure; to FEMA canine specialist Lynne Engelbert, California Task Force 3 (CA-TF3), who was my "point person" with the FEMA handlers— I had so many questions, and you were always there with a smile, right down to the last comma and period; to FEMA canine specialist Ann Wichmann, Colorado Task Force 1 (CO-TF1), who also provided contact information, moral support and sage advice—your guidance was invaluable (I'm glad your wonderful Jenner got to run and swim on our Missouri farm); to Bruce Berry, New Mexico Task Force 1 (NM-TF1), search team manager, for guiding me through the Pentagon maze; to Heather Roche, Bay Area Recovery Canines—you are as amazing as your dogs; to Debra Tosch, SDF program coordinator, for your "search" guidance with the Foundation handlers—you have the patience of a saint; to Bob Sessions, Pennsylvania Task Force 1 (PA-TF1), formerly of Maryland Task Force 1 (MD-TF1), for generously granting permission to include his article on air-scenting canines; to Rue Chagall, who understood firsthand my obsession with this book; to Bruce Barton, Northeast Search and Rescue (NESAR) director and search coordinator; to John Charos, DVM; to Officer Roy Gross, Suffolk County Society for the Prevention of Cruelty to Animals (SCSPCA); to Cindy Otto, DVM, PhD; to Sonny Whynman, New Jersey Task Force 1 (NJ-TF1); to Jodi Witte, Veterinary Medical Assistance Team (VMAT) technician; to Alexis C. Morris, study director, University of Pennsylvania; and to Daphna Straus, project manager, DOGNY, American Kennel Club. You are one terrific bunch!

Finally, and once again, to "my" handlers— you have added another dimension to my life. You folks are the absolute best!

Introduction

When first approached with the prospect of writing a book on the search and rescue dogs who worked at the World Trade Center after the terrorist attacks, I said, "Absolutely not!" September 11 was so tragic and horrific, and I was afraid of the emotions I would experience during the writing process. But after a little research and a lot of soul searching, I realized these were stories that had to be told. These extraordinary dogs (and their equally amazing handlers) deserve to be recognized and honored for their service to America during those tormented days. Without their contribution, hundreds of victims' families would not have found the peace that comes with the return of a family member or beloved friend. The skill of these dogs, their courage and their perseverance brought much-needed closure to those families and friends who lost loved ones on that tragic day. That contribution is priceless.

It was indeed a privilege to work with the K-9 teams who served our country. I was moved beyond words upon hearing about their experiences and the feelings that those memories rekindled in the handlers. And I am honored by their trust that I would handle their stories with integrity and respect. The phrase I most often heard was "thank you." These dedicated volunteers were so grateful that their dogs were being recognized.

I say they have it backwards. We are the grateful ones, and we stand in awe of their contributions to our country and, more specifically, to the victims of the terrorist attacks.

With almost one voice, most of the K-9 handlers said they do not consider their canine partners heroes: their dogs are just doing a job they love, and they do it for the love of the people at the end of their leashes. It is America on the end of the leash now, and it is America that has crowned these canines as our heroes.

We also salute the families of the canine teams, the spouses who are "dog widows/widowers," married to K-9 handlers who are gone many days and weekends to maintain their dogs' specialized skills, and the children who grow up learning about rubble piles instead of sand castles. Their sacrifice of precious family time also contributes to the K-9 resources that serve America.

It has been estimated that about 250 to 300 canine teams contributed to the search effort during and after the 9/11 disaster. From the moment of the first attack, search and rescue volunteers from state and local agencies stepped in with their canines for search assistance while the New York Police Department formulated a disaster search plan, using dogs from their own K-9 units and recruiting FEMA USAR task forces nationwide.

It is true that during a time of tragedy and chaos, good intentions sometimes overwhelm common sense. Urban disaster search is a highly specialized and demanding discipline, and some of those early volunteer handlers and their canines were ill prepared to work under such extremely dangerous conditions. Inevitably, there were some mishaps and unfortunate incidents that involved untrained dogs who posed a risk to themselves and those around them. However, those incidents are not representative of the skilled disaster search K-9 and the job he is trained to do. As testament to the USAR dog's superior training and ability, not a single FEMA-certified dog was seriously injured during his or her tour of duty. (The only documented K-9 fatality was the Labrador Retriever Sirius, a Port Authority of New York and New Jersey bomb-detection dog who was in his basement kennel in the South Tower when it collapsed.)

Not all of the dogs deployed to search for victims and survivors during the 9/11 crises were disaster search specialists and live-find dogs. Dozens of cadaver-search dogs successfully located victims' remains, enabling families and friends to bring their loved ones home.

The author is honored to be the mouthpiece of the handlers who shared their 9/11 stories with me. I hope that my rendering of their thoughts and words captures some of the significance and emotion each story deserves.

It was, of course, impossible to identify and locate all of the canines who served so honorably during 9/11 and its aftermath. Some handlers who were contacted did not respond, and a few declined the interview for personal reasons. It was therefore with deep regret that I faced my book deadline knowing that there were many 9/11 search and rescue dogs and their handlers

FEMA director Joe M. Albaugh thanks FDNY members for their ongoing efforts in the rescue mission following the 9/11 attacks.

who would not be recognized in this book. We hope that the canine teams profiled on these pages will speak for all of those who served.

Portraits in Courage

T en years after the devastating terrorist attacks of September 11th, the mission of this book remains the same—to honor the canine heroes who served America during this tragic time and to recognize those who continue to serve whenever and wherever they are needed. There is no machine, no computer, no manmade creation as valuable to humankind as the canine—to search, to protect, to comfort and to heal the heart. It is our hope that this recounting of their courage and dedication during the 9/11 recovery mission and their continued service will serve as a reminder to all Americans. We cannot…must not… *will not* forget.

The World Trade Center

When two hijacked airliners crashed into the World Trade Center on the morning of September 11, 2001, America watched in disbelief as the Twin Towers collapsed into a pile of smoking ruins. Feelings of overwhelming grief and helplessness gripped the nation, indeed the entire world, as the tragedy unfolded in ever-greater horror.

As Americans wondered how and why, New York City's Office of Emergency Management acted swiftly, requesting assistance from FEMA and state disaster search and rescue teams. Most of the men and women of the Fire Department of New York's own FEMA task force had perished when the towers collapsed, depleting their most valuable local resource. From all corners of the country, highly trained USAR task forces collected their gear and waited for the notice to deploy. Most had trained for years to respond to urban disaster scenes, but September 11 was beyond anything they had ever imagined.

At the WTC worksite, known as "the pile" at Ground Zero, the search teams faced a mountain of smoldering debris seven storeys high…jagged metal, twisted steel beams, broken glass and concrete, and knee-high layers of thick dust, spread over 14 acres of Lower Manhattan. Smoke filled the air, turning daylight into dusk. Small fires glowed in hot spots across the soot-covered landscape.

Giant cranes, bulldozers, generators and other heavy construction equipment created

a deafening din. Overhead, huge floodlights illuminated the ruins. Hundreds of rescue workers dotted the rubble area, combing through the wreckage. It was a sight no one could ever have imagined, and certainly one no dog handler had ever anticipated.

New Jersey Task Force 1 arrived at the disaster site within hours of the call. Bused into the city that same afternoon, they set up their base of operation at the Jacob Javits Convention Center in Midtown Manhattan. They would be joined there by eighty FEMA Canine Search Specialist teams, who would rotate through the WTC during the next three-and-a-half weeks. The NYPD K-9 Unit also sent in patrol dogs that were cross-trained for live find and cadaver search.

As the rescuers grasped the enormity of the task ahead, the USAR K-9s thought otherwise. Trained for years on ladders, tunnels, cliffs and unstable jungles of metal, wood and concrete rubble, they looked at the pile at Ground Zero and their inner switches turned "on." It was time to go to work.

Most of the K-9 teams rotated on twelve-hour work shifts, assigned to designated areas around the site or on the pile. The dogs worked without leashes or collars as they scaled huge mountains of debris, clambered across the twisted steel beams and crawled into voids and dark spaces, searching for survivors. They also worked "barefoot" without booties because they are trained to use their feet and toes for traction.

Safety workers and FDNY firefighters accompanied each working team to rescue any survivors found by the dogs. If a dog showed interest in an area, a second dog was called in to confirm the find. Firefighters and police officers constantly called the dogs: "Search over here!" or "K-9, check here," hoping desperately to find their fallen brothers still alive.

After each work shift, the dogs were taken to one of the veterinary-care tents at the worksite or the Javits Center to be thoroughly examined, "deconned" (decontaminated) with a bath and have their eyes and ears flushed. Only after the dogs were cleaned, fed and ready to rest did the handlers look after their own needs. Their dogs always came first.

Once it became apparent that there were no survivors to be found, the search effort shifted from one of rescue to one of recovery. After the last USAR team was dismissed in early October, several NYPD K-9 teams continued the search for the next five months. Only after their dogs no longer found any human remains did the NYPD reassign their search teams and conclude their mission at Ground Zero.

Ground Zero photos courtesy of NE-TF1.

At work at Ground Zero are (CLOCKWISE FROM TOP LEFT) Kaiser, Polly, Argus, Thea and Kita.

President George W. Bush addresses search and rescue workers in NYC; included are Golden Retriever Bretagne and her handler Denise Corliss of TX-TF1.

Abby searches while the FDNY firefighters watch...and wait...and hope. Abby's indications brought four families closure and peace.

ABBY

Labrador Retriever

FEMA Type I, SDF

DEBRA TOSCH

California Task Force 8

As program director for the National Disaster Search Dog Foundation, Debra was attending a FEMA Canine Search Specialist (CSS) class for advanced USAR canines when the World Trade Center was attacked. Unable to deploy with the first wave of FEMA teams, she left ten days later as a part of CA-TF8 from San Diego. She and Abby spent the next ten days at Ground Zero.

"It was truly overwhelming," Debra said. "We had never trained on anything like that, and I wondered if Abby could negotiate out there. Her response, however, was the opposite: 'Oh good, I get to search a new playground!' Dogs view it so differently than we do because we make it a game for them.

"When Abby searches, her nose goes down and right back up, she doesn't stop. A few times she did stop to smell, but it was brief and very subtle. I could easily have missed it if I had not been watching my dog. There were always people around, mostly FDNY firefighters, to check out where the dogs might indicate. We did learn that she had indicated remains in four different places, so we were able to bring closure to those families. But our dogs are not trained for cadaver work. We have to put the (live) victims first.

"When Abby is searching, she completely ignores everyone. She is totally focused and has a one-track mind. But after her shift, back at our base of operation, she was a typical Lab and spent her down time doing therapy work for people who were in a lot of pain. Everyone wanted to pet her, and she loved it.

"For most of the thirteen SDF teams that were deployed to the WTC, this was their first real mission, and we were all so proud and impressed with the way our dogs worked. Our dogs were at their peak performance, almost like they sensed that this was not a normal training session. They were crisp following our commands, and many handlers said their dogs never looked better. The dogs were able to transfer the type of training we do into a situation we have never trained on, and that tells us we are doing something right.

"This was a very hazardous environment, but we knew our dogs would be safe. Before we send them into a void, we have the air down there monitored. We have a structural engineer to make sure that the void or space will not collapse. We never put our dogs in situations where they would be at risk.

"On our last day there, back at the military base waiting for the bus to take us to the airport, there was a big open field. Our dogs had been working so hard, and the five of us decided to just let our dogs be dogs and run around. Suddenly the entire task force was watching. They were laughing so hard at these dogs racing around, doing their body slams on each other, with the Border Collie trying to herd them all. It was very comical and such a good stress reliever for our task force. It was an amazing way to end a very sad deployment."

ANA

Golden Retriever

FEMA Type I, SDF

RICK LEE

California Task Force 7

Seven hours after the airliners crashed into the Twin Towers, Rick and Ana were on their way to New York with California Task Force 7. With teammates Randy Gross and Rob Cima and their SDF Golden Retrievers Dusty and Harley, they were among the first USAR teams to report to Ground Zero the following day. Rick recalled the eerie vision as they first approached the worksite.

"As we moved closer to Ground Zero, the color of life faded slowly to black and white. Thick dust covered everything in sight. We rounded the corner to our staging area and there it was: smoke billowing from a collapsed building on the edge of the World Trade Center. Several storeys high, the exterior wall lay at about a 30-degree angle. It was all twisted steel that was so compressed I could not imagine how anyone could still be alive. But there are always voids and spaces, so we had hope.

"Most of the FDNY at the site had been lost during the attack, and there was understandably some chaos. Our dogs were like the point men in Viet Nam, out there making decisions whether or not someone was alive in there. These dogs have to be perfect; there is no room for error when they are making those decisions. I realized that we had to shut out our surroundings and stay focused, and treat each search mission like it was a training session back at Sacramento.

"Ana and I worked backup for Randy and Dusty, and we had assignments all the time. Whenever the K-9s were searching, it became very quiet. I would look, and all of the rescuers would be watching us work our dogs. It was like someone had turned off the sound. After our K-9s had covered their search area, we would have to tell the FDNY that we were sorry, but there were no alerts. An hour later, that same street that had been teeming with workers became just another dark corner with no lights, rescuers or equipment. It was as if God had spoken. Until that moment, we never realized that we had so much responsibility.

"In the beginning, Ana would just have to stand or lie on the ground, and I looked for something she could lie on and grabbed this sheet of black plastic. But she refused to lie on it. Then I realized it was a body bag and quickly put it back.

"As we walked around Ground Zero between search missions, the destruction seemed endless. The FDNY firefighters who we passed all had the same look of despair on their faces. Sometimes they would stop briefly to pet Ana or Dusty. One day, while I was waiting for our team to assemble, an FDNY firefighter came up and just started petting Ana. He loved animals and told me about his hobbies and his animals. It was good for both of us to talk about other things even though we were about 100 feet from total destruction. It reminded me that she was here not only to search but also to provide some avenue of relief.

"Ana is an awesome search dog. She flew across that rubble pile like it was grass. I watched her gracefully manipulate the twisted terrain as if it were another day in the park. It was hard to keep her from tripping the firefighters as she moved so freely and naturally over the twisted steel. She made her way through debris so thick and holes and voids so deep that she had to find her own way out. At times it seemed like she was gone for several minutes. Then suddenly she would pop out as if to say, 'Well, what do you want?'

"She was so full of energy all the time. Her personality is comparable to the Tasmanian Devil's. I am a type A person, but Ana is a triple A. I would be tired and exhausted, and she was bouncing off the walls with energy.

"The firefighters were amazed at the K-9s' skill level. They had no idea that our dogs could do these things. At one point, one of the firefighters warned me that we were about to cross an area that had a hot surface with smoke billowing from it. I picked Ana up and started moving on past the area he pointed out. He asked me incredulously, 'The dog will just let you do that?'

"We placed our K-9s in an unimaginable environment that tested their agility and skill level beyond their training, and they excelled above and beyond. They had no fear when we commanded them to scale the twisted beams and hazards. They were driven by a pure desire to please. These dogs had more than proven their place as a valuable tool in the search efforts at Ground Zero. I am very proud of Ana's performance at Ground Zero. She is a top gun in my book."

"What motivates me the most is that Ana is such an awesome dog."

*"Our K-9s actually outskilled us moving across the pile;
I could not keep up with Ana....The hardest thing I did in
New York was telling the firefighters on a daily basis
that our K-9s were unable to locate anyone alive."*

Ana checks an underground area with Rick, but sadly she does not alert.

After Rick and Ana returned home to their family, the two of them drove up to Rick's favorite mountain getaway to renew their spirits. "I just had to see that the beauty of nature was still alive," Rick said. "That the world still had color and the sounds of peace. Without a soul around, the wind blowing through the trees and the sound of the river, I released Ana to run and be free of commands. She ran right to the river and found herself a rock for entertainment. The five years I spent training her are unquestionably worth more than gold. I have no doubt that if there had been survivors to be found, she would have located them. I am proud and honored that she and I and our task force were part of the rescue efforts. It has changed the way I look at life, as it should for everyone. God bless America."

Portraits in Courage   **33**

ANNA

German Shepherd Dog

Live Find

SARAH ATLAS

New Jersey Task Force 1

Sarah and Anna arrived at the World Trade Center with NJ-TF1 on the afternoon of the attack.

"Anna's emotional state that first day at Ground Zero was hectic; we were desperate to find a survivor," Sarah recalled. "She later calmed down and worked in a less frenetic way. After our shift was over, we would march past the hundreds of eyes, all wondering if we had found one of their brothers.

"After the first day, Anna became quiet and her attitude went down because she was finding only human remains. I believe because I was tired and drained, she picked up on my emotions. Anna was also a certified therapy dog, and getting hugs and pats from the firefighters, police officers and other rescue workers helped keep her spirits up."

Anna was trained as a live-find dog, but she also had some training in cadaver work. "On our last shift, she had two confirmed finds in a stairwell that were later identified as the bodies of FDNY firefighters," Sarah said.

"I believe all the dogs that worked at the World Trade Center were true American heroes," Sarah reflected, "and that includes the many therapy dogs that were available. My dog's search work made me realize how proud I was to live in this great and free country. These dogs worked tirelessly, never quitting. They were our companions, our working partners and our strength."

Anna was pictured in a memorial quilt made in honor of NJ-TF1. The quilt became a part of a traveling show displayed in New York City and Japan.

BEAR

Labrador Retriever

FEMA Type I, Certified Cadaver Search

JOHN GILKEY

Pennsylvania Task Force 1

From the moment that John witnessed on television the second plane slam into the World Trade Center, he knew it was going to be a rough couple of weeks. He had no idea it would be the experience of a lifetime. "The third plane crashing into the Pentagon sealed my fate," John recalled, "and I left work to get Bear. On my way home I received the official page from my task force."

"During the bus ride to NYC, a task-force leader informed us that we would be one of the first task forces to arrive at the WTC and to prepare for the worst," John said. "A sense of calmness came over me as I tried to prepare mentally for the job Bear and I were about to do. I'm sure Bear had a lot to do with that…he just lay on the seat next to me and put his head in my lap. During the next eight days, he was my only link to the way things used to be.

"The rubble pile at 'Zero' reminded me of the moon; dust several inches thick covered everything. Walking between our first and second search problem, I tripped on a ladder. A few more steps, and I realized I was standing on top of an entire fire truck; what I thought might be ground level was actually 10 to 15 feet of rubble.

There were so many hazards everywhere, things that could hurt Bear. Yet I couldn't believe how easily he moved over that pile. He got only two minor scratches and worked the entire time with no shoes on his feet. I couldn't have lasted five minutes out there in bare feet."

Because Bear is cross-trained for live alerts and cadaver indication, he worked well regardless of what he found. "He didn't care, as long as he was receiving praise for making the cadaver indication," John said. "I believe we indicated at forty or so different sites where cadaver material was found. If nothing else, we brought closure to those families.

"I think the dogs might get frustrated, but not depressed, if they are not rewarded in some way for showing cadaver," John said. "I also believe they react to the handler's mood, so if the handler is upbeat, the dog will be, but he will get down if the handler is depressed. We did hide other members of our task force in short search problems so the dogs would make live finds and get their rewards."

Bear was also a "counselor" to the other rescue workers. He got plenty of leash time because there was always a rescuer who wanted to take Bear for a while. "I remember Bear falling asleep in a firefighter's lap," John said. "People would stop and pet him on the pile every day. They would discuss their dogs or ones they had owned, and for a brief minute or two, they had left the terror of that massacre. [Bear] helped them as much as he kept me grounded during our tour.

"I did catch him dreaming the first couple of nights after we got home; his feet would run and he barked softly. Maybe deep down he wished he had found people alive...maybe he knows more about what's going on than I give him credit for.

"Bear is not a 'hero.' Those firefighters and police officers are heroes...they knew they might not be coming back and still climbed into those towers. That's not to say I'm not extremely proud of Bear's actions at the WTC. He worked hard and would have probably worked until he fell over if I had not regulated his work cycles. He did as he was trained and he showed great trust in me. We worked as a team, and anyone seeing us together knew that we were a team and that he was my dog. All I know is that this is the job for me. There's no other position on the task force that I want to be in, volunteer or not. All that time I put into training Bear paid for itself a hundred times over in those eight days."

"Working on the pile at Ground Zero did not faze Bear," John said. "It was like going around the block for him."

BELLA

Border Collie

FEMA Type I, SDF, Certified Cadaver Search

DERESA TELLER

California Task Force 1

Deresa and Bella were deployed to New York with two other NDSDF graduates with California Task Force 1. They arrived the afternoon of September 11 and went to work immediately. Deresa's first view of Ground Zero left her in disbelief.

"It looked like a special effect in a science fiction movie like *The Terminator*," she said. "The amount of destruction was unreal. It was amazing how the dogs did not associate it with the real thing even though they were exposed to so many different things."

After the first thirty-six hours, Deresa and her teammates were assigned to work the night shift. "Sometimes the lighting was not as good, and I was concerned about the voids that were 20 and 30 feet deep," Deresa recalled. "Many times I

"After one especially long work shift, Bella did not eat, and she is a pig. But after a two-hour nap, she was fine again and ate."

would walk across a girder in front of us and then call her to me. She was pretty agile even though she was nine at the time. I don't recall any time when she slipped or fell.

"Once we got there, we realized this was going to be more of a recovery mission. Bella was one of the few dogs certified in both disaster and cadaver. I first gave her the command to search for live and then would switch to cadaver after that. My command for cadaver is 'Dinosaur.' When alerting, she would go over and sit. It was far enough away that we did not think it was live people she was alerting on.

"During our down time at the Javits Center, Bella was fine with the other handlers and rescue workers. She was very low-key and didn't seem to be bothered by all the stress and was always happy to see everyone and play with her toy. I didn't use her toy reward when she was searching. I was afraid it would fall into a void and she would go chasing after it and fall in! Her attitude was fine for the entire ten days we were there. There were times when the firefighters would seek her out and, vice versa, when she would go to them. She would bring her toy to people to toss for her, and she got lots of hugs and petting."

Bella's contributions to the search and rescue world go beyond the search missions she worked. Six of her puppies have been trained at SDF, and several others work in wilderness and cadaver search. Although Bella is retired, she is still the top dog in the Teller household. "Of all my other dogs combined, none can compare to Bella," Deresa said. "I am closer to her than I ever was to my two ex-husbands! Bella is my best buddy."

After his work shift,
Mike took Billy back
to the Javits Center
to be decontaminated.
Unlike many of the
other search dogs,
Billy loved getting his bath
every day.

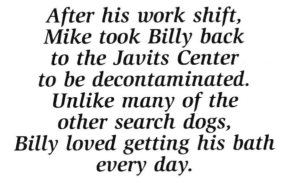

BILLY

Labrador Retriever

FEMA Type I, SDF

MIKE SCOTT

California Task Force 8

Mike and Billy were in Seattle attending the FEMA Canine Search Specialist (CSS) course when the World Trade Center was attacked. He was immediately deployed with his CA-TF8 teammates, but due to the emergency flight restrictions, they did not arrive in New York City until September 19.

"The first sight of the pile at Ground Zero was horrifying," Mike said, "but for Billy it was just another day of finding his toy....The dogs had no reaction at all." Mike recalled, "It was like climbing on a huge jungle gym, and we both had to go very slowly and search for pathways that were negotiable. Billy is very deliberate and has good agility. But he is also bold and has no fear, and he will cover an area very meticulously. We spent all of our tour searching at ground level in the plaza center court, over canyons that were five and six storeys deep."

Mike is a professional firefighter from Sacramento and had worked with the USAR task force for several years prior to 9/11. "We know from experience that people can survive in a void for up to two weeks," he said, "but after being there a few days and seeing the devastation, it was pretty hard not to feel the obvious. Yet we had to keep the dogs from feeling our own hopelessness travel down the leash. It's just part of our professionalism, and we deal with the emotional issues later. Billy would slow down and stick his nose into the dust like he smelled something interesting, but I had to keep moving and focus on this as a recovery mission."

After day eight or nine, Billy developed a bit of a droopy tail, indicating he was ready to go home. "I don't think dogs get depressed," Mike said. "'Demotivated' is a better word because there is nobody out there to find, and it's our job to remotivate them. We have to remind them that their job is fun."

Like the other search dogs, Billy served a dual purpose, becoming a companion and therapy dog to anyone who approached him. "He loved having people pet and hug him. There's something about interaction with a dog that people can identify with," Mike said. "They would talk about their dogs at home and how they missed their dogs...

"When Billy goes to work, he tends to find a way to pace himself and conserve his energy. But he always wants to go somewhere...anywhere. He always has that interest. At the SDF, we joke about many of the SAR dogs as having 'attention-deficit disorder' because they are so full of energy. They require our help to exert that energy in productive ways and focus it on their job."

"The rescue workers were amazed at the skill of our dogs," Lorrie said, "especially the FDNY."

BLITZ

Border Collie

FEMA Type I

LORRIE CLEMMO

New Jersey Task Force 1,
Northeast Seach and Rescue

Lorrie and Blitz responded with NJ-TF1 to the WTC disaster on the afternoon of the attack. She later reported to the Fresh Kills landfill on Staten Island with her other Border Collie, Claire, for a total deployment of seventeen days.

Assigned to the day shift at the WTC, she and Blitz worked twelve-hour days and sometimes longer. Blitz worked hard and was always on task, but as the days went by, the hours took their toll.

"Sometimes when we worked the pile, we could not get off the pile to rest. The fire chiefs and firefighters were all requesting a dog to check high-probability areas, and the dogs were the only hope they had to locate the scent of survivors or to make a recovery in a timely fashion.

"Each squad was given a section of the rubble to search. As we took our first step onto the pile, we saw the reflective tape on the turnout gear from the hundreds of firefighters that were already searching for survivors and battling the areas of fire and smoke that were still uncontrolled. Generators ran lighting apparatus where fires no longer blazed, keeping the area lighted for the hundreds of rescue workers searching through the rubble.

"Our team made its first find within our first fifteen minutes on the pile on the night of 9/11. We told the firefighters where to dig, pointing to a precise location. Within minutes, under a foot or so of compacted rubble, they unearthed a boot, then a leg, then the body of one of their own. From there on in we never stopped. The dogs had proven their worth.

"The firefighters were so grateful for these animals and their abilities. We learned the real meaning of brotherhood among the FDNY, and it was for them that we wanted our dogs to find the bodies of the deceased as well as the living. But, realistically, we knew there was little hope for any survivors; the smoke and fire were just too intense.

"The level of dedication in training a dog to perform this service is one of almost obsession. We want them to be the best because of the life-and-death situations they are trained for. The dogs don't know that...but the handlers do. And now America, too, knows more about the capabilities of these remarkable animals.

"My dog is not a hero. He is my partner and my search tool. He loves his job and does it mainly to please me. The real heroes are the ones who lost their lives, especially the men and women who took down the plane over Pennsylvania."

Peaceful dreams and contentment...

BRETAGNE

Golden Retriever

FEMA Type I

DENISE CORLISS

Texas Task Force 1

Brit naps between work shifts, dreaming of a soft blanket and a steak.

When Denise and Bretagne ("Brittany") were deployed to the World Trade Center on September 17, Denise prayed that she and her dog would be able to stay focused on the difficult job ahead of them.

She need not have worried. One look at the disaster site, and Brit shifted immediately into work mode. "Everything we did was an automatic response from all those weeks and weeks of training," Denise said. "Doing search work is a game for her. She gets excited over all of the cues…when I'm in uniform or put on my boots and helmet. She simply sees the environment as a place to work." Brittany remained in high gear for the next ten days.

"Our FEMA mission statement is to find live, but unfortunately there was none to find. The pressure was so great to find survivors, with everyone watching you, especially the firefighters, who were hoping you would find one of their brothers. When we walked up to the pile, there would be a sea of firefighters, like the parting of the Red Sea, watching you go to work, hoping you would find someone." Although Brittany is trained specifically for live find, she did indicate with her body language, just a turn of her head, a brief pause, that there was "something" there. "I just learned to read my dog," Denise said.

Physically tired from twelve-hour work shifts, Brittany learned to settle down and rest in her crate between shifts. Her behavior also changed dramatically when she wasn't working. "Sometimes she would leave my side and go sit next to a firefighter," Denise explained. "Not just anyone…she was very deliberate about who she chose. One time, there was a firefighter sitting against the wall; he was very solemn. Brittany went over to lie next to him and put her head in his lap. I tried to call her back, but he said 'No,' to leave her there. He petted her in silence, then came over and said thank you to both of us.

"I was really surprised at the unexpected role we played. A lot of our time was spent with people coming by to pet the dogs. One man especially stands out. He started petting Brittany and told me he didn't even like dogs. He knelt down beside her and told me that his best friend was missing. His friend really loved dogs and would be very upset if he didn't pet this dog."

BUDDY

Labrador Retriever

FEMA Type I, SDF

KELLY GORDON

California Task Force 8

Buddy's original name was "Happy"—a name befitting his upbeat, "ready-to-go" attitude during his 9/11 tour.

Kelly and Buddy and CA-TF8 were a part of the second wave of FEMA task forces deployed to the World Trade Center on September 22. Kelly said she was unprepared for what she first saw at Ground Zero.

"The first sight of the pile was overwhelming for me," she said. "The news media did not even begin to show the true level of destruction. Our hope was that we would still find victims alive, and I was ready for that mission."

Buddy, however, did not share Kelly's perception of the pile. "His reaction was the same as in normal training," Kelly said. "Buddy was originally named 'Happy' when he first came to the SDF, and at Ground Zero he was happy and true to his first name. Although he got tired due to the long hours and extended period of time away from home, he was still always ready to go to work. I just tried to keep his job fun for him.

"By the end of our ten-day tour, fatigue and emotional exhaustion had set in for me, as had the reality that no one was left alive. Although Buddy did not make any live finds, I believe the families and friends of the victims knew that everything possible was being done to locate their loved ones. One firefighter came up to Buddy and put his arms around him and just started crying. He thanked me for the work my dog was doing.

"My dog really loves his job. The work that he and the other K-9s do provides an incredible service to our country. No machine or person can give victims a chance to live another day like these dogs can."

"I never had a bit of trouble with Cholo at Ground Zero. He knew this was the real thing," Joanne said.

CHOLO

German Shepherd Dog

FEMA Type II

JOANNE REITZ

Texas Task Force 1

Joanne and Cholo reported to Ground Zero with their task force on September 17 and spent the next eighteen days searching for survivors who did not exist. Still, Cholo was calm and very serious about his work; he knew this was not just another training exercise.

"I truly realized how much he understands during disaster situations," Joanne reflected. "He was so careful and serious, even when the situation was extreme. The search site was certainly not ideal, especially with the number of workers surrounding your dog. It reminded me of a high school fight after school was out. Everyone was circled around, hundreds it seemed, watching your dog. Cholo did make a few indications into areas where some of the firefighters had gone down. But that was after the bodies had already been recovered. He also located one rescue worker underground, not a victim, but a firefighter who had not cleared the area after the call-out. But Cholo didn't know that; he thought he had found someone. He is very proud when he works and knows when he does a good job. He has a remarkable work ethic."

Like most of the other search dogs, Cholo received a lot of petting from many of the rescue workers. "He became a much-needed therapy dog to those guys," Joanne said. "I remember many times he would be petted on both ends at the same time. He's a very social dog, so he got a lot out of it too."

"Cholo was given to me as a gift," Joanne said. "Despite his working pedigree, he was a puppy most people would have passed over. But he has proven to be the best dog I have ever owned or worked with and surpasses my other dogs in health, endurance, search work and overall intelligence. From those humble beginnings, he has shown us all what he is made of. I couldn't have asked for a better partner."

A USAR colleague wrote about the special partnership between Cholo and Joanne. "Theirs was a path to making life better through search and rescue."

After Cowboy ran off the pile, Dave took him to VMAT and they gave him fluids to rehydrate him, but he still behaved very strangely. "We tried different things to perk him up, but nothing seemed to work," Dave remembered. "Then someone found a squeaky toy. That was all it took; he was back to okay again."

COWBOY

Border Collie

FEMA Type I, Certified Wilderness Avalanche and Water Search

DAVE RICHARDS

Utah Task Force 1

Cowboy was born on a ranch in Idaho, a pup from championship herding lines. Dave bought him as a youngster because he wanted an ultra-marathon companion. Their future together held much bigger challenges.

The two were deployed to the World Trade Center on the day of the attacks, but transportation problems delayed their arrival until September 16. Together with their UT-TF1 teammates, they worked at the site, searching for survivors until September 27.

"Border Collies are not 'bulletproof' like Labradors," Dave said. "When Cowboy first got to the pile, he went into sensory overload with all of the strange sounds and smells, heavy equipment and new people. But he understood that his job was to search and went right to work.

"There were remains all over; they were like pieces of a carpet mixed in with all the debris, and the dogs were trying to sort through it all to find live. When Cowboy found remains instead of a live person, he would sniff at it and his ears would go back. It was easy to spot the difference.

"When Cowboy is searching, he is totally focused and cannot be distracted from his work.

But one day while we were in the middle of the pile, he just ran off, past our team leader and several firefighters, and jumped into a Gator utility vehicle that was passing with two NYPD female officers in it and sat down next to them. I asked to be excused and took him off the pile. My teammates offered two possible reasons. The firefighters had just made access to a stairway where there were many bodies, and the overwhelming scent of death may have freaked him out. Also, we were over a huge void at the time, and the pile may have shifted and he sensed that.

"Ground Zero was filled with acrid smells, smoke and dust, and noise and death all around. Still, if you walked past someone with a dog, everyone wanted to pet the dog, and life somehow would be normal for a couple of minutes.

"Cowboy loved the firefighters. He always found a piece of wood or a stick and would throw it down in front of them, wagging his tail, and demand that they play with him. It was amazing how he found so many sticks wherever we were resting. They all started calling him 'that Cowboy dog.' He really did his part in making those firefighters forget their sadness for those few minutes every day."

"Cowboy does not relax; if he's awake, he thinks he should be searching."

"During his career in narcotics detection, D.J. had many finds and kept a lot of drugs from hitting the streets," Tim said.

D.J.

Belgian Malinois

Certified Cadaver, Man-trailing, Narcotics Detection

TIM SWAN

New York Federation of Search and Rescue Dogs

Photo: Photos by Dart

Tim began D.J.'s career as a police narcotics-detection canine. His great love for search work with Tim led them into other areas of search and recovery. Tim was a Pennsylvania state constable when the NYPD called them to assist in the recovery effort at the World Trade Center.

D.J. is a fearless and athletic worker who leaps across barriers with great ease. But at Ground Zero, Tim feared his dog would jump too far and fall down into the deep pits below them. "As a precaution, I sometimes worked D.J. on a harness," Tim explained. "I used two helpers with long ropes attached to him in case he jumped or slid as he searched and moved from one twisted I-beam to another."

After three days, when K-9 teams trained in disaster search had arrived, Tim's group of police K-9s left the worksite. Two weeks later he and D.J. were called again, this time with Pathfinders and the New York Federation of Search and Rescue Dogs, to report to the Fresh Kills landfill on Staten Island.

"The Staten Island site was much harder for the dogs to work in," Tim said. "Cadaver scent was on everything. The collapsed building material and human remains were mixed together in the move across the bay, then mixed again when offloaded at the landfill and mixed once again when it was laid out for the dogs to search. Weather was a big factor; several days it rained. And there was so much chaos, huge pieces of machinery that were so big that the ground shook when they moved. Still, the dogs just wanted to get onto the piles.

"One time D.J. almost collapsed; his legs got wobbly, his tail went down and his ears laid back. I was so afraid for him; I scooped him up and took him immediately to VMAT. They rehydrated him with IV fluids and we sat with him for several hours to make sure he was okay. The vet teams at VMAT and the Animal Planet Mobile Unit were always so good and caring to all of the dogs.

"I think this moment in history has left scars on all Americans, but the scars for the families and the rescue teams run much deeper. But if any cloud can have a silver lining, one of the good things that happened to me was that I learned how to cry."

Duke is Howard's teammate and partner twenty-four hours a day. Duke used his natural abilities and training to go above and beyond during his 9/11 mission.

DUKE

Labrador Retriever

FEMA Type I, SDF

HOWARD ORR

California Task Force 8

Howard was on his way home from a Canine Search Specialist (CSS) class in Seattle when the California Office of Emergency Services called him to prepare for deployment to New York. He and Duke arrived at the World Trade Center with CA-TF8 on September 18 as a part of the second wave of FEMA USAR teams.

"Duke saw that pile as the biggest sandbox he had ever seen in his life and could not wait to get to it. His transition from training to something of that scale was amazing. With his size and agility, he would search areas of rubble that I could not physically get across. On one search, he shoved his head into a hole and I saw his two hind feet poised on a piece of half-inch rebar. There's no way you can train them to do that. These dogs are less concerned about what their feet are doing than what their noses are telling them.

"One of the voids we searched was no more than 100 feet from the main point of entry to the plaza, and we were asked to search there. Duke went in and showed a lot of interest. I said, 'There's something in there.' I found out the next day that they pulled out three firefighters. The irony is that probably thousands of rescuers had traveled over that spot and no one knew those firemen were in there. But the minute they brought in the dog, they found them.

"Duke did indicate cadaver a little more strongly because we were willing to take that challenge. Once the FDNY knew you were willing to work your dog on cadaver, they were lined up like dominoes; as soon as you finished one search, they had another area ready for you. We made about five different searches that way. Then, all of a sudden, Duke started looking back at me like he was confused, and I said, 'Okay, we're done,' rather than come home with new issues to train my dog. This dog is my tool and if I break my tool, I can't help you any more. And everyone was very appreciative of that and what we were doing for them.

"My normal mode of operation with Duke is very businesslike…no one plays with the dog when he is working. But one night on our way to the pile, three guys from FDNY came up and asked if they could pet the dog. Now I was at a crossroads. Normally, the answer is no, but the reality is that, for them, a minute with Duke far outweighs our following the usual procedure. So I said, 'Sure, take your time.' So we would see these same people every night when they came to pet him. It was a mental break for these guys, who were away from home and sleeping on a corner of the pile, and petting the dog gave them a bit of relief. Initially, we didn't see this as part of the dogs' job. Yet here was this benefit of being a therapy dog. Again, Duke did very well. He was all business on the pile, and off the pile he loved all the attention.

"At home, Duke is with me 24/7. We're not making these dogs do something they don't want to do. When you see your dog having a good time and actually enjoying his work, that's what makes it all worthwhile."

DUSTY

Golden Retriever

FEMA Type I, SDF

RANDY GROSS

California Task Force 7

Dusty was one of three disaster search dogs in the National Disaster Search Dog Foundation pilot program. Randy and two fellow firefighters from Sacramento were paired with SDF-trained Golden Retrievers four years before the attacks on the World Trade Center. All three teams were deployed to New York the night of September 11.

Randy and Dusty worked the night shift with teammate Rick Lee and his SDF Golden Retriever Ana. For ten days, Dusty worked at top speed, never got depressed and always wanted to work and "win the game" to get her toy.

"Dusty uses a focused bark to indicate live human scent and pinpoint the area of greatest scent," Randy said. "She is not trained on cadaver, but she still worked the scent cone like it was live scent. When she got close, she raised one paw, slowly put her nose down to sniff, then turned away and kept on working. We alerted the workers to check the area, and they would tell us later what they found. Most of the time it was unrecognizable body parts.

"Dusty never got down or depressed. She had extreme drive and was always pulling me toward the pile to go to work. We did do a couple of search problems and hid someone for our dogs, but that was for our own personal motivation to help us keep our dogs upbeat, just in case. But we didn't have to worry…they never lost their desire to keep going.

"One day, we searched a subway area that was five floors below grade. Dusty was navigating the train tracks and stepped off onto what looked like solid ground but was actually 3 feet of black sooty water. She swam back over to the train rail and tried to climb out. I fished her out and wiped her face, eyes and nose and set off to VMAT to decon her. Even covered with all that goop, she kept pulling to go back to work. She was so covered with black soot that our team didn't recognize her. Even the VMAT techs thought she was a black Flat-Coated Retriever. It took three baths with Dawn dish detergent to get her clean.

"Our dogs performed better than we ever could have imagined. They flew across that terrain like it was a football field, in some of the most incredible areas where at any point they could have slipped and fallen into a black hole full of torn metal. There were areas that were considered unsafe for rescuers to go into, but our dogs went in and moved from place to place with no problem.

"I never gave up hope, even until the last day. I knew with our team, with the dogs we had, that our dogs would find them if they were there. When some of the other dogs were tired and beat, our dogs were still working. We were asked by more and more task forces to help them with their searches. One task force team manager said he couldn't believe how our dogs were working. He said, 'I want dogs like that…how do I get one?'

"Dusty was great with other workers, too. Things were very traumatic and emotional at times, and when you got a little down time, it hit you why we were there. Dusty and the other canines were a source of comfort and companionship for everyone. Sometimes I would find her sleeping next to someone else.

"The Foundation provides the highest quality dogs in the country. When Wilma Melville found Dusty, she was wild and full of all kinds of energy and would have been euthanized. The Foundation's trainer, Pluis Davern, didn't know if she could train her. But a few days later it clicked, and she said, 'This is one special dog.'"

"Our dogs went down into spaces and moved from one place to another when we couldn't figure out how we were going to get there ourselves."

DUTCH

Portuguese Water Dog

FEMA Type I, Cadaver Wilderness Search

CONNIE MILLARD

Missouri Task Force 1,
Gateway Search Dogs

Dutch is the only FEMA-certified Portuguese Water Dog in the USAR system. Known for its extreme intelligence, cleverness and ability to think through an action toward a goal, the Portuguese Water Dog is an adaptable and nimble breed and, when focused on an object, is able to generate many different approaches to achieving that goal.

Dutch was curled up on the couch in Connie's office when she received the call from her task force manager. He told her to go home and collect her gear. It was time to go to work. Dutch was more than ready. Working with Connie in search work is what he lives for, which explains his upbeat attitude during his eleven-day deployment at Ground Zero.

Connie's task force was divided into two shifts. Connie and Dutch worked during the day. "The real work of actively searching the pile was a turn-on for Dutch," Connie said. "He has an on/off switch and is either alert and lively or asleep. He would curl up and rest in the middle of all of the noise, dust and confusion, but when I'd say 'Let's go to work,' in a flash he would spring alive. He worked for all he was worth during his mission at Ground Zero. When we got back home after our tour, safe and sound, we were both about a hundred years older.

"One of Dutch's missions was to clear the top twenty-one floors of the World Financial Center in the Dow Jones-Oppenheimer building. One entire side and a portion of another had all of the windows blown in; there was glass inches deep in some places. His job was to work all of the rooms on each floor first, while my teammates, myself, Ohio Task Force 1 and a couple of National Guardsmen waited at the stairway.

"To clear a large room with many desks, Dutch systematically worked every row, double-checking under any desk that he found interesting. I about swooned when he was in the window row, and I exhaled only after he successfully completed that dangerous row. I did a quick check of his pads after every big window room to make sure that his paws were not cut.

"Like any good firefighter, Dutch always works a building search to the right, and he goes *fast*—now you see him, now you don't! Sometimes his mission was a specific area of the pile, sniffing debris to recover missing persons. Sometimes he and I were lowered into subterranean voids to work recovery missions. After each mission, I would check his feet, water him and rest him in a dust-free place while the others did their visual search. We had just worked our way to the uppermost floor when we were ordered to descend ASAP for another mission. So back down forty-two floors, double-time back to our forward base of operation, then onto another clearing mission."

As hope began to fade that any survivors would be found, Dutch's cross-training to find non-live became very important. He was able to find bodies and body parts of many victims, thus allowing the grieving families to have closure and be able to bury their loved ones. "At one site, I recognized one of the FDNY firefighters," Connie said. "He came up to me and said, 'I know your dog...yesterday he found my brother.'

"Make no mistake about it, these dogs volunteer their services. A USAR canine must raise his paw and volunteer for service. He can never be made to do this work by coercion. He works because he wants to. Dutch worked willingly at the WTC and continues to dedicate his life to the service of humanity. He is imbued through and through with the will to serve. He is a great dog."

Even while working as a disaster search dog, Dutch has competed in water, tracking, agility and obedience events. Ten days after returning from the WTC, he won a trophy and ribbon in the Portuguese Water Dog National Water Trials in Rhode Island.

"The actual work of searching the pile was a turn-on for Dutch. It was the resting and waiting that took their toll."

Much more than a "hound dog," this Elvis is a hero. "From his first day at Ground Zero until the last, Elvis was always willing to hit the pile and go to work," Mark said.

ELVIS

Labrador Retriever

FEMA Type I

MATT DAWSON

Massachusetts Task Force I

Elvis and Mark were among the first responders to Ground Zero, arriving with MA-TF1 late on the night of the attacks. Assigned to the night shift, they went immediately to work, setting the grueling pace for their next eight days of deployment.

"During his entire time working the pile, Elvis never looked back," Mark said, "and he never gave up looking until I told him it was time. His love to find was his driving force. He knew his job, and I just needed to get him into the search area. Elvis was always focused and worked extremely well under those unbelievable conditions." Like many of the other handlers, Mark used short search exercises with his teammates so that his dog could make a "live find" and be rewarded. Elvis was always eager and willing to go back out onto the pile.

"On one mission, we were asked to go with a FDNY truck company into a large space where the only way down into the void was on a ladder. The captain asked whether I wanted his guys to carry my dog down the ladder or if I would do that myself. I told him Elvis would climb down by himself. We put the ladder at a 45-degree angle. I went down first and then commanded Elvis to come down. Elvis got on the ladder and climbed down. The fire captain looked down at both of us and said, 'Now I've seen it all. You guys can do whatever you want.'

"Elvis also gave comfort and reassurance to all of the FDNY personnel he met. He is an incredible search dog and, after so many years of just training, it was awesome to see it all pay off. It was the dogs and what they did that pulled us all through 9/11."

Retired from search work at nine-and-a-half years of age, Hawk still does some public speaking. (And yes, Cathy said that Hawk does the speaking.) "He still gets excited when he sees my red deployment bags packed."

HAWK

Australian Shepherd

FEMA Type I, Human Remains Detection

CATHY SCHILTZ

Missouri Task Force I

Before he was deployed to the World Trade Center after the events of 9/11, Hawk had worked the Oklahoma City bombing, an F-5 tornado and two FEMA deployments. Now he and Cathy would work the night shift at Ground Zero from September 12 to September 20, twelve-hour shifts that often stretched into fourteen to sixteen hours.

Hawk is cross-trained for human-remains detection as well as live find, so he was eager to search regardless of the task. "We would rather have found live victims, but since Hawk is also trained for body recovery, that is what our mission became," Cathy said. The firefighters and police at the worksite quickly learned that when Hawk made an alert, they would make a find, and they soon began asking for 'that Hawk dog.'

"One night, we had to leave a search area where Hawk already had made an alert. Some of the firefighters felt there were no victims in that area and wanted to stop digging. One of my teammates who knew Hawk and his work convinced them to keep trying. After the workers had dug waist-deep into the debris, they found a hand. Then after digging deeper, they found two officers who had been buried in their squad car.

"Many nights, I had so many people asking us to check an area that Hawk would become very tired and need a rest, but it was so hard to tell them no. My search-team manager would have to run interference for us so that Hawk could get a break. We never ran out of work, and it was very hard to leave on September 20 because there was still so much to do.

"I do think Hawk is a hero, but he was just doing his job. Even though we did not find anyone alive, I hope that we gave those families some closure with the body parts of their loved ones that were found."

Hawk retired from active search work six months after the WTC and now enjoys being a pet and keeping his eye on the new recruits.

"Ivey doesn't care about being recognized for her work. She is very dedicated to her job and only wants to please me," Nancy said.

IVEY

German Shepherd Dog

FEMA Type II

NANCY HACHMEISTER

Utah Task Force 1,
Rocky Mountain Rescue Dogs

Finding people is Ivey's calling, and she'll go to any height to accomplish that task.

Nancy's canine partner, Ivey, is a working dog of many talents. In addition to certification in urban disaster search, she is certified in wilderness search, tracking/trailing, water search, avalanche search and cadaver and evidence search.

As a search professional, Ivey has two loves in her life: search work and stick fetch. But she will gladly drop her fetch toy whenever she is called to work. During her six-day tour of duty at Ground Zero, the six-year-old German Shepherd became known as the "Energizer Bunny®" because, work or play, she was always raring to go. "During one of our down periods, she had been playing fetch for a couple of hours, and another rescue worker asked if she wouldn't be too tired to go to work. Just then, we got called to search what was left of the Marriott Hotel. Of course, she immediately dropped her stick and went right to work."

Ivey's sticks became therapy tools for the other workers. Between search missions, she would get bored and find a stick or anything that resembled one. She would then try to entice the firefighters into a game of fetch by placing her stick-toy at their feet and staring at them, begging them to give it a toss.

While there were no survivors to be found at the World Trade Center, Ivey's cross-training in cadaver search enabled her to locate many of the victims' bodies and body parts. "She brought closure to this tragedy for those families," Nancy reflected. "The dogs' work also raised community awareness of the importance of these dogs in search work.

"At Ground Zero, Ivey was just doing something she has been trained to do all her life—find people," Nancy said. "She is a true professional, and nothing bothers her when she is working. She has had rabbits and feral cats run under her feet while working a rubble pile or during a search problem in the wilderness, and she just ignores them. She is always ready to work and has never been wrong in her scent work. The true heroes were the people who risked their lives trying to save the people who were in the towers."

JAKE

Labrador Retriever

FEMA Type II, Certified Wilderness Search

MARY FLOOD

Utah Task Force 1,
Rocky Mountain Rescue Dogs

Jake is a rescued Labrador who on 9/11 became the rescuer. He was a sick, homely fellow with a dislocated hip when Mary adopted him when he was one year of age. After hip surgery left his right rear leg 2 inches shorter than the left leg, Mary wasn't sure whether he would have the stamina for search work.

Jake would resolve her doubts. One year later, he was certified in wilderness search with Rocky Mountain Rescue Dogs, showing an incredible work ethic and unrelenting stamina. By June 2001, he also had earned FEMA certification and, fortunately, was ready to help on 9/11.

At Ground Zero, Jake knew his job was to find live victims. Yet his experience in wilderness search enabled him also to alert on human remains. "Of course, we all wanted to find live people," Mary said, "but we also knew that helping recover the bodies helped the family members. For the survivors, the finality of finding the remains of their loved ones is so important. That was one of the positives that Jake helped bring about.

"In fact, he helped us all stay positive in our work. Jake is a very intense worker, and my teammates told me that he did a great job of pinpointing on remains, thus saving them many, many hours in their recovery process."

Mary's teammates also got to know Jake better as he taught them how to play with him...and just how much he liked to play tug and fetch. They said his playful spirit was a big help in keeping them motivated during those difficult days.

"I remember one morning in particular," Mary said. "It was raining and we were all dirty and muddy, but Jake was clean from his VMAT bath. We had to walk across a muddy section to get to our bus. Our doctor, a guy about 6'7" tall, was kind enough to put Jake on his shoulders and carry him to the bus. We were some filthy, smelly, tired people and one tired but clean dog going home in the early morning almost-light. Dog almost asleep; people likewise.

"Jake is such a role model for me," Mary confided. "He is basically a disabled athlete, yet he has such a positive approach to life, his work and all the people he meets. In many ways, he is a SAR 'Everydog.' He's a black Lab who loves to hear the pager go off and see me gear up for a search. It's an inspiration to witness his generosity about sharing everything (except for food!) and his belief, as evidenced by his actions, that the cup is almost always full to overflowing.

"I don't think it matters whether you have a wilderness dog, a disaster dog, a specialist or an all-around dog. All trained search dogs work to find human scent. And we all have the same goal: the humanitarian cause of saving lives. That's what makes us keep our packs ready and put our lives on hold. We want to help save a life wherever and whenever we can. I want to thank Jake and all the service dogs for all they bring into our lives and all they do so that others may live."

"Jake works in heat, cold, long hours, tough conditions, almost any situation imaginable and always keeps his cool and work ethic going. And at the end of the day, he still has energy to play and steal some food."

"I love him because he is such an incredible search dog."

Jake is the recipient of a Humane Society of the United States grant that provides funding to help others train their disaster dogs. In 2003, he also was selected as a National Search and Rescue Dog Association nominee in the first Paws to Recognize program, a program to educate people about how service dogs help people throughout the world. That's not bad for a disabled rescued dog that became a search and rescue professional.

"Jenner has helped train many new handlers and been a fine mentor to younger dogs. The most important thing I did was to hug him and tell him how good he was to do this work for me."

JENNER

Labrador Retriever

FEMA Type I, Wilderness Search

ANN WICHMANN

Colorado Task Force 1,
Front Range Rescue Dogs

Ann was an instructor at the FEMA Canine Search Specialist (CSS) course in Seattle when the World Trade Center was attacked. The instructors were asked to complete the course, and Ann was able to return home on September 18. She and Jenner deployed with CO-TF1, first to Rapid Intervention Team (RIT) at Fort Dix in New Jersey, then to New York on September 24.

When Ann and Jenner first arrived at Ground Zero and walked around the worksite, she thought, "There is no way a dog can search that rubble pile!" Yet Jenner dug into the pile with great calmness and confidence and worked in a very serious and deliberate state of mind.

"Jenner seemed to understand our role at the WTC, which, unfortunately was to locate human remains," Ann said. "When we arrived, I was hopeful that we would find a live person, but that was clearly not to be. Jenner had some experience in human-remains detection and seemed to adjust quite well to the task.

"He was very careful negotiating the pile, although he scared me to death a couple of times. I remember seeing Jenner out on a steel beam that was hanging above the pit. He looked back at me with the most horrified expression in his eyes. I believe that dogs can distinguish individual human scents, and I think the overwhelming amount of death was just devastating to him. Jenner was a very experienced disaster dog at the time of 9/11. He has a wonderful work ethic and so was able to keep on searching.

"At times, we would be called to different areas of the rubble to check out possible scent sources. Jenner would check the area we were requested to search, then move off another 10 or 15 feet and indicate another place to dig; from reports, those areas did yield human remains. At one site, he lifted his nose and followed it across the rubble and disappeared from sight behind a ridge of metal. He popped back out and just looked at me—that find turned out to be the intact body of a firefighter. One fire captain approached us and thanked me, saying that the dogs were finding all of the remains. Knowing that was a huge comfort for the rescuers as well as the families of the victims.

"In reality, Jenner never rested during his down time. If he wasn't searching, he was comforting, very sweet and gentle with the other emergency

"My big fear was that Jenner's commitment to following the scent would get him hurt or killed. I watched him very closely, and his very good obedience was a huge help," Ann said.

workers. He seemed to understand the deep grief that pervaded everyone on the site. He has big soulful eyes and is a very soft, gentle dog with strangers. He simply extended himself to everyone. He would sit very patiently and respectfully while strangers came and talked to him. Almost everyone would kneel and hug him and talk about friends they had lost or a dog they had when they were a child. The dogs were literally a beacon of comfort and healing…even the priests stopped for a hug with Jenner.

"One NYC firefighter who was trudging by suddenly dropped to his knees and hugged Jenner. He did not speak to me at first, but talked quietly to Jenner. After almost a minute, he looked up at me with tears in his eyes and said, 'I lost fifteen of my best friends here.' I think it was the first time he had said those words to anyone.

"Jenner loves his work and loves finding people. His tremendous courage, strength, agility, intelligence and gentleness have made him a remarkable searcher and partner. He has devoted his entire life to working as a search dog, doing both wilderness and disaster missions, and has literally risked his life over and over to find people. When he worked the Fort Collins flood disaster in 1996, he was swept through 1,500 feet of an underground water system. He came out ten minutes later, barely alive. He is truly a heroic dog and a true friend and partner."

Jenner's contribution to the USAR world extends beyond the perimeter of Ground Zero. His brother, Merlyn, also worked at the WTC, and his son, Ronin, worked at the Pentagon disaster site. He also sired twelve search and rescue dogs, all FEMA-certified, with eight of those FEMA Type I.

As the sire of twelve FEMA-certified search and rescue dogs, Jenner has contributed his heart, soul and genes to the world of USAR.

KAISER

German Shepherd Dog

FEMA Type II

TONY ZINTSMASTER

Indiana Task Force 1

As Tony and Kaiser rode the bus to New York with IN-TF1 on the evening of September 11, his wife Annette and her USAR K-9 Max were boarding a C130 at McGuire Air Force Base with Missouri Task Force 1. They had just celebrated their twentieth wedding anniversary. Reaching the Javits Center the next morning, Tony was assigned to work the twelve-hour night shift; Annette worked days from 7 a.m. to 7 p.m.

A military truck delivered Tony's task force to Ground Zero, and they walked the remaining four blocks to the worksite. "The scene was surreal," Tony said, "Ankle-deep gray dust, black smoke, white smoke, fires burning, three cranes, two dozers, five claws and five hundred workers, working just on our corner of an 80-foot tall rubble pile.

"It was chaos at times, but Kaiser seemed happier when he was working. When a dog really loves his work, in a stressful environment he almost takes solace in doing his job, much as we do," Tony said. "We concentrated on doing a professional job, which helped us focus on the task at hand rather than the enormity of the event. I had to continually monitor the status of my dog, and if he seemed a little dull, a few search exercises would bring him back to a high gloss."

Kaiser kept that upbeat attitude back at the task-force rear base of operation, where he played with the other rescue workers and kept them company. "Everyone was lifted by his positive attitude, and it was good for me too," Tony recalled. "One FDNY firefighter came up to Kaiser and just gave him a big hug. No words were spoken by anyone. They all knew what each other felt. Then there were the four firefighters who decided that Kaiser needed a drink. One cupped his hands while one poured water into them, and the other rinsed Kaiser's face and back. They wanted to accommodate us, and like any gracious guest, I enjoyed letting them."

The School of Oriental Medicine in New York had set up an area at the rear base of operation to give the dogs and handlers massages, acupuncture and chiropractic care. "Kaiser and I would go there, and both of us would get the full-meal-deal by some really nice people."

Although Kaiser suffered a major slice to his right front carpal pad on his second day of work, he was bandaged up and went right back to work every night for the next five days. "Professionalism, selflessness and bravery in the face of great stress is my definition of a hero," Tony said. "When a dog works a pile like that...wow! Just doing 'what feels good' could not carry a dog through that."

"He did what he was
trained to do with a
good attitude that
was infectious to
everyone he met."

Lean and leggy, Kenji dwarfed even the German Shepherds at Ground Zero.

KENJI

Labrador Retriever

Wilderness Live Find

DAVE PERKS

Utah Task Force 1

"Kenji is a very deliberate dog," Dave said. "He searches the whole area and does not run out of energy. He just works and does not give up."

Dave and Kenji were notified by pager to deploy with UT-TF1 on the morning of September 11. But like several other FEMA task forces, they were grounded for a week and did not arrive in New York until September 17. No survivors had been found, and hope was fading that anyone was still alive.

Kenji is a big dog, 125 pounds at that time and 29 inches at the shoulder, but Dave adds, "...he is very agile. He moved through the rubble and debris without any trouble. The pile didn't faze him at all; of course, we humans had more reaction than our dogs did.

"By the time we got there, the mission had pretty much gone to the recovery-of-bodies stage and they were asking for cadaver dogs. We couldn't find anyone alive, yet that's what we were there for. Kenji is basically a live-find dog, but he will indicate on cadaver. He would sniff and push with his nose...but he never got depressed over not finding live.

"There were times when we were on a strike team in case of secondary collapse. Kenji got to rest, and the firefighters were always willing to watch him for me. Sometimes people would just curl up with him or put their heads on him to sleep. It was nice to have him there to break the tension and help get their minds off what was going on around them.

"Kenji did make an impression on the police department back there. They all wanted to know 'where that dog came from.' He's a very solid dog. He's so big, he made even the German Shepherds look like midgets.

"The dogs were used to the maximum that we could use them. It was such a hard place to search. The fact that there were so few injuries to the dogs is testimony that our dogs today are so well trained. We don't do much else besides train our dogs, plus we have two weekends a month for training meets. You have to put the hours in. People's lives are in your hands, and you can't make a mistake."

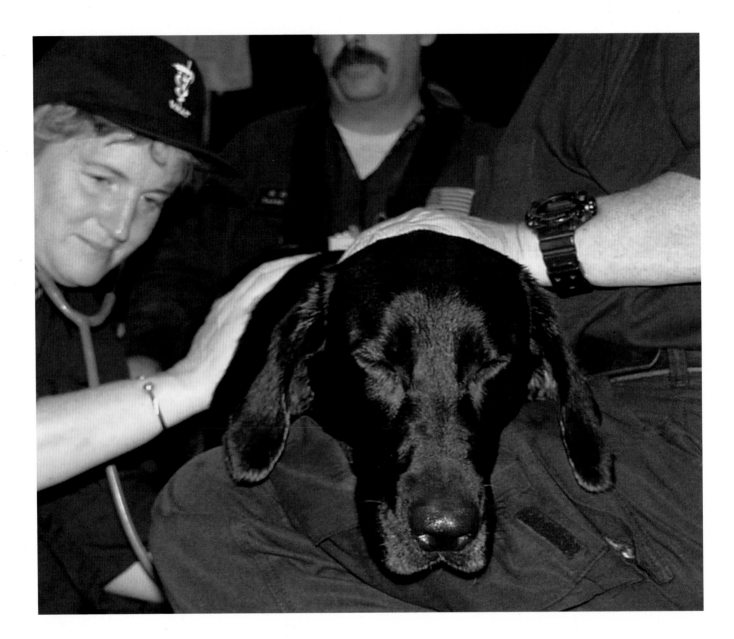

KINSEY

Labrador Retriever

FEMA Type II

BOB DEEDS

Texas Task Force 1

"We got to serve our country…it doesn't get any better than that," Bob Deeds summed up the eleven days that he and Kinsey worked at the World Trade Center searching, hoping to find survivors of the terrorist attacks.

Kinsey is herself a rescued soul, saved by the Dallas-Fort Worth Lab Rescue Group. She was found on an elementary-school playground popping dodge balls with the kids. As a rookie volunteer with TX-TF1, Bob was looking for a dog to train, and Kinsey needed a job. They had been together about a year when they were called to work at Ground Zero.

Bob and Kinsey were assigned the night shift, working from 7 p.m. to 7 a.m. Most of their search assignments were underground. "Sometimes we were sent out right away, sometimes we waited for hours," Bob said. "Kinsey would get bored… she wanted to find someone alive, and she would bark and nip at me in frustration." Bob asked the FDNY firefighters to participate in mock searches to keep her attitude upbeat between work shifts. Those firefighters became her good friends, and she always perked up when they came to visit her. She was always wagging her tail and happy to greet them. "Kathleen Antona, Special Agent, FBI, came around each night just to hug Kinsey," Bob recalled. "I saw her again on the Space Shuttle *Columbia* search mission, and she told me how much those nightly hugs from Kinsey meant to her. Kinsey was treated several times at VMAT for cut pads. Yet despite the injuries to her paws, no matter how tired she was, she was always ready to go back to work.

"Kinsey lost a lot of weight at Ground Zero but has since gained it all back. She's like an Energizer Bunny, still going strong…she's a once-in-a-lifetime dog."

The VMAT team treated Kinsey's injured paws, but she was always ready to get back on the pile.

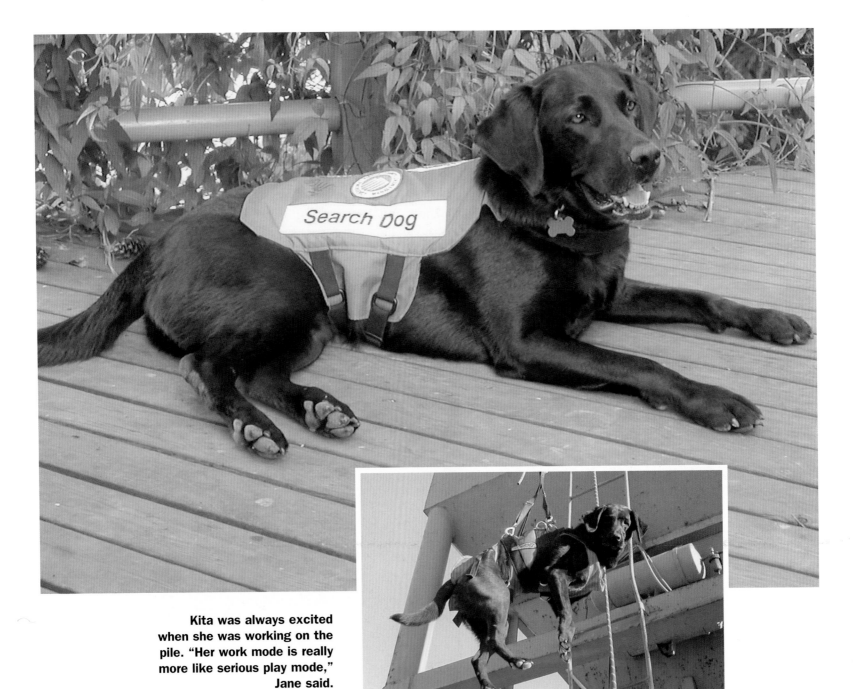

Kita was always excited when she was working on the pile. "Her work mode is really more like serious play mode," Jane said.

KITA

Labrador Retriever

FEMA Type I

JANE DAVID

Washington Task Force 1,
Northwest Disaster Search Dogs

Jane and WA-TF1 were placed on alert on September 11 but ended up "standing down" until they were deployed a week later as part of the second wave of search teams sent to the World Trade Center. When Jane and Kita first arrived at Ground Zero on September 19, Kita was calm and relaxed...until she got to the edge of the pile. Then she switched immediately into work mode, anxious for the opportunity to get on there and find someone.

"Kita is certified as a live-find dog, but unfortunately there were no live finds to be made at the WTC," Jane said. "Yet she showed me through her body language that she had found some human remains. She has no aversion to the scent of human remains; in fact, she is very interested in the scent. I would reward her with fairly low-key praise, and we would play tug after she left the pile. I hope that identification of those finds was possible, as I cannot imagine the emotional pain of never recovering anything of a loved one.

"We spent most days waiting for calls from our search-team manager to search a particular spot in response to indications that there were human remains present in those areas, and we also searched some void spaces for living victims. Since there were no live finds, in a sense she was set up for failure. However, since we weren't actually searching very often, she did not experience the frustration that can occur when a dog searches for hours without finding anyone and therefore gets no reward.

"The dogs were great stress relievers, both for our own teammates and for other rescue workers at the disaster scene. Each day I spent some of our on-site down time walking around and talking with the local firefighters. They seemed to get some measure of comfort and stress relief just from petting Kita and telling me their stories about the horrors that they experienced on 9/11. Many of the rescue workers were curious about how Kita learned to search and what her capabilities are. I was touched by the concern of many firefighters for her welfare while she was on the pile. There is something about seeing a search dog work in the midst of such devastation that brings a great sense of hope and warmth to the human heart.

"If Kita was capable of self-reflection, I don't believe she would describe herself as a hero. She would see herself as a dog who just loves doing her job. However, I think that disaster search dogs are indeed heroic because they overcome their instinctive fear of a hazardous environment, trusting in their handlers to keep them safe while they follow the command to search. They are high-spirited and bold and show great fortitude and heart in carrying out their work. Kita loves what she does, and she will always be ready to search wherever needed, as long as her body allows."

"Everyone would stop to see the dogs and pet them and just talk," Rose remembered. "It was a huge relief to talk about something other than the tremendous loss of life."

LOGAN

German Shepherd Dog

FEMA Type II, Certified Cadaver, Wilderness Search

ROSE KELLER DELUCA

Pennsylvania Task Force 1,
American Rescue Dog Association

When Rose first heard the news of the attack on the Twin Towers, she left her office at Smith Barney to "wait for the call." Her task force was deployed that day and worked the first nine days of the disaster.

As Rose and Logan headed toward Ground Zero with their teammates on the night shift, New Yorkers lined the streets, clapping and holding signs. "It is one of my most moving and special memories of the tragedy," Rose said. "Logan stood up on the rails of the bus and barked; the more people cheered, the more she barked. It was as if she was telling them, 'Don't worry, I will save them!'

"Once we arrived at the site, we would start to work immediately," Rose said. "Rescue workers would call for 'K-9! K-9! K-9!', and even when we headed back for a break, more workers would see us and ask for help. The work was exhausting, but no one was giving up. We were all convinced that there had to be survivors.

"From time to time, Logan would 'find' a rescue worker who was working beneath the pile, and we would hear her barking. I will never forget an excited fireman coming out of a hole with my dog, saying, 'I think she found someone!' But

I could tell from the way Logan was looking at him that my dog thought she had found him. After sending her back down alone to confirm that there was no one there to rescue, I explained to the fireman that she thought he was 'fair game' since he was below the surface of the pile. Our disappointment was profound, but Logan was happy; she felt she had done her job. The terrain of the pile was very difficult, and she was more physically tired during the last days."

Logan continued to bark and carry on to the crowds every time she and Rose headed in to go to work, and the people would cheer louder, which lifted Rose's teammates' spirits as well. ("Thank goodness she doesn't bark while she's actually working!" Rose exclaimed.) Logan likes to share her toys, and she would take her toy to each person in the group, drop it at his or her feet, then stand and stare at the person she wanted to play with. Then she would move to the next person so everyone got a turn. Rose said that Logan's pushy, playful attitude was a huge relief from the ugly task of searching and the despair in the days that followed.

"I am so thankful to have this happy dog as my friend and partner and proud that she was able to do the tremendous job that was asked of us all on 9/11. I could never have done it without her. She is a trooper that never gives up.

"We were the first federal task force at the WTC, and when our tour was over, it was so hard to leave because the job wasn't done. I will never forget the tributes written in the dust on the walls, file cabinets or any glass that was still intact. 'Remember the fallen brothers...we will never forget.' It was like signatures in a yearbook, but ghostly, written in dust that would eventually be gone too."

The author submitted this photograph to her editor, Andrew DePrisco, for a book on the Golden Retriever. He was so overwhelmed by the image that he phoned her and said, "Do I have an idea for a book!" And you're reading its second edition.

LOUIE

Golden Retriever

FEMA Type I

AMY RISING

Nebraska Task Force 1

When Amy heard the news of the first hijacked airliner on her car radio, she immediately headed for the closest TV set to follow the events. Within the hour, she was put on alert, checked her pack and prepared to leave. Then she waited thirteen days before she and Louie were deployed with Nebraska Task Force 1. Amy and her teammates were assigned to work the West Street site between the Marriott Hotel and the North Tower from September 24 to October 1.

"We had to walk several blocks to get to the worksite," Amy said. "On the way, Louie's nose was already up, sniffing the air in anticipation of the work that lay ahead of him. He looked up at the rubble of the fallen towers, and I could tell from his body language that he wasn't afraid."

Amy released him into the rubble without a leash or collar, using only her hand signals to guide him through the fallen debris. "There was so much noise from the bulldozers and large cranes that Louie could not hear me; he could just see my hand signals: Go left, Go right, Stop and Come. Sometimes it was just out of the corner of

"He was eager and intense and ready to go."

his eye that he saw my signals while he worked. I believe he reads my body language and understands that when we are working in a dangerous environment he should pay extra attention to my directions. Once he started working and reacted in such a responsive manner, I was no longer anxious about working him in such a harsh environment. All the thousands of hours I spent training with my dog paid off!"

Louie's alert for live finds is a bark, but there was no occasion to bark at Ground Zero. During their down time at the Jacob Javits Center, Amy heard Louie bark in his sleep, dreaming of finding live people in his search missions.

Every evening before their work shift, Amy and Louie visited the VMAT tent, where he enjoyed homemade dog biscuits baked especially for the search dogs by the hundreds of volunteers who were concerned about their welfare. Between work shifts, he visited with other rescue workers. Louie loved to be petted and enjoyed being a therapy dog when he wasn't working.

"He met one firefighter who petted him for the longest time and whispered something in his ear," Amy said. "I believe he was asking Louie to help find one of his friends. He also gave Louie a pin bearing the image of a firefighter with an axe, helmet and angel wings. Another gift was from a police captain, who gave Louie a replica of his police badge to pin on his collar, and an emergency-room nurse gave him a patch with the Twin Towers on it to wear on his vest. These are Louie's special treasures."

Amy wanted to say thank you to the man at the Minneapolis airport who looked at her and Louie and told her, "You only get one like that in your life."

"I hope he is wrong," Amy says. "I am one of the luckiest people on earth to be able to work and live with such a fine dog."

"She's smart, she's overbearing, she's a true bitch, I'll tell you that. And that has absolutely nothing to do with her gender."

LUCY

Border Collie

FEMA Type I, Certified Cadaver Search

LYNN ENGELBERT

California Task Force 4

Lynne was an instructor at the FEMA Canine Search Specialist (CSS) training course in Washington State on September 11. Once she returned home, her own task force, CA-TF3, had filled its roster. She was assigned to CA-TF4 and deployed on September 27. By then, the search effort had become mostly a recovery operation.

From the moment that Lynne and Lucy stepped onto the site at Ground Zero, Lucy knew that it was more than a training mission. She was serious and focused, making her first human-remains find within minutes of her arrival at the West Street site. "Lucy's first find was very important to our entire task force," Lynne said. "The fact that she was responsible for finding numerous remains, including one firefighter in the rubble of the Marriott Hotel, also meant closure for a few families who might not otherwise have been afforded that comfort.

"She really impressed a group of NY firefighters who watched her work the rubble of one building, searching the site with no direction from me…just doing her job as she had done for years. Their comments were along the lines of 'Look at that friggin' dog work!' in a New York accent. I'll always remember that moment. It was a tiny sliver of silver in a big, black cloud.

"Lucy more than did her job of locating human remains, but the visits she had with other workers on the site brought the kind of comfort only a dog can give…a soft shoulder to bury your face in, a little wet 'kiss' and perhaps a few tears shed without anyone thinking any less of you. Lucy was able to open up conversations with fellow searchers with the NYPD and FDNY that I alone could not have initiated. The dogs back at our base of operation were a comfort to our fellow task force members too.

"Lucy is an honest dog who would work until she dropped if necessary. Besides the WTC, she also worked the Oklahoma City bombing and the Space Shuttle *Columbia* recovery mission and is responsible for locating the remains of two murder victims and a drowning victim in our local counties. She helped put one very bad guy away for the rest of his life.

"She has been an incredible gift, not only for her ability to search and her dedication to her job but also for allowing me to help people when they most need it. I've been a very fortunate handler to be blessed with a dog like Lucy."

Lucy worked as hard on the last day on the site as she did on her first day. "I'm not sure what I'll do with her active brain when her aging body is no longer able to run a rubble pile…of course, I wonder the same thing about myself!"

"When Manny is working, he's not interested in being petted. He just wants to do the job he has been trained for, to find someone he cannot see." Here's Manny (RIGHT) with his Border Collie friend Dawson and handler Ron Weckbacher.

MANNY

Border Collie

FEMA Type I, SDF

RON WECKBACHER

California Task Force 8

When Ron was paged by his task force, CA-TF1, he was in Seattle at the FEMA Canine Search Specialist (CSS) course. He was later deployed to the World Trade Center with CA-TF8 in the second wave of USAR teams from California.

From day one of their ten-day mission at Ground Zero, Manny viewed the pile as any other obstacle course and went instantly into search mode. "The first time one of the firefighters took me to our search area, I unclipped Manny and hooked his leash to my belt," Ron said. "When I looked up again, he was already gone and out there, ready to search the pile. It was amazing how Manny and the other dogs did with their agility on that pile. This was not something you really train on, with all that metal and twisted steel. At times, it seemed like he was going straight up. As someone who sees the dogs work on a daily basis, I was in awe."

By the end of their mission, Manny was starting to tire. "It was tough on the dogs when there was nothing to alert on. We did runaways and hid people for them to find, but the dogs know the difference."

Ron had high praise for the VMAT vets who patrolled around the pile. "Manny and I were sitting against the wall, trying to catch some rest; he was covered from nose to tail with dust when the med vets came rolling up in their Gator. They asked if this was Manny. Then they climbed out and cleaned him up and cleared his nose and eyes."

In addition to searching for survivors, Ron said Manny and the other dogs performed a very important personal service. "People were away from their families, and just having the dogs to hug and pet was a real psychological bonus. The dogs were always an attraction, with people wanting to pet them. When the dogs are working, they can't have that interaction, but there were other times when you knew the rescuers needed that little something from the dogs. Some of the firefighters just buried their faces in their fur and sobbed.

"For the dogs, this work was a game and all about the fun. I train five or six days a week, and every day the dogs can't wait to get out of their kennels to do whatever we do that day, be it obedience or agility; it's all about the game for them. The desire to work is programmed into the genes of all working dogs, and at SDF we have the high end of those dogs. Manny was ready to work when he was called. It was great to know that all of our training had paid off."

"Our day began at 5 a.m.—feed Max, then myself, collect our gear and board the bus to Ground Zero. At 8 p.m., back on the bus, decontaminate both of us, feed Max, then myself, go to bed to wake up and do it all again the next day."

Annette and her husband Tony both served at Ground Zero with their dogs Max (FAR LEFT) and Kaiser (FAR RIGHT). In the middle is Thor, Tony's first FEMA-certified dog, who was retired at the time of the attacks.

MAX

German Shepherd Dog

FEMA Type II

ANNETTE ZINTSMASTER

Missouri Task Force 1,
Marion County USAR Task Force

When Annette and Max reported for work at Ground Zero with MO-TF1 on September 12, they joined Annette's husband, Tony, and his USAR dog, Kaiser, who had been deployed with IN-TF1 that same day. Tony, Annette and their German Shepherd Dogs were one of only two or three family teams to work at the World Trade Center disaster.

Once Max hit the search area at the pile, he was intense and motivated to go to work, and for seven days he did his job just like any other trained professional. "When we first attempted to enter the pile, there was a secondary explosion in our assigned area, and things were very stressful," Annette remarked. "Yet Max ignored all the noise and confusion and did not let any of that keep him from doing his job. From puppyhood, Max was trained to deal with stress and to understand that working is the best part of life. Under the worst of circumstances, his great temperament and training shined through.

"Later during our tour, some firefighters were searching a void and were asked to leave the site so that Max could work that area. We thought everyone was out of the area, but one person had not yet left. When Max started to alert at the void site, that firefighter popped out, so Max had done his job and did it well. So he got rewarded big time even though his 'find' wasn't missing. The fire chief came over while Max was alerting and told him, 'Good job, Max.'

"During our down time between searches, our team would set people out for him to find and keep his attitude up. Those motivational search problems helped to keep him working well. And so many firemen and police officers gave Max tons of petting, which was comforting to him as well as to the rescuers. Then there were times when people wanted to feed and water him as we walked to our search areas, but I couldn't allow that because he was working.

"Max was always ready to hit the pile and go to work. He loves doing this kind of work. He's a great partner and did his very best in helping find people during the 9/11 disaster."

OHLIN

Labrador Retriever

FEMA Type II

ALFRED FRANK

Washington Task Force 1,
Northwest Disaster Search and Rescue

Ohlin was ten years old and heading for retirement when he was called to work at the World Trade Center. Al was attending the FEMA CSS class in Washington when his task force called up their canine teams. He and Ohlin left for New York on September 18.

Search work has always been a game for Ohlin, so he thought his tour at the WTC was just ten more days of playtime. "Once at the pile, you would stand by until someone requested a K-9, then you would go to work," Al said. Between search missions at Ground Zero, Al walked Ohlin around the rest areas so that other workers could pet his dog. There was always someone needing a dog for comfort. "If we weren't working, I would run water and equipment out to the other workers. Back at base camp, I put Ohlin, then myself, through decon, we ate and played, then went to bed with some 200 people in the same room.

"For all of the K-9s, firefighters, police officers, USAR members and civilians who helped with 9/11, it was a tragic day, but we were able to make it better," Al said. "Yes, Ohlin is a dog that loves his job and had a chance to do his part. But the true heroes are the people who never made it home."

Ohlin did one more search mission after 9/11—a house fire in Monroe, Washington. He then retired to live out his senior years in the comfort he deserved while Al carried on with Zara, Ohlin's daughter.

Photo: Michael Rieger/FEMA News

"Ohlin's attitude never changed from his first day searching to his last. He loves his work and so do I."

Orion loves his work, and Bob's main challenge was keeping him in the search area. "With so many people and lots of machinery, it was not safe for the dogs to be out of our sight."

ORION

Golden Retriever

FEMA Type II

BOB MACAULEY

California Task Force 4

Bob and Orion and CA-TF4 were the last USAR task force to arrive at the World Trade Center. By the time they reached Ground Zero, it was apparent the search was now one of recovery. But Orion was ready to go to work, regardless of what the mission had become.

"When we first arrived, I took us for a leash walk around the entire site so he could get used to the smells and the noise," Bob said. "I had to be cautious around all of the machinery, but Orion was eager to get started right away.

"We were assigned to a very limited search area," Bob explained, "and I have a dog that wants to keep going and search all of New York. We searched the roof of one of the financial centers, and debris had collected on the roof. Orion had never been exposed to human remains, but he did make three forensic finds. One was obviously human, the others were just masses. When he finds live, his tail goes around in a corkscrew. This time he just stopped in place, put his nose down, stood very still and took three or four deep breaths, as if to say, 'I am not sure what I am smelling here.' He did not react to anything else that way. I did not give him a big reward since it wasn't a live person, just a pat and quiet 'Good dog.' How best to reward is a bit of a challenge for the handler.

"Orion never got down or depressed. He is very much a typical Golden and such a sweet dog. He always wants to rub against you and did that with the workers every day. Greeting all of the rescuers was lots of fun for him.

"I don't know what they did with the remains he found, but they might have been the only remains of those people who died, and it was something tangible for their families. I hope they knew that people from all over the country cared enough to help them. They were New York and we were California and it didn't matter a darn bit. We gave them a hand up...we don't know you, but we'll be glad to help you...that's part of our response. For the victims' families, it is important for them to know that if someone is trying to terrorize us, instead of cowering, we stand up for them."

"Osa and I walked in a single file to Ground Zero with the other K-9s and handlers from my team. Ahead lay the most horrible destruction and mayhem, more than I could imagine in my worst nightmares, and we were walking smack into the middle of it."

OSA

German Shepherd Dog

FEMA Type II

LAURA LOPRESTI

New Jersey Task Force 1

Laura and her K-9 partner, Osa, arrived at the World Trade Center on the afternoon of September 11, called up with the NJ-TF1 Rescue and Recovery Unit. About 10 p.m. that night, they received their clearance to enter the search area at Ground Zero.

"Gray ash covered everything; the smoke was thick, and breathing was difficult," Laura said. "I was concerned about our dogs. We were wearing masks, but there was not much we could do for our dogs except pray."

The firefighters called on Laura and her teammates to check different areas for victims, everyone hoping that the dogs would bark to indicate that someone was still alive. "But no dog barked that night or during the next ten days of our deployment," she said.

Their team was assigned to continue working on the night shift. "Osa is a live-find dog, so when she is on command, she will ignore everything else, including cadaver," Laura said. "But during our 'off' time on the pile, she hit on the bodies, or pieces of bodies, by digging and scratching. She did help to recover some remains. She was always eager to search, but she was cautious, so I would sometimes hide people for her in mock searches because she was not finding anyone alive.

"Osa loves people. While we were waiting between calls for 'we need a dog over here,' workers would approach and ask if they could pet her, and I would agree if she wasn't working. She would wag her tail and give them kisses, and they would tell me about their dogs at home. Some would just hug her and tell her their secrets. She was always patient and seemed to actually give them her attention. Our dogs became therapy dogs before the actual therapy dogs came to the WTC.

"Osa finds people because she genuinely loves people and wants everyone to play with her. She gets so excited when she sees me put on my uniform. She is loyal and courageous and a true friend. I couldn't ask for a better partner."

Osa truly loves people and enjoys being around the other handlers and emergency personnel.

Sonny recalled the bus ride over the bridge into Brooklyn. "We could see the smoke and empty space that used to be the WTC. A young firefighter sitting across from me looked out and said, 'Omigod, my heart just got torn out of my chest.' All of a sudden we were in each other's arms, crying."

PIPER

German Shepherd Dog

Certified Wilderness Search

SONNY WHYNMAN

New Jersey Task Force 1

Actor Peter Gallagher spent time with Piper during a visit to Lower Manhattan.

Sonny and Piper and NJ-TF1 were among the first USAR teams to arrive at the World Trade Center on the afternoon of September 11. After unloading at the Javits Center, they were bused to within a few blocks of the worksite and walked the rest of the way to Ground Zero.

"When we first arrived, it was like walking into hell," Sonny remembered. "People were running in all different directions. There were dozens of firefighters and they were all pleading, 'Bring your search dog over here.'

"I said to Piper, 'Go find.' He would paw or whine, and then he would look up at me. And as soon as he put his nose to the ground, the firefighters were all over him. They were so crazed to find one of their brothers buried where Piper had indicated. That's when I started feeling the deep depression they were feeling. There were ten or twelve dogs on our search team. In all, Piper and his buddies found about fifteen bodies.

"One firefighter came up to me, with hollow eyes and sunken cheeks and desperation on his face. He asked if he could pet my dog. Then he leaned down and gave Piper a big hug and whispered something in his ear. Piper looked at him and wagged his tail. When the fireman left, he had just a tiny smile on his face."

NJ-TF1 shared their base camp at the Javits Center with the FEMA teams that followed. Many slept on the floor, the dogs lying next to them, the dogs' heads propped against their handlers.

"The support the dogs received was great, from vets and chiropractors, physical therapists and nurses, all waiting to bathe and massage the dogs. Piper got beat up pretty bad. His paws were red and ragged, and his eyes were red. We had masks on when we worked, but the dogs didn't have that protection.

"My experiences with this K-9 team opened up a whole new area of my life. I know what faith really means. I have a partner who asks nothing of me except to stay at my side and do his work. And when he's tired or hurting, he works even harder. In my next life, I would like to be that good."

On the long bus trip to New York and home again, Polly would "work" the passengers, walking up and down the aisle looking for a free hand to get some petting or a morsel of food or an invite into a seat.

POLLY

Border Collie/Golden Retriever mix

FEMA Type I

MARTI VANADA

Indiana Task Force 1,
Ohio Valley Search and Rescue

Marti and Polly and IN-TF1 were among the first disaster-search teams to be deployed to the World Trade Center, arriving the day after the attacks. They spent the next eight days looking for some flicker of hope that they would find survivors.

Marti and Polly worked the pile on the day shift from 7 a.m. to 7 p.m. "The first night was the hardest," Marti said. "We worked the pile for an hour or more and then sat in the rubble that was to become our forward base. The faces of the firefighters were the worst: dirt-smudged, tear-streaked cheeks. They formed 100-plus man-bucket brigades. They would clear a small section and ask for Polly's help. She would work the area with no indication, and they would go back to digging deeper and hoping against hope. Wednesday and Thursday were almost like a street fair, with people from all walks of life offering anything a rescuer might need...socks, gloves, knee pads, masks, sandwiches. By Friday, the big machinery and security were in place, and Manhattan became almost a police state. We had a military escort when we bused in and out, with a National Guardsman always on the bus with us."

Polly was eager and ready to work for the first several days, but as the days wore on with no survivors, she lost her normal playful attitude and became more serious and withdrawn. "Her work ethic is great, so she always worked when I asked her to," Marti said, "but by the end of our deployment, she didn't show her normal interest in play and other people." Yet, despite her own deep sadness, Polly managed to comfort the firefighters, who petted her and often buried their tears in her fur. "Having the dogs present in a disaster situation helps people let go of some emotions they can't release otherwise."

Polly's Frisbee-mania also lifted the spirits of the rescuers and members of IN-TF1. "She became known as the Frisbee dog," Marti said. "Even the guards at the Javits Center recognized her because she always carried her Frisbee."

During her down time, Polly learned to sleep through anything, at any time, anywhere. Sensing that her dog needed quiet time away from the confusion of the task force, Marti slept on a piece of carpet on the concrete floor next to her.

Marti considers Polly's mixed heritage to be the best of both worlds. "At work or play, she is all Border Collie, and when she needs to chill, she becomes a sweet-natured Golden Retriever. Her focus and work ethic are amazing, and she's a great lap dog!

"I'm not sure if she's a hero, but she knows her job, and no matter what the conditions or how often, she will go to work and complete her task. She has not been wrong yet; I trust her completely!"

QUEST

German Shepherd Dog

FEMA Type II

PENNY SULLIVAN

New Jersey Task Force 1,
Ramapo Rescue Dog Association

Penny received the initial page from NJ-TF1 at 9:18 a.m. on the morning of the attacks on the World Trade Center. Deployed that same day, she and Quest worked the night shift at Ground Zero, searching for live victims in the mountain

Quest was assigned to search some of the damaged buildings surrounding the WTC.

of debris. Sadly, none had survived the tragedy, but the failure to find survivors did not deter Quest in the least. Although never trained for remains recovery, he was all business, confident and enthusiastic, and successfully located human remains on numerous occasions.

"His body language was unmistakable," Penny tells us. "His interest was so intense. He would nose the area or gently paw at it with great concentration. Although he did not receive his usual play reward for finding a live victim, I rewarded him verbally, and his attitude was excellent for the entire ten days." Penny concentrated her efforts on Quest's safety during their searches and on maintaining his physical well-being throughout their ten-day deployment.

"Throughout our tour, the dogs played a dual role as therapy dogs, which had a healing effect on the searchers and families who were looking for their loved ones. Quest loves people and would often try to get any person near him to play with him. He also provided a welcome respite for many of the firefighters and workers who were involved in the search effort. They would stop to pet him and the other dogs and sometimes whisper quietly in their ears. The one comment we heard over and over again from everyone was 'thank you.'

"I think all of the dogs who served following 9/11 are true American heroes. They helped bring closure to countless families whose loved ones had perished in the attack. But more importantly, the dogs provided a sense of hope, a belief in the future, for their handlers, the workers, the families and the nation as a whole."

Quest's usual reward
for indicating a live find
is a rowdy game of tug.
Sadly, during 9/11 she
received no such reward.

RILEY

Golden Retriever

FEMA Type II

CHRIS SELFRIDGE

Pennsylvania Task Force 1

Chris and Riley and PA-TF1 were notified at noon on September 11 to deploy that same day. During the trip to New York, the USAR dogs seemed to sense that this was not a typical training mission. "Riley usually wears a typical 'Hi, I'm a Golden Retriever' attitude," Chris said, "but this time he knew something was up." They arrived at about 10 p.m. and were on the pile the next morning.

"Riley kept dragging me to the pile; he knew there was something to do in there. He was never formally trained as a cadaver dog, but there were times he would sniff intently at an area and paw the ground. A couple of times, he actually dug bones out of the debris.

"During our first couple of hours, we were bounced all over until we finally explained to the rescuers what our dogs could do. We had to educate them. People would tell us that they could smell something in a certain place. I explained that the dogs were here to find people who were still alive and that if they could smell it, they did not need the dog.

"About mid-tour, the FDNY were looking for one of their deputy chief's cars, and several times they asked us to search a certain area. Riley kept going back to the same spot, and I told them to check in there, but they had no luck. One day, during a search in that area, Riley was hot and tired, and he went in under an I-beam in a shady area and lay down. I thought he was tired and called him to come out, but he wouldn't come. So I crawled underneath the debris about 5 feet down, which was at street level, and put his collar on him and tried to pull him out. He surprised me because he wouldn't budge and just growled at me. So I said 'Good boy' and told them to look right there. Ten minutes later, they found who they were looking for. It was the same place he had indicated several times before. We learned to trust our dogs.

"We didn't have time to take the dogs off-site to play hide-and-seek for motivation. So if we saw a firefighter go into a void, we would send one of our dogs in after him and tell the dog to 'Go find.' When the firefighter came up, we told him to give the dog his Frisbee, and the dog would prance around with his toy and be happy. Without that, our dogs would feel our feelings travel down the leash."

Riley's most memorable moment came four days into their mission, when rescue crews called

Riley's well-deserved fame continues, as this photograph graces the cover of our book.

Portraits in Courage **103**

US Navy Photo: Journalist 1st Class Preston Keres

"Normally when we send a dog, the handler goes with him," Chris explained. "This time we decided it was more practical to just send the dog." Three months after 9/11, Chris and Riley visited a couple of firehouses in NYC. "One firefighter said, 'Hey, we know your dog—that's Riley!' The fire captain showed me the picture of the three firefighters raising the flag, then said that Riley's was the second most famous picture."

for a dog to search the top of what was left of the North Tower. Chris and members of PA-TF1 set up a Stokes basket to transport Riley over a canyon 60 or 70 feet deep. "He was strapped in with his harness on, and for the first 30 seconds he was not real sure about it," Chris recalled. "Then he just lay down and waited while he was transported across the void, and I went around to street side and met him." Riley's photo in the Stokes basket (facing page) has appeared on websites and in publications around the world.

Chris said that the very presence of the dogs seemed to help people come full circle. "Whenever they passed by, they all bent down to pet him. You could see the people change from being very down to wearing little smiles on their faces, even for just ten seconds.

"Riley has been a great friend and partner, and now he gets to spend time with my two-and-a-half-year-old son. He sure has earned that reward."

Some of Sherman's proudest moments were at Steve's daughter's school, when her classmates gave him cards that said "I love you, Sherman!"

SHERMAN

Labrador Retriever

FEMA Type I, SDF

STEVE SWANEY

California Task Force 1

On the morning of September 11, Steve's CA-TF8 teammates were in Seattle at the FEMA CSS class. Because of the demand for FEMA advanced-level dogs, Steve and Sherman were deployed immediately with CA-TF1. They arrived in New York the following day and worked the next thirty-six hours without taking a break.

Steve recalls, "The first few days, there was no organization or controls. There were civilians all over the pile. The firefighters were concentrating on the tower area where they lost their command post, and we worked a lot on the perimeter. After a few days, it was more organized and controlled, and there was a joint effort with the FDNY. They would assign a sector for us to work, and our task force would grid it off. We chose to work all of our dogs together, and we backed each other up. One of our teammates had a dog that was cross-trained for cadaver, and if our dogs showed any interest, we would send him in.

"Sherman is very animated and energetic. It's not hard to tell if he is interested. He might just slow down and circle; a couple of times he tried to penetrate a little bit. Sometimes the dogs made alerts because scent drifted up from a rescuer in a void below us. We had to watch our dogs to figure things out. Our technical search team had cameras and could look around below. It was a good team effort.

"Sherman didn't react to the pile at all; he didn't know the difference between that and normal training. He was fine, maybe even a little too energetic. He's incredibly fast and has a ton of energy and drive. On the second day, it started raining and things got slippery. I fell down right after I let him go and slammed my leg. Sherman didn't care...he was just out there covering a huge area.

"Sherman made friends with everyone. Every time we came off the pile, everyone had a hand on him as we walked off. People would come over and sit down and ask to pet him, and he got all this extra attention. But petting is not what drives this dog. He is totally focused on his toy. After working the dogs for as long as I have and training other handlers and their dogs, I am still amazed at what they do and offer up—and all for this stupid little toy.

"I was hoping we could find someone alive. But in the absence of that, there were a lot of those pieces of paper that could be taken down... those handwritten signs that said 'Have you seen this person?' We were able to aid in the recovery of those people and those heartbreaking signs were not there any more. And now the families have some closure.

"Sherman has gone to my daughter's school, and after Ground Zero all those kids made cards for him that said 'Thank you, Sherman' and 'Sherman, we love you!' It makes my daughter very proud."

STORM

German Shepherd Dog

FEMA Type II, Certified Cadaver Search

DAVID SANABRIA

New York Police Department K-9 Unit

David and Storm were attending the Canine Search Specialist course in Seattle when the planes hit the World Trade Center. Delayed because of flight restrictions, David, Storm and several USAR teams finally arrived in New York on September 14, thanks to a private jet owned by the General Electric Company. All reported directly to Ground Zero.

David recalled the chaos of those first days. "Everyone was calling 'K-9, we need you over here!' Within our first fifteen minutes there, the NYPD K-9s had found six bodies. Initially, I would send Storm in for live find with his command to 'Locate,' and he would go out and come back with nothing. Then I gave him the command 'Body' for cadaver, and he would hit right away in three different spots. It was like that nonstop the first couple of weeks.

"In the beginning, everyone was working twenty hours at a time. There were no typical shifts, you just kept going. Our breaks were walking from one area to another. The rescue workers knew that any time Storm indicated, they would find someone. They told me once that he got seven guys out of one search area; they pulled up a beam where he had indicated and found the bodies lying there.

"Storm was like a mountain goat up on some of those piles. Even I was amazed. I called him down and he went after the scent and just kept climbing. That's when you see how valuable all that training is.

"In one void we were searching, he started backing up. He had passed by some beams and they were actually glowing. He knows that when it's hot, he must back off. When I got closer, I could feel the heat generating.

"During one of our searches, Storm found two cops. One of them was a guy we used to work with. Joe loved Storm and used to play with him and pet him. His father lost both of his sons: our co-worker, Joe, and the other son, who

"In the beginning, Storm would find people and we would just move on. Later, someone would tell us that was a Port Authority cop. You just never knew…"

David believes that Storm "really has the gift." As a search dog, Storm was never mistaken.

was a firefighter. After we found Joe's remains, his dad asked me to put Joe's shield on Storm. He's wearing that shield right now."

David said that rewarding Storm became a catch-22. "Any time he gave an indication, I had to praise him, but I also had to be discreet. All the while, you're feeling sad because everyone you found is dead, yet you have to keep your dog peppy."

Storm gets a tug toy as a reward for finding. "The first day out, I realized that wouldn't work because he would get saliva all over his toy, then drop it and get ashes and asbestos all over it, so I had to throw it out. So I compensated with a plastic water bottle. Empty it, throw it for the dog, then throw it away. There were hundreds of them all around. Unfortunately, now he thinks it's his real toy and any time he sees a water bottle, he wants to play with it.

"In the beginning, it was easy for the dogs because there was so much to find. But later on, when the finds were 6 and 7 feet under, that's when Storm would indicate and the others could not. He really has the gift. I knew any time I sent him out he would find something, a body or body parts. I always had the hope that by some miracle we would find someone alive in a void or trapped somewhere, but after about two weeks, reality hit that we might not find anyone alive. At the end, Storm was coming back with nothing, and after two or three days of that, I knew it was over.

"Storm and I were down there for eight months, long after they had sent everyone else home except for five or six NYPD K-9 teams. In February, they tried to break us up and give us some time on patrol, but I wanted to be down there because I knew my dog was the best at it.

"These dogs are a tool we really can't do without. Their noses are amazing. In such a tragic situation, everyone wants to come and pet the dogs. Just petting the dogs helps them get through the next couple of hours. That's an important part of their job, too."

"When our task force arrived at the worksite, the search-team manager, the Hazmat technician and two dog teams would go to the assigned area. After the voids were checked for air quality, our dogs were sent in to search."

Photo: Andrea Booher/FEMA News

SUNNYBOY

Doberman Pinscher

FEMA Type I

SHIRLEY HAMMOND

California Task Force 3,
California Rescue Dog Association

Shirley, Sunny and CA-TF3 were deployed to the World Trade Center on September 19 after waiting eight days on alert. Shirley was a veteran K-9 handler who had worked in searches at Mexico City, Loma Prieta (California) and Oklahoma City. Still, she was shocked at the enormity of the disaster site at Ground Zero.

"The first day was mind-boggling," she began. "The air smelled strange and acrid, and the pile vibrated like an aftershock. Once or twice a day, the workers would remove one of the large steel beams, and flames would burst into the area. We had to focus on the assignment and just do our job.

"Sunny is a live-find dog. Although he did not find any survivors, he did make one accidental live find, a firefighter who was still in an area that Sunny was sent to search. Sunny 'found' him and of course was rewarded for doing so. He also indicated on the location of one of the fallen firefighters. Those remains were recovered several hours later, and we were informed that Sunny was correct in his indication."

Between searches, Shirley and one of her teammates took their dogs to a vacant building and set up finds for them. "Dogs need their paychecks for searching to keep them motivated, especially as the week wore on and the dogs were getting tired. Setting up motivational search problems is part of the handler's job."

Sunny is a very large dog, 95 pounds and impressive, so he attracted a lot of attention from the other teams. "If he was between searches and hanging out, they would often visit Sunny," Shirley said. "He became a therapy dog for the other teams. He was frequently invited to come to the forward base of operation, where they had cookies for him and lots of petting, and he gobbled it all up. Typical comments were, 'He looks like he could eat you, but he is such a love. I can't believe he is so nice.'

"I think he made life a little easier for a lot of firemen and Port Authority guys who were really tired and stressed to the limit. He made a difference in each of their lives, and in the life of the family of the recovered fireman. It was important for the family to be able to complete the grieving cycle. . .

"I would like people to judge Sunny on his behavior and his contributions to mankind. I have done search and rescue work with my Dobermans for twenty-seven years. We have found live victims and those who did not survive. Dobes are wonderful friends, loyal companions and great working dogs."

"I wanted an off-the-wall, happy dog who would be crazy to work," Lee said. Tara is every bit of that and more.

TARA

Labrador Retriever

FEMA Type I

LEE PRENTISS

Massachusetts Task Force 1

As members of MA-TF1, Lee and Tara were one of the first USAR teams to arrive at the World Trade Center on the day of the attacks. They worked the pile on the day shift for the next eight days. "The dogs had a feeling this was not a typical training exercise," Lee said. "Even when you stay calm for the dogs' sake, they still feed off everyone around you.

"When we first arrived, I thought I would have to give her some down time to handle all of the confusion…the machinery and noise and people all around…but she didn't need it. She took it all in stride and worked her twelve-hour shifts without ever losing her desire to search.

"On that first day, within our first fifteen minutes on the pile, our dogs had found a body. After that, the firemen worked with us like crazy, trying to find their brothers. This was such a large-scale incident and so widespread that someone was always calling for a K-9 to check an area and the dogs were bouncing all over. But everyone showed great respect for the dogs when they were working.

"The love for the dogs was incredible down there. Everyone wanted to pet and hug them. They always asked if they needed water and had water ready when the dogs were resting or on breaks.

"Tara is trained to find live," Lee said, "but we have spent so many years together that I could read her body language. She would drop her tail, show interest in an area and start to circle around it. I would give her a pat and tell her she was a good girl. I couldn't praise too much or it would upset the reward for finding live."

After her first three days on the pile, Tara developed a stress-induced urinary-tract infection. "I rested her for a day, but after that I kept her quiet during breaks to minimize her stress. We had so much work, but it was important for her to rest, not just for her health's sake, but so that she would not be tired and maybe make a mistake that could be harmful or even fatal. The dogs have to be calm and rested walking over steel beams and wobbly surfaces.

"I always took care of my dog first, before I took care of myself or did anything else. She is my most valuable tool and, more importantly, she's my best friend."

The bond between a handler and her search dog cannot be conveyed in words, but it can be photographed with utter eloquence.

THEA

Labrador Retriever

FEMA Type I

ELENA LOPEZ DE MESA

Florida Task Force 1

Elena was on the FL-TF1 roster for deployment when the airliners hit the Twin Towers. She and Thea arrived at Ground Zero on September 12 and worked the pile for the next sixteen days.

"My first impression of the pile was shock," Elena said, "A lot of fire and burning steel. All I could see was hate. But Thea acted like a kid in Disneyland. It was so comforting to know that the dogs had no idea what kind of tragedy lay in front of them; they were just there to perform and enjoy their work."

Thea worked twelve to fifteen hours on the day shift, sometimes searching, and many times "hurrying up to wait." During her down time, she waited patiently for the next assignment and another opportunity to search.

Despite the length of her deployment, Thea maintained her typical enthusiasm from the first day to the last. Her tail was always up and wagging. "My team's effort and support kept Thea positive and always ready to work. Between searches, we played with our canines back at the convention center to keep them (and ourselves) energized. Playtime was a big reward for all of us. The other workers usually loved our dogs; it made them smile to just pet the dogs and talk to them.

"I don't think my dog's a hero," Elena said. "This is a job she loves, and it is one big game for her. I feel honored to be able to do this with her. I believe in what our canines do, and any exposure they get helps to support our efforts. We were happy to be able to help our country in one small way during such a terrible disaster."

"Thea and all of the dogs were ready to work all the time, with their tails up and wagging."

Thea with Elena and FL-TF1 on the streets of Lower Manhattan.

"When is it my turn to go to work?"

Confident and people-oriented, Willow exemplifies the hard-working, sweet-natured Labrador Retriever.

WILLOW

Labrador Retriever

FEMA Type II

BOBBIE SNYDER

Pennsylvania Task Force 1

Bobbie was watching *Good Morning America* when the news broke of the attacks on the World Trade Center. Several hours later, she and Willow were on the bus on their way to New York with PA-TF1. They spent the next ten days working the recovery effort at Ground Zero. Despite finding no survivors, Willow remained her normal happy Labrador self throughout their deployment.

"Willow faced that huge rubble pile—with fire and very hot, dangerous conditions—and never questioned what I asked her to do," Bobbie said. "She thinks if mom's okay, then she is okay, too. Our work shift was twelve hours and sometimes more until our relief team could get to us. Sometimes the NYPD would close the streets to Ground Zero, and the relief teams would have to wait for clearance from the military before they could enter. But despite the long hours, Willow always did her best to complete her task because she loves her job." Bobbie's teammates often commented on Willow's calm demeanor under such extreme conditions.

"Willow is trained to bark for a live find, but I could tell from her body language when it was

cadaver," Bobbie said. "Sometimes she will even urinate when she finds dead."

At home, Willow is also a therapy dog, so she fell naturally into that role at Ground Zero. She was always ready to play ball with rescue workers or snuggle up for petting, a huge comfort for everyone who met her.

"Willow is a real 'people person.'" Bobbie said. "She's a very positive and confident dog. She was there to do her job, and she did it to the best of her ability and would do it all over again if her country needed her."

Isn't that what heroes do?

Willow's training on simulated rubble piles helped prepare her for the job she faced in the aftermath of the 9/11 attacks. Willow is pictured making a "find" during a training session.

Zack celebrated his eighth birthday on September 23 while working at Ground Zero.

ZACK

Labrador Retriever

FEMA Type I, SDF

JEFFREY PLACE

California Task Force 4

Jeff was put on alert through his dispatch center at the Fremont Fire Department. He and Zack were deployed to the World Trade Center eight days later and searched for survivors until October 2.

Despite the conditions and the pervasive death, Zack never got depressed and never slowed down when he was working. "He just pushed forward and kept on searching," Jeff proudly recounted. "He had no reaction at all to not making live finds." Zack usually is rewarded with a tug toy when he makes a find. "I just rewarded him verbally and kept a positive attitude to keep him motivated."

Jeff and Zack worked twelve-hour periods on the day shift. "He showed some signs of sluggishness after the first day, but he was better after he was rehydrated with fluids by the VMAT team," Jeff said. "Once the initial stress was over, he was able to cope with the conditions and worked much better. He stayed in his kennel at our forward base of operation until he was called to work. But he handled the down time really well."

Between work shifts, Zack was rewarded with plenty of petting and hugging from the firefighters and rescue workers. "A lot of people commented on his friendliness and how he reminded them of their dogs at home. The firefighters always took time to play with him, and that helped them in their healing process.

"Zack comes from a line of field-champion bird dogs and is in great shape. We are together twenty-four hours a day, seven days a week, and we are ready to respond anywhere we are needed."

Photo: Shutterstock/Frontpage

The Pentagon

At 9:38 a.m. on September 11, a third hijacked airliner struck the Pentagon in Washington, DC, killing 189 people: 125 military personnel and civilian employees and 59 airline passengers as well as the 5 terrorists. K-9 task forces were deployed on 9/11 to the emergency operation at the Pentagon to search for survivors and remains. Within two days, the 27-acre complex became a federal crime scene and was secured by the military, FBI and Secret Service. On September 15, the Pentagon officially activated the search and recovery.

The FBI coordinated the overall recovery operation. They called in FEMA task forces to assist in shoring the collapsed structure and to search for any victims still alive inside. Unfortunately, the devastation was vast, and it soon became apparent that no one had survived.

Officer Jim Lugaila, cadaver search dog handler from the DC Metropolitan Police Department, orchestrated the recovery/cadaver canine operation. Lugaila contacted the cadaver search teams to assist in the search for victim remains.

Security at the Pentagon was at its highest level. When the canine teams reported to the Pentagon, they were escorted to the Secret Service tent, where they obtained color-coded photo ID badges that restricted their access to only certain areas. Badges were constantly checked and rechecked each time they entered their designated areas.

The massive destruction at the Pentagon site did not hinder search and rescue dog Otto of VA-TF1.

The debris from the collapsed building was trucked down from the upper-level impact site and spread out in the north parking lot to be sifted and then searched by the cadaver dogs. The dogs would find the DNA evidence necessary to identify all 184 victims and the 5 hijackers.

The DC Metro PD K-9 force under Officer Jim Lugaila coordinated the cadaver dogs' daily tasks and provided the handlers with any necessary supplies for themselves and their dogs. They also set up and helped staff the decon tents, where the dogs were examined and bathed.

"They drove us to the hot zone in Gators, directed us to the piles and looked after our safety while we worked," said Heather Roche, who worked her three Labrador Retrievers at the Pentagon. "They watched our backs...literally." Heather and the other K-9 handlers credit the success of the K-9 recovery efforts to the hard work and dedication of Jim Lugaila and the DC Metro K-9 officers.

"On a scale of one to ten," Anne Rehfeld said, "the performance of Jim Lugaila and the DC Metro PD was at least a twelve!" Rehfeld was an emergency medical technician (EMT) from Maryland who assisted with peer support, offering psychological assistance to the K-9 handlers. "The recovery teams' positive success was verified by the families' responses at the conclusion of the Burial of Unidentified Remains ceremony

A memorial on the Pentagon crash site pays tribute to the Pentagon employees and Flight 77 passengers killed in the 9/11 terrorist attacks. Pictured here is one of the 184 memorial units, one for each victim, which consists of a bench onto which the person's name has been inscribed, positioned over an individual reflecting pool.

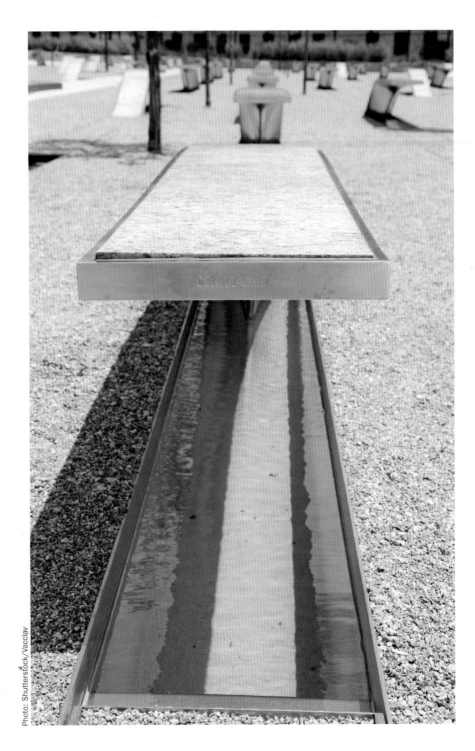

Photo: Shutterstock/Vacclav

held at the Arlington National Cemetery in September 2002. Several K-9 teams were present for the service, and the family members were deeply moved that the dogs were there. Some families had observed the recovery operation from a knoll above the recovery site and knew the date and time when their loved ones' remains had been found, and the names of the K-9s who had found them. Immediately after the service, there was a spontaneous meet-and-greet with photographic opportunities for the families to pose with their heroes, the recovery K-9s."

F ernando Fernandez, Belgian Malinois Gerry's handler, reflects on their time at the Pentagon: "Some after-noons we watched buses carrying the victims' families to a prearranged location so they could observe the impact site from a distance. I felt bad that they might see me walking my dog to or from the piles. I don't know why...common sense told me that I was just doing what we were trained to do. But common sense was no comfort.

"Some in the 'dog world' criticized us, after the fact, claiming that we jeopardized our dogs and their health by subjecting them to the conditions at the Pentagon, that a handler's first duty is the safety and welfare of his canine partner, and inferred that we had failed in our duty. I don't disagree, but I will say that, along with the many other handlers there, we responded to an unprecedented event in our history, filled with issues and situations never encountered before. Faced with those situations, we took every precaution possible to ensure our dogs' safety and respond to the challenges before us.

"On December 15, 2001, the United States Police Canine Association honored the dogs, handlers and support personnel who were involved as part of the K-9 Search and Recovery Team at the Pentagon. They dedicated the ceremony to those who had worked 'to bring home to their families those American heroes that were senselessly slaughtered during a terrorist attack on the United States of America at the Pentagon on September 11, 2001.' That's exactly what the dogs did at the Pentagon."

Anne Rehfeld recalled one Sunday when the Outback Steakhouse donated meals for all the workers, including the canine units. When the handlers received their meals, they found steaks included for their dogs.

Pentagon heroes Tucker, Glory, Otto and Nikko with their handlers and a member of the support staff.

A gathering of Pentagon heroes, including Smokey, Alley, Thor, Nikko and Maverick.

ALLEY

Labrador Retriever

Certified Cadaver Search

HEATHER ROCHE

Bay Area Recovery Canines

Heather was called to the Pentagon when the DC Metro Police Department contacted Bay Area Recovery Canines to assist in the search and recovery effort. She took all three of her cadaver search dogs, Cassy, Alley and Red, so each could contribute to the search effort. Although Alley was the "middle" dog with less experience, she turned in a most exceptional performance.

"When I took Alley to the piles in the north parking lot, I knew immediately why this dog was in my family," Heather said. "She was born for this mission. Alley usually works fast and far away from me, so I expected to have to work her on lead. She dragged me to the pile and placed her nose between her feet and began to walk—slowly—in straight lines. I unhooked her and let her go to work. She would work each pile in rows and then work the larger items on the pile's edge. I could not have trained that behavior or that search pattern. She was perfectly meticulous and intensely focused. The range of items she found in that first pile set the pace for the rest of her recovery efforts. I knew then that this was her calling in life: to serve our nation and those families affected by the terrorist attacks.

"I will never forget how Alley searched those piles. She found so many sources in piles that already had been searched by a dog, then raked and sorted again by several agencies and were declared cleared, yet she still found numerous items. Her intense desire to locate even the smallest source kept her going until our very last day.

"Nothing stops this happy little dog. Her desire to search is the driving force behind her career. She works without any thought to things that are happening around her. She even works without being given a command, because finding sources is part of her core being. She is unbelievable to watch. Searching is what she was born to do."

Heather explained that the mortuary staff learned to read the dogs and would be right there when they started to hit. At the end of a rotation, they would often run over to the dogs when they couldn't determine if some particle was human or not. "It was then that I knew my dogs had been properly trained and had overcome the odds to be successful in these harsh conditions," Heather confided. "A couple of FBI agents joked that they wanted to 'kidnap' Alley because they loved her work ethic and ability. Her whole being is about being happy to work."

Heather's three dogs were also great stress relievers for the other workers. They were always eager to get through decon because they knew there would be someone waiting who needed a friendly dog to play with or to share his or her meal with. Heather would simply drop the lead and let the dogs visit with the crew while she finished her own decon process.

"What touched me most was a conversation I had with a couple of Red Cross workers who were flight attendants and friends of the crew that

"Alley's work ethic amazed me every day. She was a black dog working in direct sunlight on hot asphalt with her tongue hanging out until I pulled her away to decon. I am lucky to have such a dog to work with!"

perished that fateful day," she remembered. "They had helped those families collect hair samples for DNA just in case, and they were counting on our cadaver dogs to help bring closure for their friends. Before this, I knew that families talked about closure, but I didn't realize how much it meant to them or how much they needed that. I know that Alley and the other dogs helped dozens of families who lost their loved ones, and I am honored to have been a part of that."

In November 2001, Heather received a short note from a family friend who was an Air Force general. He wrote, "…very few people know what you did for those of us who work here. Through your efforts, and those of your dogs, the victims' families have a chance at closure. On behalf of all of us, a simple but heartfelt thanks."

Heather concluded, "I couldn't help but think that this special dog came into my life to do this for our nation at a time when her amazing skills and determination were needed. She was put here for a reason, and I believe she is fulfilling it.

"My dogs just do their jobs. It just happens that their job is to help the community find lost loved ones. Through all of our work, we brought everyone home."

Given Ayla's drive and sense of accomplishment, Marilyn did not find it difficult to praise her for a job well done. Ayla was not emotional about not finding live victims.

AYLA

German Shepherd Dog

FEMA Type I

MARILYN ARWE

Virginia Task Force 1

Marilyn was teaching a patrol-dog class when she heard that the World Trade Center had been attacked. A fellow task force member gave her the news that they were being deployed to Washington, DC, and to leave immediately. She and Ayla worked at the Pentagon for the next seven days.

Arriving at the Pentagon, Marilyn was struck by the emotional impact of the disaster site. "Although the size of this disaster was physically small compared to other disasters we had been deployed to," she said, "it was emotionally shocking because of the location and the fact that the terrorists had come this close to paralyzing our country. But dogs do not exhibit the same types of emotions as humans, so it is not a fair analysis to say that Ayla was emotional. It was another day of work as far as she was concerned. We worked the interior of the building for several days."

Although no one had survived the crash, Marilyn said that Ayla did not view the no-find as a failure. "That would be a human emotion. Dogs are in hunt drive when they are searching for a victim, and I give her appropriate praise for doing a good job of hunting. Normally, she will search harder when asked to look again. She is driven by the fact that if she makes a find, she receives her toy. Ayla is also very social and is a good therapy dog for other team members when we are on deployment."

After searching the interior, Marilyn was assigned to shoring operations and to assist in removing rubble. By the end of their tour, she and Ayla were exhausted. "But that is normal when we are deployed on any mission," Marilyn said. "We learn how to manage stress. Ayla would unconditionally risk her life to look for a human being."

Working in close proximity to other dogs was challenging for some teams, but not for Boomer. He just went about his business and paid no attention to what was going on around him.

"The sense of accomplishment and the admiration of the victims' families is the only reward we need."

BOOMER

Labrador Retriever

Certified Cadaver Search

MICHAEL REHFELD

Gamber & Community Fire Company

Mike and Boomer from Carroll County, Maryland, joined the recovery operation four days after the plane hit the Pentagon. They traveled to the worksite in Mike's 1991 Ford Explorer, better known to the Gamber Fire Company as the "Boomer Mobile." For the next ten days, they searched for human remains in the Pentagon north parking lot.

Each day, Mike and Boomer went through rigid security checks before reporting to the "pit boss," who assigned them to a worksite, a 100- by 100-foot rubble pile. Boomer was always excited and anxious to go to work. "Search dogs don't know the difference between finds and no-finds as long as they get their reward at the completion of their work," Mike said. Boomer always got his Frisbee, so each work session was a "play time." Mike and his teammates played with him often to keep his attitude upbeat between search periods and work shifts.

When he's working, Boomer apparently lives up to his name. His trained indication when he finds something is to jump on Mike and then show him what he found. Mike stated that 85 pounds of Labrador jumping on you is only for the young!

After Boomer would indicate on remains, the mortician detail recovered, marked and tagged them for DNA sampling and identification. "Many people just don't understand the importance of having something to bury," Mike submitted.

"Boomer sometimes got very frustrated waiting in his Boomer Mobile to go to work. He learned to put his chin on the window and look unloved in order to get someone to come and pet him. He became an important part of stress management as a therapy dog for the other rescuers. He would play and love them, which really helped them cope with the event."

During one rest period, two police officers came by the vehicle to play with Boomer. While they petted him, they told Mike that they had been refueling their police cars when they saw the plane impact the Pentagon. "They had rushed to the scene to help with the severely burned patients. This was the first time they were able to relax and wanted to play with a search dog. That was really something," Mike said.

After the intensity of the work and the work environment at the crash site, Mike said that Boomer needed a period of retraining to allow him to refocus on small amounts of scent instead of the large amounts he encountered at the Pentagon.

"I don't view my dog as a hero. We were just doing a job that we both enjoy, helping others with their assigned jobs. Boomer is very focused on his task, with little interest in anything but pleasing me, and he sure has done that. It was our pleasure as Americans to serve the families of so many who sacrificed their lives for the cause of freedom. We had a sense of helping families get something back from this horrible attack on their loved ones. I only wish we could have done more."

CASSY

Labrador Retriever

Certified Cadaver Search

HEATHER ROCHE

Bay Area Recovery Canines

Cassy was almost ready to retire when she and her two search partners, Alley and Red, accompanied Heather to the Pentagon. Although Heather worked mainly with Alley, she made sure that Cassy also got to do what she loves best.

"Cassy searched many piles and found many items that helped bring closure for the families," Heather said. "She was trained with an active indication versus a passive indication like my two younger dogs. But she seemed to know that at this scene she should not touch the sources, and she did not. I was really proud of my old dog. She stayed focused and was thorough. It's always nice working a dog you've spent so many years with in the field. The partnership is deep, and it shows with results.

"Cassy was eager to work each day and was comfortable with all of the noise and commotion… she's been around it for many years. The devas-tation was so great to everything that sometimes you could not imagine what you were looking at. But the dog is just using her nose, so she doesn't experience that confusion.

"Cassy, Alley and Red rose above this difficult situation to pinpoint scent sources amid the debris and strong gas and burn odors. I was amazed at how well they did. It made me feel that all my hard work training these good dogs paid off instantly. I was glad I had dogs that specialized in human-remains detection, because we were able to do so much for the victims' families. It was an honor to be there when America needed us." Surely, Cassy concurs.

Cassy was an old pro at twelve years old when she worked the Pentagon. She knew the drill and always kept her focus despite the machinery that sometimes came very close to her.

Like all of the search dogs working at the Pentagon, Dusty worked tirelessly to the best of his ability to meet that challenge.

DUSTY

Labrador Retriever

FEMA Type I

MARY BERRY

New Mexico Task Force 1

When the World Trade Center was attacked, Mary and NM-TF1 were notified by FEMA to report to the Pentagon disaster site. They arrived on September 16 and were relieved of duty on September 22. Mary and Dusty worked the day shift, rising at 4:30 a.m. for breakfast and bus transport to the Pentagon and their 6 a.m. work shift.

"We were in the 'hot zone' by 7:30 a.m. and searched various areas of the building according to our assignments," Mary said. "The area was burned and wet, and there was twisted metal and broken glass everywhere. We would work for about an hour, then leave for rehab…decon, food, water and relief…then return for more search activity. Around noon, we would leave the hot zone again for lunch and the required decon of our Tyvek suits and boots and a bath for our dogs. We returned to the hot zone for more searching until about 5 p.m., went through another decon and were debriefed at our base of operation until our shift was over at 6 p.m. We finally got to bed about 10 or 11 at night.

"Dusty is not remains-detection certified, but he had been 'imprinted' in beginning-level training. The Pentagon was devoid of distractions such as dead animals and other smells, so whenever he sniffed an area intensely, I marked it as a possible remains site for our certified cadaver dog to check out later. It turned out he was always right.

"He worked happily and excitedly from the first day to the last, I think because I kept an upbeat attitude for his sake. Our team set up live finds for the dogs and gave them fun, happy exercises to keep them positive and upbeat. And he loves to be petted, so he interacted well with the other workers. People were often amazed at how calm and well mannered he was when not working.

"Dusty has a very strong and serious work ethic. Because of his work, numerous human remains were found, and we brought closure to those families. He just does his job the way he has been trained, and he loves doing it."

Reflecting on one of the lesser known benefits of the disaster work, Mary said, "…the dog's work brought new respect to our K-9 unit from the non-dog-handlers on our task force. And the other rescue workers learned a lot about search dogs and developed more respect for their abilities and level of training."

"…along with the many other handlers there, we responded to an unprecedented event in our history, filled with issues and situations never encountered before. Faced with those situations we took every precaution possible to ensure our dogs' safety and responded to the challenges before us."

GERRY

Belgian Malinois

Human-Remains Detection

FERNANDO FERNANDEZ

Senior FBI Agent: Elizabeth City, North Carolina

When Fernando arrived at the Pentagon with his canine partner, Gerry, at midday on September 15, he was completely unprepared for what he was about to experience.

"The various news media reports did little to accurately reflect the site and its impact," Fernando said. "In the parking lot, we were exposed to a mixture of overwhelming smells consisting of aviation fuel and decomposition, which drifted over to us from the debris piles. I saw several dogs, including Gerry, raising their heads and 'winding' toward the piles.

"I don't believe you can coin words to describe the dedication, sacrifice and tenacity exhibited by the dogs and their handlers. Neither the breed, size or specialty of the dogs, nor the affiliation of the handlers, whether law enforcement or volunteer, ever mattered. Everyone had the same sense of urgency, the willingness to contribute and get the job done to the best of his abilities.

"The dogs were stretched to their limits, and whether guided by a sense of urgency passed down the leash from their handlers or by the very drive we come to expect from them, they rarely let us down. As the shifts progressed, you could see them tire and even lose a little of the wag in their tails, but a quick rest period in an air-conditioned car, some water and even a little play seemed to regenerate them. They continued to return to the piles, conduct their searches, go through decontamination and repeat the process all over again throughout the course of their shifts.

"My own dog, who was relatively young at the time, very athletic and considered to be extremely high drive and hyper, would routinely end his day by lying down in his air crate, his head hanging out of the door while he consumed his meal from his bowl. As soon as he finished, he curled up and went to sleep until the next morning. He dreamed out loud as some dogs do, moving his legs as if he were running and softly barking. I hope those dreams were of happier experiences, like chasing a ball in an open field or running with a pack of his friends and getting into mischief.

"It was the combined perseverance, performance and tenacity of all of the dogs and handlers that made the Pentagon effort so successful. The mission was clear—to recover and identify the remains of all of the victims of this tragedy—and each dog and handler met and surpassed that goal. We wanted to bring closure to the families of the victims and to do it as thoroughly and professionally as we possibly could. That is what we train for.

"The fact that many of us worry about the health of our dogs based on their exposure to the terrain and search conditions is a reality. The long-term effects of such exposure are unknown. After losing my first K-9, Charo, to cancer, I pray each and every day that K-9 Gerry enjoys a long and fruitful life with me in retirement."

Gus was three years old and running field trials when the Oklahoma City bombing occurred. Ed decided that he wanted to help, so he trained Gus for search work and joined the Tennessee Task Force. Now Gus gets his training bumper as a reward for finding human remains instead of ducks.

Photo: Jocelyn Augustino/FEMA News

GUS

Labrador Retriever

FEMA Type 1, Certified Cadaver Search

ED APPLE

Tennessee Task Force 1

Photo: Jocelyn Augustino/FEMA News

Ed and Gus reported to the Pentagon as part of the seventy-six-member TN-TF1. They went to work two days after their arrival, after the engineers had mapped out the areas that were safe to search.

"We did some searching while they were still tearing apart the collapsed structure on the center slab," Ed explained. Gus moved easily amid the debris and indicated many areas where the teams should search for victims. "Inside the collapsed area, he found several places where they had removed remains prior to our arrival. When Gus alerted, he would give a bark and dig. The FBI would flag the spot and send in another team to search by hand, so Gus and I were not there when they made the find. I was told that in one place they found four victims, one of whom was a four-star general.

"Several times, when they were tearing apart a structure, they would see what appeared to be clothing or fabric, and I would send Gus up to search for any remains. If he walked right over it, that meant there was nothing there."

Unlike some of the working dogs, Gus never dragged Ed to the pile. "Gus is a former field-trial dog," Ed explained, "and just like any good trial dog, he's always under control and he always heels right next to me. But when I ask him to go to work, then he gets all excited."

Well, not always under control. "Gus loved the other workers, and it got so bad that when I walked through the compound, if anyone made eye contact with him, he would run to them. The FBI agents loved him, and he was good therapy for all of the workers. It was so devastating for everyone there. Our chaplain had to be replaced after three days because he just could not handle it any longer."

Ed decided to train Gus for search work after the Oklahoma City bombing in 1995. "Gus was about three at that time, and I decided I wanted to help. These field-trial Labs work like they are going after a flyer duck. You can't build that kind of drive into a dog. They are either born with it or they don't have it. Gus has done everything I've ever asked of him. You can't do any better than that."

Pentagon

JAKE

German Shepherd Dog

FEMA Type II

SAM BALSAM

Maryland Task Force 1

Called up on the FEMA Task Force Hotline, Sam and Jake reported to the Pentagon shortly after the attack and worked the search effort for the next eight days. Due to the fire conditions at the scene, Sam was often absorbed into rescue squads to assist with structural stabilization, so Jake's actual search time was limited. Yet despite being kenneled when not working, he always had a "ready-to-go" attitude and did everything Sam asked of him.

During breaks, Jake worked in other important ways. He was "Mr. Friendly" and always wanted to play with the other workers. "He came with me whenever I wasn't working," Sam said, "and we would play tug during breaks. He's a very upbeat dog!" Jake suffered minor burns to his feet from searching areas that were still hot from the fire, but that never stopped him from doing his job.

"I believe that all of the families and coworkers of the victims know that everything possible was done to save those that could be saved. The fire department deserves a tremendous amount of credit for fighting what most of them will never again see in their careers.

"Jake is no more a hero than any other disaster, police, arson or wilderness canine. He had a job to do and did it without any reservations...all for his toy. Like all other FEMA dogs, he is the product of years of intensive training. Of the highest caliber dogs, only a few successfully complete the FEMA program. It is the dedication of the team members at all levels that makes their success possible.

"These canine handler volunteers incur tremendous expenses to train and maintain these dogs during their careers. They have to purchase their own kennels, training and communication equipment, hearing and vision protection, disaster gear and special boots and vests, plus the cost of travel and lodging to attend training seminars to maintain the certification status of their dogs. When their dogs retire, they have the added expense of pain medications, joint supplements and extra veterinary care."

In 2000, Sam founded a nonprofit 501(c)(3) organization called Search and Rescue Assist to help SAR volunteers with the training of their dogs. The organization hopes to offset some of the expenses and thereby increase the quality of those dedicated teams.

*Jake is very calm and professional while working,
but he's a "regular dog" between work periods and is always willing to play.
Hugs are one of his favorite "rewards." He's proud to be one of
the multitalented, dedicated members of MD-TF1.*

"Maverick was the stress reliever of our group. On our last day while I was in the field, my teammates dressed him up and took his picture. The whole team had smiles on their faces, and I did too when I saw Mav. He just stood there wagging his tail with that smile on his face. He was very special to our team."

MAVERICK

Labrador Retriever

Certified Cadaver Search

ROSS RANDLETT

Prince William County Police

Ross was called up by the FBI Evidence Team to work the Pentagon disaster site. Maverick was nine years old and pushing retirement, and this turned out to be his last mission with Ross.

"We worked twelve-hour days," Ross began. "Mav was concerned and concentrated on his job, but otherwise he was his usual laid-back self. We had areas of debris to search and then would take a break while the next dog did the same thing. We mostly worked as a team, helping each other. Mav loves to work. He would work all day and all night if I asked him too. The only thing he ever wanted was to make me happy.

"On the third day, he cut his pad, so he stayed at staging for a couple of days and gave comfort to others. He was very good at putting smiles on people's faces and making them feel good. He has a knack for that. He is gentle and caring and loves to be loved. He was special to the whole team.

"*Hero* is a very strong word. Mav and I were just doing what we were trained to do. There was nothing in it for either of us. The heroes are not the ones who cleaned up this mess; they are the ones who died in this mess. Even so, Mav is my hero for having the will to do what he did. I was just along for the ride because he needed someone to drive him! He is just the finest dog, friend and companion that anyone can ever have. I am a lucky guy to have a one-of-a-kind dog like Mav."

Pentagon

NERO

German Shepherd Dog

FEMA Type I

ELIZABETH KREITLER

Virginia Task Force 1,
Search and Rescue Dogs of Maryland

As Elizabeth sat on the bus, awaiting security clearance, smoke was still billowing from the Pentagon impact zone. She recalled past deployments to Nairobi and Turkey. "It was unbelievable to be gearing up for a national disaster here at home," she said. Nero was her new canine partner, replacing her retired USAR German Shepherd, and this was their first mission together.

"Despite the heavy smoke, Nero never hesitated, and I was pleased with the way he dealt with such a stressful situation," Elizabeth said. "We went from very hot, smoke-filled offices to areas of charred, waterlogged, unrecognizable debris. Some debris was almost 2 feet high, like wet charcoal amid twisted metal, and there was a strong smell of death. Later, as we searched other offices, the pictures, slogans and artifacts gave a glimpse into the character of the people who worked so hard for the safety of our country, and I felt great pride in their dedication.

"Nero was very determined in his work, climbing over and through all the charry paste, which was sometimes 12 to 15 inches deep. Working deep in one pile with Nero, I found fifteen color photos, virtually undamaged. Nearby were pieces of human tissue.

"Nero's primary mission was to find live victims, but the fire and impact made that hope impossible. Still, he indicated parts of corpses that were sometimes unrecognizable and thus helped bring closure to some families. By the time the scene had been declared a recovery situation, Nero's job was finished, and special cadaver dogs were brought in to complete the search.

"Taking our first real break about 3:30 a.m. late that first night," Elizabeth recalled, "I remember that the sky behind me was clear and star-filled, and in front of me it was blurred by a heavy haze of smoke. To the left of the impact zone, the firefighters battled a blaze on the roof, and to the right, on the roof, waved the American flag that had been raised that afternoon. Next to me, Nero was lying down but upright. Occasionally, he would put his head down, but he stayed awake, watching, the rest of the night. I never did catch him sleeping.

"As on other deployments, the canines become great stress relievers for the other workers. Thus they get very little true down time, as people constantly come over to talk to them and give them a pat. This is just another part of their job, but it does make play for the dogs during their down time that much more important. The helpers at the decon station showed great care and concern for all of the canines, not worrying how wet they got from the water flying off their coats.

"When VA-TF1 was ready to leave, our team with our K-9s walked in formation to the collapsed area. A Navy chaplain said a prayer, and we all recited the Pledge of Allegiance. As we left, our colleagues from the other task forces and special disaster teams lined our route and clapped. It was very moving to be so honored by our peers."

Search dogs must possess intelligence, agility, perseverance and dedication, but their most important quality is courage.

NIKKO

German Shepherd Dog

Certified Cadaver, Water Search, Wilderness
Live Find

SONJA K. NORDSTROM

California Rescue Dog Association

Sonja and Nikko were contacted by the FBI to assist in the recovery and search operation. They worked September 20 through September 27, the last week of the recovery effort at the Pentagon.

"At first, Nikko, like many of the other dogs, was confused by the overwhelming odor from the disaster," Sonja said. "Cadaver-detection dogs are trained and tested on minute amounts of blood and body fluids, and in a disaster scene such as this, human scent was everywhere. To help Nikko deal with this, during the first morning I supported and reinforced him with enthusiastic praise when he made a find. By afternoon, he was working through all of the distractions without a problem. Once he understood what was expected of him, he hunted strongly and enthusiastically.

"We were both very mission-oriented, motivated and positive," Sonja said. "If I had shown negative emotion, Nikko would have fed off my attitude. It is a fallacy that dogs get 'depressed' working such a scene. Depression is not a part of the equation for a dog. If a handler does not behave as the dog expects, with the same enthusiasm as in training, then the dog will start to shut down because the handler is not reinforcing the dog's indications.

"Every time we went to work, Nikko pulled me out to the search area, jumping and barking in anticipation until I released him to go to work. We were tasked with finding human remains to be used for DNA identification. Nikko found many remains from an unknown number of victims."

Nikko's days were twelve-plus hours long, structured and routine, and he rotated through about four search sessions a day. When he was working, he was rewarded with a rousing game of tug. "He loved it, and I'd usually leave the search area covered in muddy pawprints from him playing and jumping on me," Sonja said. "He was very happy and driven. Some of the other workers remarked how he was not distracted around all of the noise, heavy equipment, people and commotion. At night, we went back to the hotel and hit the sack. During the night, he sometimes barked in his sleep as if he were still searching.

"One of the best compliments we received was from another handler who watched us from the edge of the pile as we worked. She remarked that Nikko and I seemed to feed off each other when searching, that together there was positive electricity flowing between us. That is what I strive for with my working dog—a connection, a mutual admiration and satisfaction through our work.

"Working at the Pentagon and being able to contribute during the most horrific attacks on this country was one of the most memorable and valuable things that Nikko and I ever shared. It was a privilege for us to serve there. That experience alone validated Nikko's life and all the effort I put into his training.

"He was my partner, my buddy and my protector…he served the people of the United States with undying enthusiasm and dedication, without complaint, in sometimes miserable and physically painful conditions."

Sonja called Nikko her "little wonderdog." He worked with an "all-business" attitude and was always ready to serve, any place, any time. His most important mission was at the Pentagon with Sonja. "My emotions ran high as I watched him work with such motivation, precision and dedication to his job," Sonja said.

The Pentagon mission was the first time Otto's specialized wilderness, human-remains detection and urban disaster skills were utilized in one mission.

OTTO

German Shepherd Dog

FEMA Type II, Certified Cadaver Search

SONJA HERITAGE

Virginia Task Force 1

"Our typical work day was 0700–1900 hours. Suit up. Wait for an assignment. Work your site. Decon. Repeat. Repeat. Repeat. Repeat."

Sonja was an instructor at the FEMA CSS course in Seattle when she saw the TV news report of the first plane hitting the World Trade Center. When the skies finally opened for flights, the General Electric Company donated a Learjet to transport disaster-search canine teams to the East Coast to deploy. Sonja and three teammates from Virginia headed for the Pentagon.

By the time Sonja and Otto arrived in Washington on September 13, the mission focus had changed to one of recovery, requiring Otto's human-remains detection (HRD) skills to be integrated with his urban disaster search work.

"Otto is cross-trained for HRD, and there were many finds," Sonja said, "so Otto remained highly motivated during the next two weeks. He helped bring closure to many of the victims' families, who deserved more, but I know we helped them in the long run. It was also very therapeutic for me, just knowing we could help.

"People would just stand back and watch Otto work. He's a big handsome dog, the type you remember; he has a presence. He knows his job and worked well off lead with very little input from me. He is a professional, and I am always amazed by his performance under pressure. He is honest and steadfast and true, and if a search problem doesn't work out, it's always my fault...always. He drives *me*.

"We, the handlers, know what we are getting into. These wonderful dogs are there because we brought them into this chaos. They work out of trust and love of 'the game.' That drive is pure, and it demands respect. Otto has changed my life. He has made me step up to the plate and deliver as unselfishly as he does."

PACY

Golden Retriever

Certified Cadaver, Wilderness, Water Search

JEANIE MARSHALL

Chesapeake Search Dogs

Jeanie was called to the Pentagon when the DC Metropolitan Police Department requested help from the canine teams of the Chesapeake Search Dogs. During her twelve-day tour, her Golden Retriever Pacy celebrated his second birthday. There was little time to celebrate, however. Assigned to work the 3 p.m. to 11 p.m. shift, Pacy had a more important job, searching for the remains of the victims who perished in the attack.

"Pacy was always focused on his task and never lost his enthusiasm for the search," Jeanie said. "He was more tired toward the end of our deployment, but he never lost his desire to search. He is a true partner and can often sense things about me that no one else can."

When Pacy wasn't working the debris piles, he was his typical Golden Retriever self, providing therapy for the other rescue workers. "The dogs gave them a sense of home. They identified our dogs with their own pets, and that gave them some much-needed comfort during such a difficult time."

Pacy is also a certified therapy dog. Jeanie is a special-education teacher and takes him to work with her to help with the children. She and Pacy also go to pediatric wards in hospitals to visit the young patients there. "We tried to go to nursing homes," Jeanie said, "but being a Golden Retriever, Pacy had a difficult time ignoring the tennis balls on the bottom of the walkers."

Pacy and his teammates enabled 184 families to bury their loved ones. Thanks to the dogs' work, the victims' families were able to find closure.

"Whether my dog is a hero is not up to me to say, " said Jeanie. "Pacy was there doing what everyone else, human and canine, was there to do...what he was trained to do. He is a true partner and best friend."

Behind that sweet Golden Retriever face lies the heart of a true search professional. Pacy loves to work and never gives up on the job.

Pentagon

"At first, the mortuary staff was skeptical, but as each day went by, they learned to read the dogs and would be right there before you even had the chance to tell them the dog hit. By the end of the rotation, the workers would often run over to the dogs when they couldn't decide if something was human or not."

RED

Labrador Retriever

Certified Cadaver Search

HEATHER ROCHE

Bay Area Recovery Canines

Red was newly certified in cadaver search when she, Heather and canine search partners Alley and Cassy were called to the Pentagon on September 16. This was Red's first real mission and, although she bowed to the experience of her teammates, she proved to Heather that she could handle a tough job when necessary.

Like her two Lab partners, Red was eager to work each day and was comfortable from the start with the noise and commotion. "I wasn't sure how she would do with the overwhelming scent picture, but she was able to pinpoint sources even though she was not as experienced as my other dogs," Heather said.

"We were directed to each pile by a 'yard boss,' who kept track of which pile was ready for a dog after the other agencies had finished spreading it and sifting through for evidence. Red ignored the other workers and kept her focus despite the machinery that sometimes came very close to her. At times, she would smell a larger source in a nearby pile, and I would have to convince her to keep working the lesser-scent pile. Sometimes I couldn't tell what the source was, so at times I didn't believe my dog, but she was

always right. The old saying 'Trust your dog' can get blurred when you just can't imagine what you are looking at."

Red and Heather worked the day shift, and it was hot on the parking-lot asphalt surface. "Because of health issues, water was at a minimum while we were working on the piles. They didn't want us drinking water that might be contaminated with airborne particles. The dogs fared better since we rotated out every few piles, and they were thoroughly washed every time they left the hot zone." After decon, Heather and Red would go off to toss a toy just to take a mental break from the work. "The dogs needed that fun time, too," she said.

"September 11 was not about the world knowing who my dogs are and what they do. I know what they have accomplished and who they helped. These dogs and their handlers train hard and dedicate so much of their lives to being ready when the pager goes off."

Ronin instinctively knew the seriousness and magnitude of his job at the Pentagon. He is a very sensitive Labrador Retriever, described by Jeaneen as "all heart."

RONIN

Labrador Retriever

FEMA Type 1

JEANEEN MCKINNEY

New Mexico Task Force 1

In addition to his career with New Mexico Task Force 1, Ronin is an important member of the Scottsdale, Arizona, Police Department K-9 Unit.

Five days after the 9/11 attacks, Jeaneen's task-force pager summoned her to the Pentagon. With NM-TF1, she and Ronin worked at the site from September 16 to September 23.

"As we were walking into the Pentagon, it was pitch black inside the building, and I had this awful feeling of 'Omigosh, I could lose my dog in here!'," Jeaneen recalled. "But Ronin? He was fine, all excited and ready to go.

"Before we went in to work the building, we suited up in Tyvek suits, goggles, respirators, gloves, boots and masks. Ronin just looked at me with big eyes, and his ears perked up. I realized he had never seen me quite like this. Even my voice was muffled by the mask. I leaned down to pet him and said his name, and he wagged his tail.

"Ronin is trained to find only live, and by the time we got there, I realized that probably would not happen. On our first time in, we followed a cross-trained dog who was hitting on many places. Then Ronin just bounded in, moving very fast, and all of a sudden he went stock still. He put his nose down and slowly traced the area with his nose. He gave me a very readable indication on human remains and basically worked that way all week.

"When he would indicate, I called out on the radio. The FBI came in with their lights and found us in the blackness and started digging. Later, they would report to our search-team manager and confirm the find.

"In some offices there were still half-filled coffee cups on the desk and pictures that were undamaged. You could feel the people who had been there. It just gave me more resolve and motivated me to search that much harder. It was really a privilege for us to be there.

"Decon was set up at the exit from the hot zone, and we had to go through immediately after each search, so the dog got his shower after each time in. Between searches, we went to the rehab tents set up by the Salvation Army and the Red Cross. When Ronin and I walked around the tent areas, the other workers would ask to pet him. He got very good at sizing people up, and when he saw a 'target,' he would slide down onto his back and roll over for a tummy rub every time. Those times were important for all of us.

"There is no way you could ever train for such a huge experience. But the dogs are more sensitive than we think, and they know when it is the real thing. Ronin helped to bring closure to the friends and families of the victims. He is all heart!"

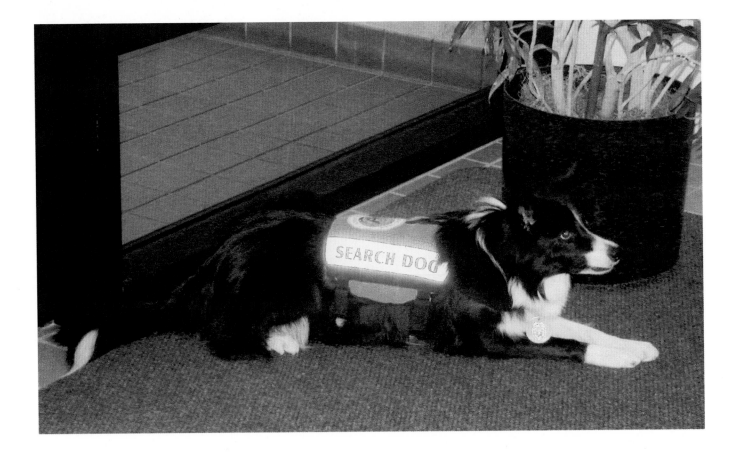

Sage came to the United States from the United Kingdom when she was ten weeks old. During 9/11, she proved that she was an All-American dog! Trained jointly by her handlers, Diane Whetsel and Dr. Kim Lark, Sage works for both with equal courage and enthusiasm.

SAGE

Border Collie

FEMA Type I

DIANE WHETSEL AND DR. KIM LARK

New Mexico Task Force 1,
Search Dogs Southwest

Sage was called to work at the Pentagon with FEMA-certified handler Dr. Kim Lark, as her owner, Diane, was recovering from an injury. Sage is one of the few FEMA-certified dogs that is certified with two handlers, doing so before she was two years old. Had she not been so precocious, a valuable K-9 resource would have gone untapped during a time when every nose counted.

Sage and Kim worked the day shift, starting at the crack of dawn and working late into the day. Police bomb-detection dogs searched the task-force buses when they arrived at the Pentagon each day. After heavy-rescue teams had secured an area, the K-9 teams went in to search. "It was all done under the watchful eye of the FBI and other government agencies," Diane said.

"I was told that Sage was in high spirits throughout the duration of her deployment," Diane noted. "Although she was more tired at the end of her tour, she has very efficient recuperative abilities, and her work ethic kept her driven to continue."

Diane's teammates also assured her that Sage was always a perfect lady and, when she was not searching, she continued to work as a stress reliever for the friends she made at the worksite. "Simply petting Sage or scratching her ears helped her human teammates settle down after a stressful day on the scene. Many of the NM-TF1 team members had never had the opportunity to watch Sage or the other USAR dogs in action. Through this tragic event, they learned firsthand the true value of the canines' search and rescue skills."

During the days following the attack, Diane, along with the rest of the nation, watched helplessly while Sage and her teammates did the jobs they had been trained for. "Sage was there to help the victims' families find closure by finding their remains. Every dog that worked 9/11 is a hero to me. The FEMA dogs are some of the best-trained canines in the world, and we can all be very proud of them and their handlers for the work they performed...I only wish I could have been there working alongside my own little canine hero."

"There's nothing that can replace the precision of a dog's nose, and absolutely nothing can replace a dog's heart." Sky remained happy and "driven" even after failing to find live victims. "She is proud to serve her country," Bob said.

SKY

Labrador Retriever

FEMA Type 1

BOB SESSIONS

Maryland Task Force 1

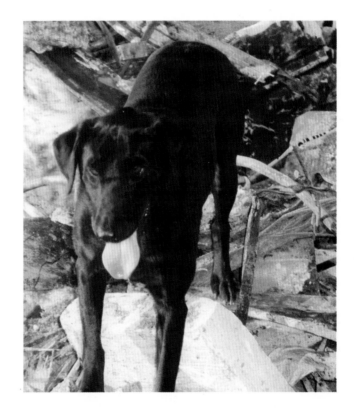

Bob and MD-TF1 were one of the first FEMA task forces to arrive after the plane hit the Pentagon. Bob worked with his two Labrador Retrievers, Sky for live find and Thunder for remains search. Bob used Sky for live find during their first three days of deployment.

"We searched the collapsed areas of the building to make sure there were no live personnel still trapped inside," Bob said. "Our shifts were twelve-plus hours long, but Sky never seemed to tire and worked well as long as I maintained a positive attitude and kept her pocket Frisbee handy."

Sadly, there were no live finds to be made, but nevertheless, Sky was always eager to continue working. There were times when she sat patiently in 6 inches of cold, mucky water, waiting with Bob for their next search orders.

"Sky was also a comfort to the rescuers, who also worked long hours," Bob said. "She loved them all and always wanted to play with them.

"We later learned that some part of all of those lost in this attack were recovered and identified. Each family now had a part of their lost loved one for burial. Sky truly embodies the American spirit."

SMOKEY

Labrador Retriever

Certified Cadaver Search

GEORGE MCMAHON

Northern Virginia Search and Rescue Dogs

George was deployed to the Pentagon on September 11 after being paged by the FBI. He searched with his cadaver canine Smokey in the parking lot and also worked as the "yard boss," coordinating the work shifts of the canine teams.

Smokey was anxious to get to work, but on his third day out he cut his paw on a piece of metal. VMAT's Dr. Keith Gold cleaned the wound and ordered antibiotics and a day of rest.

"Smokey was in no pain and he was unhappy that he was not working," George said. "Dr. Gold suggested I use a boot to protect his paw when he was searching. Well, that lasted about two minutes—the boot was gone! So Dr. Gold decided to wrap his paw with duct tape. Smokey started running around without any problems and couldn't wait for his turn to work. Each time we came off the work zone, we removed the wrap to check the wound and let it air-dry. His paw never got wet. From that moment on, everyone on the worksite called him 'Duct Tape.' Smokey's drive never slowed down, even when he got hurt.

"We had members of the Puerto Rico Military Mortuary on our assignment, and very few of them spoke English. At first, they were afraid of the K-9s, but after a couple of days, they got used to them and even asked me if they could play with Smokey.

"*Hero* is a strong word. Smokey is a dog that loves his job. Like the other canines who have been trained for rescue and cadaver search, he does it willingly and enjoys doing it. For him, this is not work; he is out to have fun. I was glad that Smokey and I could do a job that most canines are not trained for and that we could allow some families to have closure.

"One year after the event, we returned for a memorial service and burial at Arlington National Cemetery for some of the remains. The children of the victims loved playing with the dogs, and it allowed them to talk about it. We were thanked constantly by all the people there for helping them.

"The next time you see a service dog of any type, know that there are a lot of people who have put time, effort and skill into teaching the canine to do a job, and that the dog is doing it because he loves it."

> *"Smokey is a dog that loves his job," George said. "He, like others that have been trained for search and rescue and cadaver recovery, does his job willingly and enjoys doing it."*

STRYKER

German Shepherd Dog

Certified Cadaver Search

ALICE HANAN

Maryland-National Capital Park Police

Assisting the Montgomery County Police Department, Stryker located a homicide victim wrapped in plastic and buried 5 feet underground.

Officer Alice Hanan and her partner K-9 Stryker have been together since 1997, but their biggest challenge faced them on September 16, 2001, when they responded to an FBI plea to join the canine search teams at the Pentagon.

"Locating human remains is a gruesome task that can deeply affect the emotions of the search dog," Alice said. "Stryker was always focused and effective whenever he was working, but over our eleven-day deployment, he lost his normal playful attitude. Yet his courage and determination allowed him to press on. He helped his country in a time of need by doing his job of locating victims' remains, and that allowed those families to have closure.

"In addition to disaster work, Stryker works day in and day out for his community. His services have been employed to locate everything from lost children and murder victims to illegal drugs and poachers. He's been called up to search rape and murder crime scenes to find evidence, weapons and more. He revels in assisting his fellow officers whenever they need to locate something that a dog's nose can find," Alice concluded, "and he does all this for a tennis ball and a pat on the head."

Stryker is surely an all-around American hero. For five consecutive years, he was named the Maryland-National Capital Park Police K-9 Officer of the Year and has earned several other state and community awards along the way.

Stryker is a multitalented dog who is certified in obedience, agility, area search, article search, tracking, trailing, search and rescue, narcotics and cadaver detection.

Thor and the other Pentagon search K-9s have received many certificates, plaques and medals. They were also invited to attend the Burial of Unidentified Remains at the Arlington National Cemetery on September 11, 2002.

THOR

German Shepherd Dog

Wilderness Live Find, Cadaver Search

BLAIR MILLER

Fairfax County Fire and Rescue

When Blair first heard the news of the attack on Washington, DC, he felt certain that he and Thor would be deployed. Three days later, the FBI called him with orders to report to the Pentagon.

The first canine teams to arrive at the site were FEMA search and rescue teams looking for survivors. Blair and Thor were a part of the next wave and were assigned to search for human remains amid the concrete rubble, burned office fixtures, airplane parts and personal effects.

"In addition to being a live-find dog, Thor has had additional training as a cadaver dog," Blair said. "FEMA had determined that it had become unsafe for the search teams to enter the collapsed building. The debris was removed from the collapsed area and dumped onto the Pentagon parking lots. Bulldozers would spread the rubble across the parking lot, and the K-9 teams literally walked through it, searching for human remains. Some pieces were as small as a quarter. Other human material was hidden below the rubble, and the dogs had to deal with broken glass, concrete dust, sharp protruding objects, asbestos, jet fuel and occasional small fires. Twenty-nine K-9 teams worked twelve-hour shifts for thirteen straight days."

Blair and Thor reported to the decon tent several times during each work shift. With each visit, the vets gave Thor a bath and complete physical exam, checked him for cuts and abrasions and flushed his eyes to remove dust and contaminants. "It was so gratifying to come off the rubble at 3 a.m. and see the vets there, ready to take care of our dogs," Blair recalled.

"We were all deeply touched by the tremendous outpouring of support we received from so many people…cards and posters from schoolchildren, delicious meals prepared by a volunteer chef sent in by the Salvation Army, huge pallets of donated dog food for the dogs and countless hours donated by the veterinarians. So many people showed their appreciation in so many meaningful ways."

While Thor sits in Blair's front yard and barks at the school buses as they pick up the neighborhood children, he has no idea of the incredible role he played for two and a half weeks in September 2001.

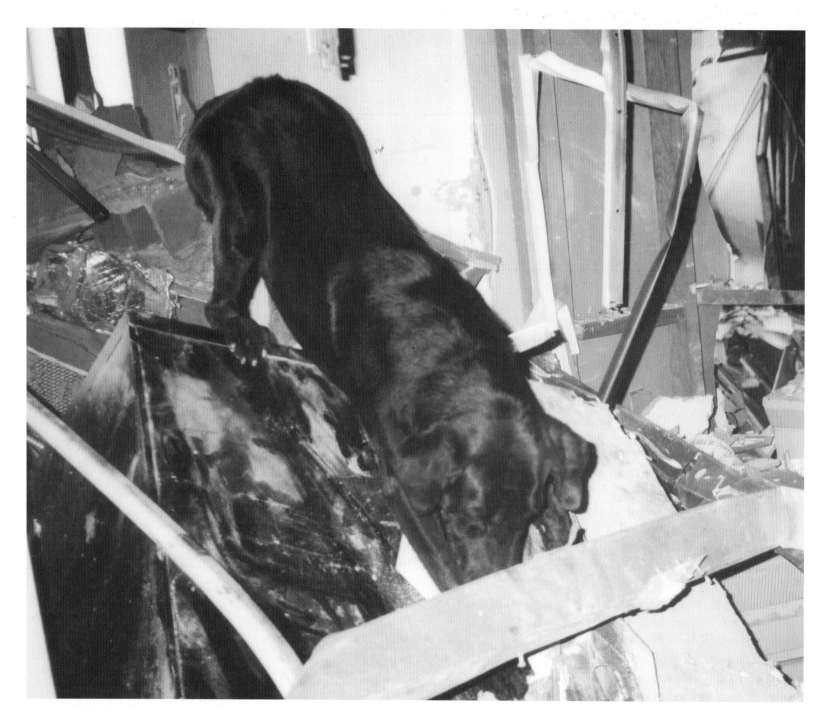

THUNDER

Labrador Retriever

FEMA Type 1, Cadaver Search

BOB SESSIONS

Maryland Task Force 1

When Bob was called up with MD-TF1 to join the search effort at the Pentagon, he brought his senior search dog, Thunder, out of retirement to work with his younger canine, Sky. He took Thunder in to work on day four of his deployment.

"Thunder turned into a younger dog again for this incident. She searched through 2 to 5 feet of charred, wet debris, looking for the remains of the Pentagon personnel who perished in the attack," Bob said. "She worked very deliberately and would thoroughly grid the debris area, then do a focused bark alert on any human remains she located, even very small pieces. She seemed to understand that this was not a typical search event, that it was indeed a 'big deal.' Like her sister, Sky, she was eager to be working, always waiting for her pocket Frisbee toy. She, too, comforted the rescue workers with her playful attitude.

"Thunder was a true veteran who also served in Hurricane Fran, in Hurricane Floyd and at Oklahoma City for ten days following the April [1995] bombing. She had many finds in police and wilderness search. She and Sky were proud to serve their country, and both dogs truly represent the American spirit of self-help and service to others."

Thunder became a television star when she was featured on America's Most Wanted *in the show's coverage of the memorial service commemorating the Oklahoma City bombing.*

TUCKER

German Shepherd Dog

Certified Cadaver Search

GAMBLE MCCOWN

Search and Rescue Dogs of Maryland

Called to the Pentagon by the DC Metro Police Department, Gamble and Tucker worked remains recovery in the lower parking lot at the Pentagon for seven days. "Tucker woke up each day ready to go to work because he received lots of rewards and praise for his search efforts," Gamble said.

"Between searches, we would play, play, play, and that kept Tucker's attitude happy and upbeat," she relayed. "A lot of the other work crews were very pleased to see Tucker work a pile, and many times we would receive literally a 'thumbs up' from some of the agencies that were working there. He just did an awesome job. He was a bit stressed on some days, when a lot of heavy machinery was operating within a few feet of us, but that improved after they stopped running the heavy equipment near the dogs while they were working.

"Tucker is a hard-working dog who was trained well and has always done his best. He was very dedicated to his task at the Pentagon, and I admire him for what he does and has done. This is why I got into search, knowing we did all we could to recover the remains of the loved ones who died so they could finally be put to rest in a respectable way. I am so grateful for being able to do this work with a dog like Tucker.

"I never thought of him as a hero. He just did what he was taught, thanks to an incredible work ethic that was instilled into him at an early age. It enabled him to step up to the plate in a very hazardous situation and do the job he loved. I don't think there was anything more that dog could have done to show his excellence.

"I have read the definition of a hero: feats of courage or nobility of purpose, especially one who has risked or sacrificed his or her life. Yes, Tucker is courageous, but he would have it no other way."

Tucker, also known as "the Handsome One," might also be called "the Awesome One" for the recovery work he did at the Pentagon.

The Fresh Kills Landfill

Canine Recovery Task Force, Staten Island, New York

Within hours of the collapse of the Twin Towers, the city of New York began the torturous process of removing the millions of tons of debris from the fallen World Trade Center. Hauled by truck, then barge and again by truck, the rubble was moved in an endless cortège across the Upper New York Bay to the Fresh Kills landfill on Staten Island. Mixed in with the labyrinthine mass were countless pieces of human remains, the victims who had perished during the attacks.

Fresh Kills is the largest landfill in the world, encompassing 3,000 acres. After fifty years in operation, it was officially closed on July 4, 2001. However, it was reopened on September 11 as the final site for the massive amounts of debris moved from the World Trade Center. Although Staten Island is actually situated much more closely to New Jersey than it is to any portion of New York State, it is one of the five boroughs that make up New York City; each of which is also a county of New York State. Staten Island is the county of Richmond.

To aid in the search for human remains, the New York City Police Department asked Bruce Barton, Director of Rescue International, Chief

of Northeast Search and Rescue, Inc. and a thirty-year SAR veteran and K-9 handler, to organize a task force of recovery-dog teams and support personnel to search for remains at the landfill. Volunteer search teams were called up from New York, New Jersey, Pennsylvania and Ohio. Several more teams, notified by their local sheriffs or their county SAR groups, also joined the effort, working under Rescue International. Barton coordinated the K-9 task force during the two-week recovery operation. Over 60 canines and 300 people responded to the Fresh Kills Landfill Canine Recovery Task Force search effort.

Barton set up a command post and base camp for the K-9 teams, including a supply tent where workers were equipped with hazardous-materials suits, respirator masks, safety helmets,

Amir Findling and his dog Radar wait for rescue workers at the Fresh Kills landfill to rake out the pile, making it easier for the dog to search for remains of the victims of the World Trade Center attack.

rubber gloves and work gloves; a large tent next to the worksite where he kept a grid map of the work areas and assigned the search teams to work shifts in specific areas; and a tent for veterinary care and decontamination for the dogs.

The canine teams began arriving on Staten Island on September 16. Affectionately called "dump dogs" by the rescue crews, most of the dogs were wilderness-search canines that were cross-trained in cadaver work and human-remains detection (HRD). In addition to the K-9 teams, 50 to 100 law-enforcement officers a day from state and federal agencies had already begun working the pile with rakes and hoes, looking for any remnant of evidence or remains.

The canines deployed to Staten Island were specialists in cadaver search and recovery and HRD. Cadaver dogs have been trained to locate bodies and body parts. The HRD canine has been fine-tuned to search large areas for minute particles, such as a drop of blood, a bone chip or a tooth. SAR handlers sometimes compare cadaver training to a high school degree and the HRD level to a PhD.

The search environment for the dogs was daunting. Huge machinery and equipment operated around the clock: sanitation trucks deposited the debris in enormous piles; backhoes removed the larger pieces; and bulldozers spread the debris out to be raked, sifted and searched. Methane gases seeped from the decomposing matter under the newly deposited debris.

Despite the heavy machinery and equipment operating around the clock at Fresh Kills, the rescue K-9s worked diligently and flawlessly.

Barton assigned one or two support people to each K-9 team—one to check for any hazards that the dogs might encounter and another to carry a 5-gallon bucket for collecting and transfering materials from the finds. When a dog made a find, it was tagged with the dog's team number and taken to the forensics tent to be catalogued for verification and future DNA identification. The handlers had to navigate around intimidating pieces of construction equipment—noisy, moving and unpredictable—while at the same time keeping their dogs focused and controlled. The dogs provided the final search for those tiny pieces of human tissue that were unrecognizable to the human eye.

Most of the K-9 teams searched at the landfill for two- and three-day rotations; only a few teams worked for the entire operation. Working twelve-hour shifts, they would spend about forty-five minutes searching a pile and then rest for about an hour and a half before reporting back to the pile. After each rotation on the pile, the dogs were taken to the decon tent, where they were examined and cleaned. At the end of each work shift, the dogs reported back to the command post for a full decon bath.

"Our biggest problem was getting hot water to wash the dogs," Barton said. "There was not much of a water supply. We finally got a heater for warm-water baths. When VMAT came, things got a lot better."

The Animal Planet Mobile Vet Clinic arrived at Fresh Kills mid-tour. The dogs finally were given veterinary exams in addition to the decon process after their shifts. Between shifts, the handlers often gathered at the command post or the Animal Planet trailer and sat on one of the many white buckets, sometimes sharing their feelings about the enormity of their task. Many slept in their cars and trucks at night. Others stayed at "Home Port," the National Guard Armory, which was set up with beds, food and showers for the handlers.

The canine search effort at Fresh Kills was disbanded on September 29. Most of the handlers who worked at that site do not consider themselves or their dogs heroes. They were simply partners with their canines, doing what they were trained to do and hoping for the best possible outcome: providing closure, allowing the victims' loved ones to say goodbye.

"The level of dedication in training a dog to perform this service is almost obsessive," Lorrie said. "We want them to be the best because of the life-and-death situations they train for. The dogs don't know that, but the handlers do."

CLAIRE

Border Collie

Certified Cadaver Search

LORRIE CLEMMO

New Jersey Task Force 1,
Northeast Search and Rescue

Lorrie's deployment with the Canine Recovery Task Force to Fresh Kills with Claire was her second tour during the two weeks following the September 11 attacks. She and her other Border Collie, Blitz, had already spent two weeks searching for survivors at Ground Zero with NJ-TF1. Now she and Claire would search instead for victim remains at the landfill.

"Claire is an all-business dog and is always ready to work," Lorrie said, "but she became tired as the days progressed. Between searches she either slept or sometimes played ball with the rescue workers. Claire loves to search and was at least able to bring closure to some of the victims' families.

"Our task force dogs train not only in scent detection but also in agility, obedience and directional commands. They all worked the disaster scenes magnificently with the limited training they have had for a disaster of this magnitude. These canines showed professionalism and did a deed that no human could have done. They saved time and man-hours in locating many bodies and human remains. Their work provided closure in a timely fashion to many of the family members and department members of the victims. There is no electronic device that can compare to the talent of these specially trained dogs."

When Lorrie pulls out her training gear, Claire and her brother, Blitz, switch instantly into search mode, ready to go to work.

Fresh Kills Landfill

CORY

Labrador Retriever

Certified Cadaver Search, Wilderness Live Find

BOB BRODY

Brighton Volunteer Ambulance Urban Disaster
K-9 Team

After working with the emergency medical team at Ground Zero for three days following the attacks on the World Trade Center, Bob was summoned by Rescue International's Canine Recovery Task Force to work with Cory at Fresh Kills. The sight of that vast rubble pile and the chaos of heavy equipment did not faze Cory in the least. She was more than ready to hit the pile and go to work.

Cory worked successfully for years after serving at Fresh Kills.

Cory is cross-trained for live find and cadaver search, so she is always eager to work, regardless of the task. "Cory is a very high-drive dog, and she has had lots of experience in search work," Bob explained. "Finding human remains is just as exciting for her as a live find. Whenever she indicated on something, my backups and I would 'praise off' Cory, then tell her to go back to work. This technique worked very well for us. She was so excited after one find, she ran over to a table located between the rows of debris and grabbed a water bottle and brought it to me so we could play fetch. Her reward at the end of every shift was to play Frisbee.

"The heavy-equipment operators and police officers were impressed with Cory's ability to work so well with hand signals and whistle commands, especially off lead around all of the noise and heavy equipment. We would work in thirty- to forty-five-minute slots, then rest for about ninety minutes before starting another search.

"At the end of her work shift, she was de-conned at the Animal Planet rescue trailer. The bath was not her favorite time! Then we returned to our base of operation on the USS *Comfort,* where my backups and I played Frisbee with Cory...on the ship's deck amid the machine guns."

Cory was always friendly and upbeat with everyone and provided some much-needed emotional relief for the police officers who were raking through the debris at the worksite. "But is she a hero? No," Bob said. "A hard worker and dedicated searcher? Emphatically yes! She comes from a line of championship duck hunters. I cannot take credit for her Olympic-quality work ethic, focus and drive. She is a gift from God, intended to help us all."

Cory was never intimidated by all of the heavy equipment. She was more than happy to hop aboard this dozer.

Nancy asked, "Please don't forget to thank the American people for all the concern, love and support they gave our dogs during and after 9/11. Semper Fido…"

JAZZ

German Shepherd Dog

Certified Cadaver Search, Wilderness Live Find

NANCY BROOKS

Ramapo Rescue Dog Association

"Search and rescue dogs and their handlers are attached at the heart, not the end of a leash."

Nancy and Jazz were called out to work at the Fresh Kills site with the Ramapo Rescue Dog Association. After three cancellations, they were finally deployed to Staten Island to work with the Canine Recovery Task Force.

Nancy said that Jazz must have sensed the tragedy of 9/11, as her emotional state was "I don't like this, but I'll do my job." Jazz has a very strong work ethic and thus was very willing to work despite the intimidating work environment.

"On her first day out, she worked well on the areas she was tasked to search. At least two of her finds were verified as human remains. In training, when Jazz makes a live find, the first thing she does is go to the subject, wagging her tail, and licks his face. Then she returns to me (just as Lassie did with Timmy), and if I ask her did she find, she will spin wildly around, wagging her tail. Then she happily returns to the subject, looking back over her shoulder as if to say, 'Come on, hurry up, let's go!'

"After all the work she did that first day, she still loved meeting all the new people. Most seemed surprised that a German Shepherd could be so friendly and loving. Some even asked to have their picture taken with her, and Jazz happily posed with anyone who stood beside her."

On her second day of work Jazz developed diarrhea, so Nancy took her off the site and spent some time working her on her second-most-important job: boosting worker morale. Jazz visited everyone assigned to her work area— US Army, NYPD, FDNY, FBI—anyone who was connected to the worksite. Everyone needed the warm and fuzzy distraction, and Jazz lapped up the attention.

Nancy said that she does consider Jazz a hero. "She is an ordinary search and rescue canine that performed in an extraordinary situation far better than any of us could have imagined, as did all of the canines that reported [to the various sites after the September 11 attacks]. We knew the dogs were good, but they surprised us all by doing the wonderful job that they did. It reaffirmed the reason to train, train and train some more, on all those freezing, hot, humid, rainy, snowy, miserable days, when we all say, 'And we're doing this because…?'. Then there's the memory of 9/11, and the complaining stops and the day's training doesn't seem so bad after all. The bond that develops between a dog and handler is one that few people would understand. It was very special before 9/11, but it has only gotten stronger since that time."

"For the most part, my dogs ignored everyone else unless the workers sought them out. Then they waited patiently while the workers petted, hugged and talked to them. Then it was back to work again."

JERRY

German Shepherd Dog

Certified Cadaver Search

SUE LAVOIE

Ramapo Rescue Dog Association

"One night, I had to give my dogs a bath from a fire hose connected to a fire hydrant. They weren't happy about that! Another night, we slept on board a ship that was docked at the National Guard Armory. The creaking noises and the ladder we had to climb to the bedrooms were something that my dogs and I had not experienced before!"

Sue was called with her unit, Ramapo Rescue Dogs, by the NYPD to deploy to Fresh Kills on September 18. She worked with her two German Shepherds, Jerry and Socks, until September 27, two days before the canine search operation was discontinued.

"I was glad I had both dogs to work," Sue explained, "because each could have a break and not have to work quite so many hours. Jerry just loves to work! Even when he was tired, as soon as he saw me put on the Tyvek suit and pick up his toy, he was charged and ready for work.

"As I saw how good a job Jerry was doing, I worked him more than Socks, and he became my primary working dog. He actually improved with each day. The positive reinforcement he got each time he found remains made him want to find more.

"At first, the work was difficult for the dogs because they were told to find human and cadaver scent, and it was everywhere, on everything, on every piece of debris. When we told them to 'Find,' they looked at us as if to say 'it's everywhere.' But within the first day, they learned to differentiate between the generalized scent and the actual remains they were to find.

"One big distraction for the dogs was all the food that was mixed in with the debris. There had been restaurants in the buildings, and we had to search through large amounts of fish, chicken and other food from those restaurants. But the dogs did a great job of discriminating and understanding what we wanted.

"One time, when I was working Jerry, we were requested to search a specific pile of debris in which a New York police officer's gun holster had been found. The other NYPD officers wanted to find their comrade's remains that were most likely in the same general area of the holster. I took Jerry to the pile and worked him while thirty NYPD officers watched. And yes, we did find remains. Afterward, an NYPD officer came over to my truck to hug Jerry and thank him for his work.

"The dogs at the landfill not only brought closure to many families, they also sidelined as therapy dogs. Many of the recovery workers came to love the dogs and to seek them out to pet them and hug them and confide in them. We had many comments on how beautiful the dogs were and how wonderful their work was.

"Jerry and Socks don't [work] to be thought of as heroes. They truly live to work. They do it because they love it. I'm happy that we were trained and ready to help when we were needed."

Kea began her search-dog education with Bob when she was four months old. He was her only teacher.

Photo: Alice Su

KEA

Belgian Malinois

Certified Cadaver Search, Water Recovery

ROBERT WILL

Northeast Search and Rescue,
Rescue International

On September 11, Bob sat in his living room and watched on television as the second plane hit the World Trade Center. That night, his search team, Northeast Search and Rescue, was placed on a call list for deployment. That call came on September 16, when he and Kea and three teammates were sent to Staten Island as part of the recovery effort.

When Bob and Kea first arrived at the Fresh Kills site at about 8:30 p.m., he was struck by the indescribable odor from the landfill. "The smell of death was everywhere; it was overwhelming," he said. "As we got closer, all we could see was debris and twisted metal piled 10 to 15 feet high as far as the eye could see."

When Bob first let Kea out of her crate, her nose went immediately into high gear. "I knew the smell was overpowering for her, and she kept trying to drag me over to where the smell was coming from. I knew how hard this task was going to be, but nothing had prepared me for what we were about to encounter."

As each truckload of debris was brought in from Ground Zero and dumped onto the debris field, a backhoe came in to spread the load and push the larger pieces out of the way. One hundred or more workers from the NYPD, the FBI and other government agencies then surrounded the piles and scoured them with rakes and hoes, looking for the black boxes from the planes and any personal effects or other evidence that might identify a victim. Afterwards, a bulldozer would push the pile out of the way and into a pile to be buried, and then the next truck backed in to dump [more debris] and the process would start all over again.

"Our job was to search the piles to find any human remains still in the debris," Bob said. "All of the workers, including the dog handlers, had to wear full Tyvek coveralls, hard-hats, goggles and respirators, and to the dogs they looked like monsters. When I suited up and put on the respirator, which completely covered my face, and called Kea out to work, she backed into her crate and growled." Only Bob's voice convinced Kea that he was "her dad."

The debris field assigned to Bob and Kea was about the size of two football fields. Five tractor-trailer trucks and other heavy machinery moved about, continually dumping and moving more debris. Work conditions were also complicated by the half-dozen tractor-trailer trucks dumping at the site, along with several backhoes, trucks, large front-end loaders that were almost two storeys high and other noisy machinery. "The 'monsters' [workers in protective gear] were throwing debris to the side and over their shoulders, and we had to duck and pull the dogs back to avoid being struck," Bob said. "They were not used to us being there and it was obviously annoying. The trucks and large machinery didn't stop for us either, and we had to move for them. Working a dog off lead

Fresh Kills Landfill

in this environment was not an option for me." Kea's play reward of a tug towel was hampered because she had to work fast and keep moving.

On their first task, Bob worked Kea gradually to get her used to the environment and other obstacles. "I let her visit with the 'monsters' so she knew they wouldn't hurt her. I took her near the trucks and backhoes so she could get used to those as well. I wanted to remove as much stress as possible.

"As we were finishing our first tour around the debris pile, Kea started an aggressive pull toward the larger piles. She took us through the piles and stopped at a large piece of what looked like a clump of mud. I picked it up and discovered

she had made her first find. It was a large piece of human flesh. Suddenly I realized that what we were looking for would be unrecognizable.

"Kea kept up her aggressive pulling and took us to the remains of what we think was an ambulance. The smell around it was overwhelming, and we felt that there were probably people inside. The area was flagged off so it could be pulled out and checked in the morning. We made it through that first night after making several more finds. At 3 a.m., we stopped and let the dogs take a break, then climbed into our cars to take a nap. We would start again at 6 a.m.

"When we first arrived at the landfill, no one talked to us. The officers working there had been through so much, and our being there with our dogs was one more thing to get in their way. But as we worked through the piles and started making more and more finds, they began to realize that they had missed so much and that we were now finding what they could not recognize. All of a sudden, we were part of them; we were accepted. As we made a find, everything would stop and they would look over what we found. After the item was removed, several officers would surround the area and get on their hands and knees and go through the rubble by hand, looking for more.

"Sometimes the dogs would hit on something that was only shredded paper holding scent or soaked with blood. If they hit on large pieces of steel and you looked closely, you could see human tissue there. In cadaver training, you teach them to pinpoint the scent source, but nothing had been like this. The dogs were doing their jobs, but some of those things couldn't be used for DNA. Sometimes you would find nothing, and other times it was overwhelming.

"This type of thing was repeated over and over during our time there. People would stop working and ask if they could take our picture. Some would come over just to say hi to the dogs. The 'monsters in the field' were now our friends. The dogs loved seeing them and were happy to go over to say hi or jump up and get a little love from them. People just couldn't do enough for us. It was amazing.

"Our first week at the landfill was from September 16 to the 19. Then another K-9 unit came to relieve us, and we went home to get cleaned up and give our dogs a break. We headed back on September 23 for another four days of work.

"There wasn't enough time to stop and reward Kea after each find...her next scent source was only seconds away," Bob said. "We had to work fast and keep moving."

This time, we stayed on a retired military support ship and could sleep in real beds instead of in our trucks. We were sent home on September 26.

"Sometimes I hear a song or see a commercial on TV that takes me back to those days at the landfill. No one can ever understand what it was like there...they never set foot on the hill I walked on. Kea and I had a mission there, and it was to find people, people who were lost and needed to get home. The families needed to know that their loved ones had been found. I will never forget my time there and the people who entered my life during this terrible time in history."

A hero brings hope to those around them: Lolli is that hero and that K-9 rescue worker. She did her job and she did it well, and Penny is rightly proud.

LOLLI

German Shepherd Dog

Certified Cadaver Search

PENNY SULLIVAN

Ramapo Rescue Dog Association

Before arriving at the Fresh Kills landfill, Penny had already spent a ten-day tour at Ground Zero with her German Shepherd Quest. Three days later, she and Lolli were deployed to Fresh Kills to search for victim remains. They worked until September 29, when the canine search at the Fresh Kills site was officially closed.

"We would check in at the worksite, don our Tyvek suits and gear, then report to the command center for our assigned work period," Penny said. The teams rotated repeatedly throughout each shift, so all of the dogs had frequent periods of rest.

"As soon as the loads of debris were spread out on the field in front of us, we would start our search in an assigned area. A support person would usually accompany each team, carrying a collection bucket into which he would place any remains found. The dogs were surrounded by numerous other workers raking through the mud and wreckage, but they seemed oblivious to the confusion all around them. Lolli was happy and enthusiastic whenever she was working. She searched carefully and methodically, checking through the twisted metal and debris. In spite of the myriad scents, she stayed focused on her task.

"Each search phase was quite limited in time. After some twenty minutes or so, bulldozers would move in to sweep the field clear, making room for new loads to be spread out and searched. The process would repeat itself throughout the day. At the end of each work period, the dogs were given health checks and shampoos before their well-deserved time out. The dogs had frequent breaks and play sessions with occasional simulated searches with positive training aids to properly reward the dogs.

"Many of the workers were amazed at the dogs' work and their ability to find even small fragments of human remains amid the mud and debris. Lolli and the other dogs also played the role of therapy dogs and offered comfort and stress relief for the searchers sifting through the never-ending piles of debris.

"I think that all of the dogs who served following September 11 are true American heroes. In addition to bringing closure to countless grieving families, the dogs provided a real sense of hope to their handlers and to other rescue personnel who were involved in the agonizing search for victims of the attack."

LOUIE

Boxer

Certified Cadaver Search

MICHELE VERRALL

Southeastern Pennsylvania Specialty Dog Unit

"Our job was done but our mission wasn't, and it was hard to walk away," Michele remembers. "Our hearts were with the people waiting to be found. This is why I train my dog, so he can send people home."

Louie was the only member of the Boxer breed to work search and rescue during the September 11 tragedy. He and his handler, Michele, were among the first four teams of search dogs deployed to Staten Island, arriving on September 16. Michele said that when they arrived, both she and Louie were overwhelmed by the enormity of the pile, the huge machinery and the overpowering smell of death.

"There were huge piles of debris covered in a blanket of ash. Seventy-five to one hundred men in white suits and respirators were raking over the piles and throwing stuff in all directions as they separated the debris. Backhoes and large dump trucks were going in every direction and rows of eighteen-wheelers were lined up, ready to be unloaded. It looked like a nuclear explosion or a scene out of the *X-Files*. A large American flag waved over the entire site."

Michele and Louie worked the night shift with her partner, Bob Will, and his Belgian Malinois, Kea, alternating their dogs so they wouldn't become stressed by the extreme conditions. "This wasn't your typical victim lying in the woods," Michele said. "Backhoes would be backing up and coming directly at the dogs while another one would be scooping up the row right next to them. All this went on while you and your dog were trying to work.

"We had to wear white Tyvek suits, helmets and respirators. We chose to wear surgical masks only because otherwise our dogs would not be able to hear us talk to them. After all, there were a hundred other men and women out there that looked just like us, and the dogs needed to be comfortable with this new look."

"This was a very special time to share with my dog. I just wish we could have done more for the victims' families."

By the second day, Louie had settled into a work routine. "When I gave him the command to search, he would take off with his nose to the ground. He wasn't afraid of the backhoes or the men; he was just doing his job. It was as if he knew the importance of why we were there."

Michele said that Louie and the other dogs earned the respect of the work crews once they understood that the dogs were trying to find their people. Kea's handler, teammate Bob Will, recalls, "There was one NYPD captain that I will never forget. He was tall and tough-looking, with a large cigar hanging from his mouth, and it was obvious he was in charge of his men. Michele was working the field with Louie, and this time out they made fourteen finds in about twenty minutes. The captain watched in amazement and, after that, whenever Michele and Louie came onto the field, he made a loud announcement: 'Okay you guys, make way and watch what you're doing. See this dog here? This is the best [expletive] dog here, you just watch him work. God, I love this dog!' He watched over them as they worked, and if anyone wasn't watching or got too close, he would order them out of the way and tell them

to watch what they were doing. He would come over and give Louie a pat on the head when he was done. He really did love that dog. By the end of the second week, we never saw him again, but we'll never forget him."

On September 19, Michele and Louie went home to rest and returned on September 23 for another four-day tour. "By then, Louie had it all down, and it was nothing for him to drag me 30 feet for a small piece of tissue," Michele recalled. "He blocked everything else out. One time, he never even noticed a backhoe coming toward him, scooping up the piles. He stopped and faced the loader and challenged it to a standoff. Even after it went by, he was still challenging it! This was a big turnaround from his first two days there."

Like many of the other dogs, Louie also helped the men and women who were working on the pile, acting as a therapy dog as well as a search dog. "So many of the workers would come up to the dogs to give pets and love," Michele said. "It was good for them as well as the dogs."

After many SAR deployments together, Michele and teammate Bob Will were married in August 2005.

MITTRU

German Shepherd Dog

Certified Cadaver Search

CHRISTINE BUFF

Cayuga County Highland Search and Rescue

Chris and her canine partner, Mittru, were activated by the Cayuga County Sheriff's Department per a request from the Canine Recovery Task Force on September 24 to respond for two- to three-day shifts at the Fresh Kills landfill. Their assignment: the recovery of human remains from the World Trade Center disaster.

"Our first rotation on the pile began at about 4:30 Thursday morning," Chris recalled. "I cannot tell you, even now...what it felt like arriving at that landfill. It was like a moonscape, the most macabre, surreal surroundings I've ever seen. Under the dark sky, with giant machinery constantly moving, 50 to 100 law-enforcement officers wearing respirators and white Tyvek suits raked through the rubble, and hundreds of white 5-gallon buckets were scattered everywhere; the portable lights over this enormous debris area created an otherworldly glow."

Once she and Mittru arrived at the pile, they both got right down to business. Mittru was full of enthusiasm and anxious to do what he loves best—work. "Less than five minutes into his first rotation, Mittru started barking, his indication that he has made a find," Chris said. "Our 'backer,' investigator Steve McLoud, retrieved the object Mittru hit on and came to me with a baseball cap. He held the cap open and said, 'Look what your dog found.' I never looked. It could have been hair, an ear, skin, etc. What I did know was that I could not, at that time, look, or that would have been the end for me.

"After that, things got easier. Despite the overwhelming smell of death, Mittru and I learned the most efficient way to 'clear' a pile. Whenever he made a find, it was tagged by a 'backer' with his team number, placed in a white bucket and taken to the forensic tent to be logged for further identification. Several times before Mittru went to work, a chaplain from one of the agencies would kneel down and bless him, and then sneak him a cookie as he blessed.

"One of the best compliments came from a respected friend and colleague about a month after the landfill deployment. He told me, '...I saw a team working well in unison, you did the job at hand and did it well.' That meant more to me than words could ever convey.

"Mittru is not an American hero...he is a search and rescue canine who loves his work and is definitely my hero! He has drive and an incredible work ethic. It is a joy to watch him work, regardless of how depressing or even frightening the circumstances might be. He's my partner and our family pet, and he never fails to bring a smile to someone's face, whether it's here at home or on a search or when I take him to my 'real job.'

"While rescue is what's always hoped for, when that's not possible, closure is just as important. People need to say goodbye. And these dogs, Mittru included, helped to make that happen."

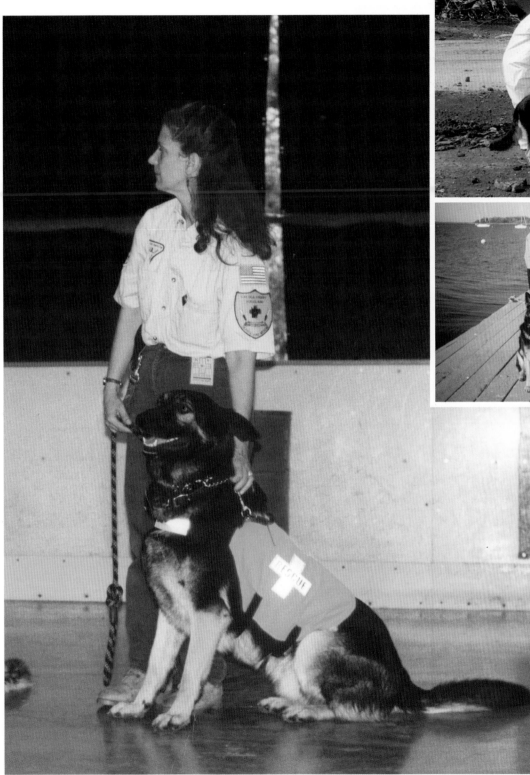

Mittru was only two years old and certified for cadaver just two months before being deployed to Fresh Kills. Chris wondered how he would handle this unparalleled task. Five minutes into the job, he made his first find, and she knew this beginner was a born rescuer.

NEMO

Belgian Malinois

Certified Cadaver Search

JOHN VALVARDI

Rescue and Recovery Search Dogs

As director of Rescue and Recovery Search Dogs, John was deployed to Fresh Kills on September 16. He and Nemo were a part of the Canine Recovery Task Force's first four canine search teams to arrive on Staten Island.

"At first, Nemo was a bit intimidated by all of the machinery, piles of debris and 'monsters' [people in Tyvek suits]," John explained. "Large bulldozers and earth-moving machines were constantly moving the debris, and it was very loud at times. But by the second day, Nemo had regained his normal enthusiasm for his job, and he continued to enjoy working throughout his thirteen-day deployment at Fresh Kills."

Working twelve-hour shifts, and later eight- to ten-hour shifts, Nemo drove hard when searching and slept like a rock when off-duty. "We would suit up and report to the command center, work the piles for about forty minutes and rest for fifteen. Then it was back out for another forty minutes or so. During our first few days, Nemo hit on ten to twenty finds each day. The other workers were amazed at how he could determine, in a 20- by 30-foot pile of rubble, that there was a small bit of human remains in the area.

"My dog is not a hero," John said. "He was just doing his job. He worked hard to get to where he is, as did all of the other dogs and handlers. Search and rescue is not just a 9/11 disaster. It is also the everyday missing child, person and victim where the dog's work goes unnoticed."

Finding is Nemo's life, and like a true hero, he seeks no recognition or reward. In most search and rescue scenarios, "the dog's work goes unnoticed."

Fresh Kills Landfill

A role model for the Rottweiler breed, Phoenix set a high standard at Fresh Kills. She worked long hours with few breaks, never faltering in her desire to "find."

PHOENIX

Rottweiler

Certified Cadaver Search

DENISE GRIMM

New Jersey Rescue and Recovery K-9 Unit

Denise and Phoenix were part of one of the first contingents of search teams deployed to Fresh Kills after the Twin Towers collapsed. Phoenix is one of only a few Rottweilers who are certified in search work. For several days, she worked twelve- to fifteen-hour shifts with few breaks, yet she remained upbeat and willing to work from the first day through the last.

On their first day out, Denise recalled that the smell was overwhelming. "Jet fuel and death is the only way I can describe it," she related. "I was worried that the smell of death would be too much for the dogs, and that they would not be able to pinpoint exact locations because the smell was everywhere. However, fifteen minutes into our first assignment, Phoenix alerted on a human bone fragment. It was then that I knew she could handle the situation.

"Phoenix worked tirelessly for as long as I asked her to. The other rescue workers commented on how diligent and thorough she was in her work. After she made a find, she simply pushed ahead and continued with her task. I rewarded with just a few words and a pat on the head. She made so many finds in a row that it was hard to reward her with a toy each time. Between searches, she was very friendly and pleasant with the other workers. She's a very social dog.

"The work that Phoenix did helped the victims' families begin the healing process and carry on with their lives after such a devastating tragedy. Most of them had no bodies to bury, only a few small body parts, and she helped bring closure to those families.

"The 9/11 work also brought the search and rescue dogs into the forefront so people could learn more about their work and how they contribute to society on a regular basis. Phoenix would do this all over again if America needed her because she loves her job."

Fresh Kills was far beyond the typical training site. Radar and the other search K-9s rose to the grisly task and helped return some of the victims to their families.

RADAR

Labrador Retriever

Human-Remains Detection, Wilderness Search

AMIR FINDLING

Western New York Search Dogs

Amir was notified by the chairman of the New York State Federation of Search and Rescue Teams to report with Radar and his Western New York Search Dog team to the Fresh Kills landfill on Staten Island.

"Radar's focus in life is his work as a search dog," Amir said. "At Fresh Kills, I believe he understood that something was terribly wrong, as he could smell death all over the place, and he quickly understood what his task was. His trained alert just did not work in these conditions, so he quickly found an alternative way to indicate his finds. I had to learn to understand what he was telling me and how to read that so we could be successful at finding human remains.

"Our reward system also had to change, as I could not reward him for each body part he indicated, which is also quite different from the way we trained. Here, there was no room for rewarding

him in the field, so he had to wait until we went back to the truck for a break. He adjusted to that quite well and even began to demand his reward as we were headed back! His work ethic was flawless, and the quality of his work was very high and consistently so.

"None of Radar's training ever came close to the conditions he faced at Fresh Kills. Who could have imagined that? Yet he understood the task, adapted to it and worked hard at making me understand how he now was indicating his finds. When things got tough, he just kept on working that much harder. His response to the call showed me that he had undergone the right kind of training. Some of the law-enforcement officers tested Radar with chicken bones and baby-back rib bones that were scattered all over from the restaurants that had been in the Twin Towers. He never even looked at those. He just indicated on human remains. Schenectady County Sheriff Harry Buffardi, who was overseeing the operation while we were there, praised Radar for his excellent work.

"In this gray mountain of ashes and despair, one star was shining for me, and it was Radar, my SAR dog! Every piece of human remains he indicated, and he found many, was one that we saved from the clutches of bin Laden. Each piece was a victory by itself and might bring some comfort to the families of the victims."

The rescue workers were constantly amazed at the dogs' ability to find tiny bits of human remains in the vast amount of debris at Fresh Kills. The canine nose is its most amazing body part!

SNIPER

Labrador Retriever

Certified Cadaver Search

ANNE DOTTORE

Barren River Area Search Dog Association

When Rescue International issued a call for search teams to assist in the recovery effort at Fresh Kills, Anne and Sniper responded with the Barren River Area Search Dog Association. They started work at 3 a.m. on September 21 and rotated out at 9 p.m. on September 27.

Although Sniper's work experience included cadaver searches in Kentucky and Tennessee, Fresh Kills was far from a typical search environment. Yet, despite the chaos, noise and constant movement of heavy machinery, he coped very well with the distractions and remained focused and happy to be doing his job.

"Many of the workers at the landfill were amazed that the dogs were able to recover what they did, as most of their finds were unrecognizable to a human," Anne said. "Many of the pieces that Sniper found not only were very small but were disfigured and covered with dust and other material.

"We worked the day shift and were up at 5 a.m. and at the landfill by 6:30 a.m. We would work for twenty to thirty minutes on the pile and then break for about forty-five minutes. We finished up at about 6 or 7 p.m. We tried to get a few hours' sleep before doing it all over again.

"Sniper did what he loves...his job...in difficult circumstances to the best of his ability. And he did it all for tennis balls! Work and tennis balls are two of his favorite things, and he got plenty of both at Fresh Kills.

"He also received a lot of attention upon our return home. His work during the disaster helped our town and local people feel that they were involved and able to contribute in a time of need. Sniper also visits area schools and helps teach the kids about search and rescue work. The children love him, too."

Fresh Kills Landfill

SOCKS

German Shepherd Dog

Certified Cadaver Search

SUE LAVOIE

Ramapo Rescue Dog Association

Whether down time or at work, Socks just wants to be with Mom.

When Sue was deployed to the Fresh Kills landfill to work remains detection, she knew that both of her German Shepherd Dogs, Socks and Jerry, would be needed in the search effort. Socks was ten years old and close to retirement, but her experience in cadaver work made her a valuable search tool.

"Because Socks was the older and more experienced dog, I started out working with her more than Jerry. Socks was always happy to be with me and working, regardless of what we were doing, but she did get tired, so Jerry became my primary dog. Toward the end of our tour I brought Socks along as a backup for Jerry.

"We worked the day shift. Each morning, we checked in at the K-9 tent and shortly afterward we were assigned our starting time. Each dog worked a twenty- to thirty-minute shift and then had an hour or so of down time. Before we hit the pile, we waited while large trucks deposited the debris on the search field. Large machines then moved the debris around, and people with rakes and hoes sorted through it to find evidence and personal effects. After the raking and hoeing, they called for the dogs, and we would work the dogs through the debris on their search command, looking for small and sometimes minute pieces of human remains. After a dog had indicated and received his reward for doing so, we put the remains in a bucket that then was transported to the forensic tent for cataloging. There were records kept on how accurate each dog was.

"In the first few days, I'd give my dogs a drink and a potty break and put them in my truck to rest. Although they were tired, they stayed awake most of the time. Later on, when the Animal Planet Mobile Vet Clinic came to the landfill, I took my dogs to be checked over after they worked. At the end of each work day, the vet would decon the dogs with a bath and clean their eyes and feet. I think the baths were the most unpleasant part of their day!

"We monitored our dogs' work shifts closely so the dogs wouldn't burn out," Sue explained. "I was happy I had both my dogs [Socks and Jerry] to work, so each could have a break and not work quite so many hours. They were both always happy and ready to go to work!"

It is said that a dog's eyes reflect what is in her soul.

"We use play rewards when our dogs make a find. When I adopted Socks at two years old, she wouldn't play with any toys, so I taught her to play with a tennis ball, which became her favorite toy. After making a find in wilderness or cadaver search, she will prance around with the ball in her mouth and act so proud of herself.

"My dogs worked many hours, searching for and finding human remains. Having been trained to find cadaver and to associate cadaver with play rewards, they had no problem staying upbeat and excited about working. They were not aware that they were finding someone's loved one who perished in the disaster. They only knew that they were finding a scent source that results in a great

play session. They stayed anxious to work right up to our last day there."

"When Socks's original owner boarded her as a pup at my home, I fell head over heels in love with her," Sue said. "I was fortunate to adopt her two years later. We worked together for eight years before she retired after the 9/11 disaster."

The temporary memorial near the Flight 93 crash site includes a chain-link fence where visitors can leave notes and other mementos, flags, a plaque engraved with the names of the passengers and crew members, a large slate cross and forty angels, one for each of the victims.

It's an American thing we should all understand!

NEVER FORGET

Shanksville, Pennsylvania

Just as innocent Americans lost their lives at the World Trade Center and the Pentagon on 9/11, a fourth plane, United Airlines Flight 93, also was hijacked and headed toward unimaginable devastation. At 10:03 a.m., it crashed in a field about 80 miles southeast of Pittsburgh.

The melee aboard the plane during the hijacking was transmitted over several passengers' cell phones and heard by family members of the passengers, 911 emergency centers and the FBI. As the plane was diverted from its original flight plan and rerouted toward Washington, DC, the passengers aboard Flight 93 decided to take a stand against the terrorists. Led by Todd Beamer, Jeremy Glick, Mark Bingham and Tom Burnett, they overtook the hijackers, and the plane crashed in a field in Shanksville, Pennsylvania. All forty passengers plus the four hijackers perished in the crash. Many people, including US Representative John Murtha of Pennsylvania, believe that their brave actions prevented another deadly attack, probably upon the Capitol or the White House.

Lou Ann Pomposelli of Crafton, Pennsylvania, and her search and rescue K-9, June, were called to the crash site with the Pittsburgh area's Air Search Rescue Team. "It was the most devastating thing I've ever seen," she said. "We were some of the first people on the scene. Originally, we were sent there looking for live people, but once we saw the devastation, we knew that was

not a possibility. There was simply nothing there, just a huge hole in the ground. Even the trees surrounding the field were charred. We did set up a command post and remained on standby for the day, but it was pretty apparent that June and our teammates were not needed. That was hard to bounce back from."

No live-find search and rescue dogs worked at the Pennsylvania crash site, which was a double-edged sword for the volunteers who were called upon. Rescue workers arrive at disaster sites with the intention of finding survivors. And while there were no "live finds" at the World Trade Center or the Pentagon, dogs were put into service for weeks to locate human remains. A volunteer on various community missions, Lou Ann explains, "…it's rewarding to be able to help the victims' families to understand what happened to them. It is disappointing when you can't bring people home to their families."

As the Pennsylvania crash was a major part of the events that unraveled on September 11, 2001, we honor the passengers and crew of Flight 93 in this book to commemorate their lives and heroic efforts on behalf of our country. We will never forget a single life lost on 9/11. Perhaps the lives lost at Shanksville, those American heroes inspired into action by Todd Beamer's now famous mantra—"Let's roll!"—are the most painful of all as there were no remains recovered, leaving a hole in the hearts of their families as large as the one left in the field in Shanksville.

KEYSER

German Shepherd Dog

Human Remains Detection, Wilderness Search

LISA LEPSCH

Barbour County Tactical Search and Rescue

Certified in multiple search disciplines, Keyser worked throughout his life to serve his country.

After 9/11, Lisa worked the Flight 93 area with K-9 Keyser. "We spent only one day at the scene and searched our assigned areas," Lisa said, "but we were unable to find any human remains. The thing I remember the most was the overpowering smell of jet fuel. I was very impressed with the professionalism of the people we worked with in such a sad environment."

"Keyser was certified in wilderness (airscent), land/water cadaver work and evidence search. He had his first search eight hours after his initial certification in wilderness. Keyser was involved in approximately thirty searches during his career as well as over fifty demonstrations. He loved the water and taught my other dogs how to swim.

"Keyser was my first SAR dog, and he excelled at his job. I learned so much from him. Despite two torn ACLs and spondylosis, Keyser continued to work courageously."

A thorough and methodical worker no matter the mission, Mangus particularly excelled in water search.

MANGUS

German Shepherd Dog

Human Remains Detection

KATHY CHIODO HOLBERT

Fayette County Sheriff's Department

When Kathy and Mangus arrived at the Flight 93 crash site, the odor of jet fuel was still heavy in the air. "The crash pit was quite deep, and I hoped that no one had felt any pain upon this impact," Kathy remembers. "We were told that a lot of human remains had been recovered from the trees directly in front of the crash site. The DMORT tables had buckets that were filled with human bones that had been burned white as snow, and I wondered about the history and the people behind each one."

"We were tasked with sweeping the open field surrounding the crash site—I think to make sure that the human searchers had not missed anything. I was flanked by my teammates, one on each side, and we spread apart in the field to do a wide grid sweep. Our dogs showed lots of animation as we walked through the crash-site area to sweep the open fields.

"Mangus worked the way he usually does— very methodically and seriously. I remember that a cowbird dive-bombed him, and he never even looked up. When we neared the tree line, Mangus alerted on a tiny scrap of seat cushion. We bagged it and turned it in. We were very thorough, working the field one way and then the other to make sure, but I don't think there were any other finds that day.

"Mangus was originally a patrol and narcotics dog before he was trained for human-remains detection. He was an exceptional water dog, and he made about thirty water recoveries during his career. Mangus was eight years old when he worked Flight 93, and he made his last water recovery at the age of thirteen.

"I know how valuable our recovery dogs are to the victims' friends and loved ones. The families tell me that what we bring to them is the path to finally start grieving, and that no matter how many days or years pass by, the grieving never really starts until they have their loved ones back."

Animal-Assisted Crisis Response: Comfort during Crisis

As first responders and search and rescue teams descended on Ground Zero and the Pentagon after the terrorist attacks, a lesser-known group of canine teams also gathered in New York City and Washington, DC. Therapy dogs, trained to respond to human emotions of grief and sadness, also arrived, prepared to offer a friendly paw and a furry shoulder to cry on. While the search dogs often functioned in that same role during their down time off the pile, teams of therapy dogs—all breeds and sizes—came daily to provide additional comfort and support.

An estimated 500 therapy dogs, most of them from animal-assisted therapy (AAT) and animal-assisted activity (AAA) organizations and Therapy Dogs International, responded to help comfort the victims' families, the injured and displaced persons and the firefighters, police officers and relief workers from the many organizations involved in the rescue effort. Aided by the Red Cross, Salvation Army and ASPCA, the therapy dog/handler teams set up at Family Assistance Centers (FACs) for the World Trade Center site at Pier 94 in New York City and Liberty State Park in New Jersey, as well as in Virginia to assist the families of Pentagon victims. Many teams remained for weeks, some for much longer, as the need for emotional relief continued for several months.

The 9/11 therapy dogs, with their friendly demeanors and often uncanny sensitivity to human suffering, offered solace and a brief respite from the overwhelming sadness of the disaster. They provided important hugging time for those professionals—firefighters, police officers and other relief workers, including the clergy—who suffered their own emotional pain while attending to the devastating pain of others. The therapy teams also performed a valuable service by assessing the needs of grieving individuals; the handlers were then able to discreetly summon the appropriate healthcare workers to assist those people, thus providing the right help at the right time.

While therapy dogs could not heal the wounds of those they comforted, they made a difference

Dogs provide comfort to our military, who serve on dangerous deployments to fight terrorism in the wake of 9/11. Army Major Tim Shaffer says goodbye to his Golden Retriever, Ali (bred by the author), before deploying to Baghdad in support of Operation Iraqi Freedom.

in the emotional lives of the grieving and aided in the reclamation of a strong self—a necessary step toward recovery. They worked for the reward of "knowing" that they provided comfort from the unrelenting chaos left by the events of 9/11.

On the following pages, some therapy-dog owners who assisted at the various FACs share particularly poignant moments that they witnessed between their dogs and those whose lives their dogs touched.

9/11 Therapy Dogs

ANNIE

Cavalier King Charles Spaniel

ELIZABETH TEAL

Giving Paws

FAC Pier 94

A nnie and Elizabeth began their work at the Family Assistance Center at Pier 94 on September 18, 2001, and they continued until January 2002. Additionally, they worked on the ferries that ran from Pier 94 to the World Financial Center, as they helped families, chaplains and mental health workers disembark and walk to the site.

"On one memorable occasion, as Annie and I walked down a back corridor at the Red Cross staging area, we passed several people just standing in a group, and there was one woman in a folding chair. As we passed by, Annie stopped rather suddenly, and I felt the leash tighten. My little partner was looking straight at me, but she was walking *backwards*. Then she sat her hip down on the foot of the woman in the chair. The woman looked down and, without saying a word, picked Annie up into her arms and began

On the sidewalk in front of the FDNY Engine 54 fire station, Annie provided comfort to passersby. The city was in a state of grief, and many individuals would bend down to pet the therapy dogs as they walked by, often being moved to tears.

to wail—deep, ripping screams. A mental health worker came immediately. I was kneeling beside the woman, and Annie was in her arms. Annie's head was over her shoulder, her body clutched to the woman. The wails subsided, and there was a moment of quiet clarity as the woman said to Annie, 'You're so alive, you're so alive.' The woman then looked into the face of the mental health volunteer for a moment and put Annie back on the floor.

"What I witnessed in the abilities of the dogs to help people reconnect and to find some small corner of solace was more profound than any dogma or creed. It often needed no words."

Photo: Lori Sash-Gail

Photo: Lori Sash-Gail

Annie and Elizabeth visited Engine 54 as part of a big group of canine therapy teams. On the wall behind Annie are many cards and notes from people of all ages and from all over the country to show support for the firefighters.

ABOVE: Squish, wearing his therapy uniform, waits to go into the FAC. ABOVE, LEFT: Gremlynne provides comfort and comedy to a delighted admirer at a senior daycare center in New Jersey. LEFT: Squish and the bejeweled Gremlynne pose for the camera.

GREMLYNNE AND SQUISH

French Bulldogs

MANDA KAPLAN

High School Volunteer

FAC Liberty State Park

Manda and Squish outside the Liberty State Park FAC. The Twin Towers were visible from this spot only a few months earlier.

Manda, owner of French Bulldogs Gremlynne and Squish, was the youngest person known to volunteer at Liberty State Park. She was sixteen years old and a junior in high school when the 9/11 tragedy occurred. With school permission, Manda, Gremlynne and Squish worked seven or eight Wednesday-afternoon shifts at the New Jersey FAC.

"Being part of the Honor Guard is a poignant memory for me," Manda wrote. "It's a military formation in which the mourners stand, one person every 6 feet, in two rows facing each other, with the procession down the middle. We stood in one of the lines while several men wheeled palettes of cartons draped with American flags down the center. Inside the boxes were urns that contained ashes from the World Trade Center. The urns were to be given out later that day at a ceremony for the family members. Gremlynne was wearing her patriotic red, white and blue windbreaker….It felt like such a noble thing to be a part of that."

"I was afraid [Gremlynne] would bark if she stood with me in the Honor Guard because of the large objects wheeling by, but she must have understood because she stood silently at attention."

HUNTER

Golden Retriever

DIANE PENNINGTON

Human-Animal Relational Therapies (HART)

FAC Pier 94

Hunter and Diane spent several months working with victims' families at Pier 94 in Manhattan. "On one of our visits, we met a child I'll call 'Bobby,' a young boy about nine or ten years old, in the Children's Corner, where he sat drawing pictures. He asked many questions about Hunter, who was performing his usual bag of tricks, eager to engage the boy. Bobby and his mother joined us for a walk, with Bobby helping to hold Hunter's leash. When other staff and volunteers stopped to ask about the dog, Bobby proudly told them everything he had learned about his new friend.

"Then he asked me to walk with him to the 'Wall of Bears' [a wall where teddy bears and other stuffed animals were placed alongside photos and flyers of the missing and notes from families], where he pointed to a flyer of his father. 'That's a picture of my dad; that's my dad,' he said. I felt my throat grabbing, took a deep breath and said, 'I see your dad.' His mother began to cry, and Bobby comforted her, saying, 'It's okay, Mom. It'll be okay.' I remember thinking, 'When? When will it be okay? Wow, this kid is taking care of his mom.'

"We sat in front of the wall for a few minutes, and I let Bobby lead the conversation as we stroked Hunter on his side and belly. Bobby continued to answer questions about the dog for anyone who asked. For that hour, Bobby had Hunter for his own.

"When they left, Bobby was holding a large white stuffed gorilla. His mother thought that 'Hunter' would be a good name for the stuffed animal. Bobby nodded his head and said, 'Yeah, I'll call him Hunter.' His mother looked at me with tears in her eyes and thanked us. That may have been the most important impact Hunter and I have ever made."

Photo: Lori Sash-Gail

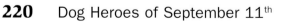

"Hunter went into 'work mode' as soon as his vest went on. He knew his job, and he loved connecting with everyone—of any age, background, of any physical or emotional state."

"Dr. Mac," with his personable nature and gentle demeanor, helped start the healing process for some of the grieving in the aftermath of 9/11.

MACHIAS

Bernese Mountain Dog

BARB BECK-WILCZEK

AAT Volunteer

FAC Liberty State Park

Machias, better known as "Mac," was a frequent consoling presence at the FAC in New Jersey. His owner, Barb Beck-Wilczek, remembers October 2, 2001, when Mac encountered a young woman who had obviously been crying for some time.

"She came to the center with her father- and mother-in-law and their attorney. She looked dazed, but immediately started petting Mac. The attorney asked that Mac accompany them into a small conference room.

"The woman's husband had worked in the WTC on one of the floors above where the plane hit. He was on the phone with a client at the time and told the client that the room was filling up with smoke. Later, the client called the wife to tell her about the phone call.

"The attorney began the paperwork necessary to avoid the court process normally required to have someone legally declared dead in the absence of a corpse. The family was asked what they had done to find him afterward and how they had reported him missing. Both the woman and her father-in-law kept petting and stroking Mac during the death-certificate application process, and Mac even nudged him a little bit when he stopped. The young wife even smiled at [Mac] a few times. On an unconscious level, I believe that Mac helped them through that time."

ABOVE: Annie enjoys a little down time during her therapy work with brain-injured patients. RIGHT: Megan played Sandy in a local theater production of *Annie*.

MEGAN AND ANNIE

Golden Retrievers

ROSE MARY LAUBACH

AAT Volunteer

FAC Pier 94 and FAC Liberty State Park

Megan and Annie waited with Rose Mary at the Pier 94 FAC on September 20, the first day that dogs worked at the center. Family members of victims arrived to seek information about their loved ones, to file missing persons reports and to submit hairbrushes, toothbrushes and other items for that could be used to get DNA samples for identification.

"It was silent except for the sound of military helicopters overhead. People avoided eye contact, but you could feel their heavy hearts. For many, it was an acknowledgment that their loved ones might *really* not be coming home.

"One woman walking toward us lifted her downcast eyes and looked at us. Megan approached her, and the woman knelt down beside her and buried her face in Megan's soft golden hair. She began to cry and talk to Megan between sobs. She talked about her fears and told her about the person she was trying to find. I did not speak; I simply let Megan do the comforting. After several minutes, the woman stood up, took a deep breath and walked away with her head held a little higher, her shoulders not quite so heavy. No words were exchanged; none was necessary."

Megan gets double hugs on a therapy visit with twins.

9/11 Therapy Dogs

PATRICK

Golden Retriever

ELAINE SHOE

TheraPet

FAC Pier 94

Patrick relaxes with a good book as a participant in the Read to the Dog program at Roselle Park Veterans Memorial Library in New Jersey.

The Family Assistance Center at Pier 94 opened six days after 9/11. Patrick and Elaine made their first visit three days after the center's opening—the first day that dogs went in—and they worked at that location for about three months.

"The pier was set up like a compound, a mini-town unto itself. A secured perimeter surrounded the building starting at the sidewalk on the West Side Highway, and there was a security clearance checkpoint and then a tented area across the front of the building and the entrance doors.

"On the first day of the Presentation of Flags and Urns, when families were presented with their loved ones' ashes from Ground Zero, Patrick and I stood just outside the building's entrance, working with the families who were waiting in line to enter. One woman in line reached for Patrick, then dropped to her knees and collapsed emotionally onto him. While she was crying out her grief to him, she would stop every so often and ask me for his name, then his age, then make a comment or laugh at herself and then begin crying again. This continued for five or ten minutes. The harder she cried, the closer Patrick placed himself to her. A member of her family finally came back outside to find her. With a deep sigh, she calmed herself and gave Patrick and me big hugs. She thanked us and told us that now she would be able to handle what she needed to do.

"My memories of those many faces and families are still quite clear and intense. I wonder if our pets feel the same."

TUKA

Chesapeake Bay Retriever

SUSAN GREENBAUM

Barking Hills Country Club

FAC Liberty State Park

Tuka and Susan spent sixty-three days at the Family Assistance Center in New Jersey. On their first night working the late shift, they stood by the rail overlooking the Hudson River.

"Two EMTs wandered in our direction. Tuka leaned against the younger man, who had the 'thousand-mile stare.' He spoke of the downtown area, with body parts everywhere…fingers, parts of arms and legs. They had walked behind a firefighter, who commanded them, 'Eyes front, don't look!' His voice broke when he said, 'Why did I look? How could I look? How could I *not* look?' Then he was silent, working his hands through Tuka's curly hair. His older partner stated, 'These things don't bother me…I've seen a lot in my career.'

"We talked of their families, their kids and wives, the young man still petting Tuka. The older man talked about his dog, who recently had died, and his hands drifted to Tuka. He rubbed [Tuka's] head and neck, then started to shake, and then tears literally flew out of his eyes. Sobbing uncontrollably, he and his young partner continued to pet and stroke the dog.

"We all stayed silent together for a while. Then they returned to looking out over the Hudson at the pile. Tuka and I left to inform mental health workers so that both EMTs could get the help they needed."

Photo: Close Encounters of the Furry Kind, LLC

Tuka worked with three-year-old Ryan and his physical therapist for a year to help the boy increase his muscle strength, control and endurance.

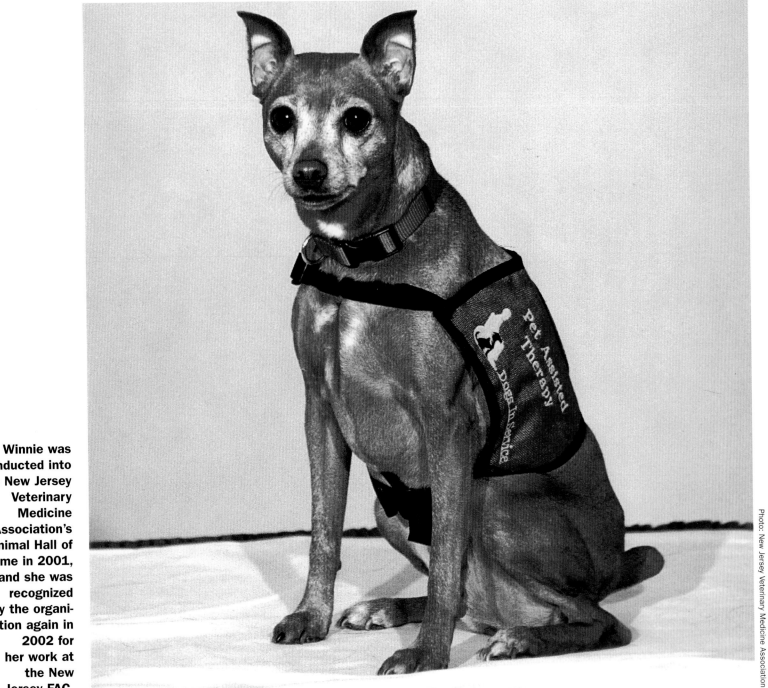

Winnie was inducted into the New Jersey Veterinary Medicine Association's Animal Hall of Fame in 2001, and she was recognized by the organization again in 2002 for her work at the New Jersey FAC.

Photo: New Jersey Veterinary Medicine Association

WINNIE

Miniature Pinscher

DONNA LUZZO

AAT Volunteer

FAC Liberty State Park

Min Pin Winnie's heart was almost bigger than her tiny body. For about two and a half months, from mid-September to early December 2001, she and Donna visited the FAC in New Jersey, consoling relatives of missing victims as well as the Red Cross relief workers, who missed their own families.

"Winnie was there for all who needed her. She consoled the grieving as they boarded and returned on the ferries that brought them to see Ground Zero. Winnie was a friend to the man who carried a picture of his son, and each time he came, he wanted Winnie to kiss the picture. She was a comfort to the four-year-old boy who used his hands to show her that the towers 'used to be this big, and now they were only this big.' Winnie stood by that boy's side, his hand stroking her head as he gazed across the river, on the day that his father and the child psychologist explained that 'mommy would not be coming home.'

"A year later, Winnie again offered comfort to 9/11 victims' families as they gathered for the one-year anniversary of the tragedy. Many called her by name, remembering the little red dog who had helped console them."

Remembering the Rescuers

We can never adequately thank the courageous search and rescue teams who searched for victims' remains during the chaotic aftermath of the 9/11 attacks. Ten years later, many of those canines have gone over the Rainbow Bridge. Some are still alive but have retired from active service; a few continue to serve during their senior years. We share the following words from handlers in praise of their canine partners—indeed, their best friends.

ABBY

BORN OCTOBER 30, 1997

Profile on pages 28–29

FROM DEBRA TOSCH:

After nine years in search and rescue, my sweet Abby is enjoying retirement and spends her days at work with me, resting under my desk or napping in her crate. Her retirement is well deserved after serving during 9/11, the 2002 Olympics, Hurricanes Katrina and Rita and the La Conchita [California] mudslide. Her final deployment was the September 2008 Metrolink train wreck near Chatsworth, California.

Whenever she is invited, Abby is happy to "volunteer" at SDF handling courses, which gives her a sense of purpose so she can pretend that she is not actually retired. She also does occasional presentations with me, but due to her aging rear end, she no longer does live demonstrations. To maintain Abby's good spirits, I have taught her to "find" my car keys, so each day she thinks that she has just completed another search. Good job, Abby!

"During Abby's career, she was called a 'ballerina,'" Debra said. "When she ran, whether on the ground or on the rubble, she was so graceful."

"I was in awe of her talent and desire to find."

ALLEY

OCTOBER 29, 1998–AUGUST 29, 2008

Profile on pages 132–133

FROM HEATHER ROCHE:

Searching was what Alley was born to do! I didn't train her; I merely let her work. She had a talent and a driving force that I have never seen in any other SAR dog. Her career was amazing, and she worked until cancer cut her life short.

We needed Alley, and she was there—at the Pentagon after 9/11. She was also sent to Texas by FEMA to help in the Space Shuttle *Columbia* recovery efforts. She worked the devastation in Bay St. Louis, Mississippi, after Hurricane Katrina. She found the buried body of a child for the National Center for Missing and Exploited Children. Alley also found several drowning victims in rivers and lakes, and she worked countless other searches in numerous states, looking for missing people. She even worked with archaeologists, proving that dogs can find historical and prehistorical remains.

I was in awe of her talent and desire to find. She was put on this Earth for a purpose, and I believe that she fulfilled that purpose. It was Alley's calling in life to serve our nation, our communities and those families with missing loved ones.

In Praise of
Their Partners

ANA

JULY 4, 1995–NOVEMBER 12, 2008

Profile on pages 30–33

FROM CAPTAIN RICK LEE:

We had absolutely no idea what we were getting into when we started SDF's fledging program—the level of responsibility, the time commitment or the impact it would have on our lives.

After four years of training, in 2001 we were deployed to the World Trade Center. By mid-afternoon on September 11, we were flying under military F-16 fighter-jet escort. The experience at Ground Zero was devastating. Life there was heartbreaking, horrific—a treacherous challenge for rescuers. During the days that followed, there were agonizing hours spent wondering where and when we would be needed. Then, suddenly we would be called when areas were uncovered that only the canines could search. Ana navigated the twisted metal, over void spaces—some so large it was like walking on a high wire, some so small she could barely fit in. As the dogs searched, all of the rescuers silently waited. The other firefighters were amazed at the dogs' skills. The endless hours of training were paying off. We never dreamed we would have had this much responsibility.

Ana never lacked confidence, not for a single moment. She had boundless energy and enthusiasm. She gracefully negotiated the wreckage as if it were a day in the park. I know that her trainer, Pluis Davern, would have been very proud to see her student fly across this debris. I know I was.

We will be forever grateful to the Search Dog Foundation for our experiences and the lifelong friendships that these experiences have given us. The new handlers will need to have a passion for the SDF program, not just for their dogs. They'll need to understand all of the responsibilities involved…someday they may be making life-or-death decisions. With their training from SDF, they'll be up to the challenge.

FROM SDF FOUNDER WILMA MELVILLE:

Impossibly energetic and active as a puppy, Ana had been thrown out of her first few homes and was eventually placed with Bonnie Bergin to be trained as a service dog. But Bonnie could see that this beautiful youngster had far too much energy for that line of work and gave me a call. That's how Ana became SDF's first search dog.

As the first canine recruited for our program, and the first to become certified, Ana and her partner, Rick Lee, set a high standard for all search teams to follow. In founding the Search Dog Foundation, I was looking for the right model of recruitment and training that would be successful and could be replicated. Ana's amazing agility, bubbly personality and "can-do" attitude were just what I wanted.

Ana and Captain Rick Lee of the Sacramento City Fire Department couldn't have been better

In Praise of
Their Partners

suited for each other. Ana was wonderfully responsive, and Rick had tremendous perseverance and attention to detail. They achieved certification after just seven months of training together, a record no SDF team has matched. They were deployed to the World Trade Center after September 11, to Hurricane Katrina and to a building collapse in Sacramento and other local disasters. They taught and supported many new teams through the years, and they set the highest standard for all to follow. Rick's wife, Luann, and his son, Kevin, loved and cared for Ana like a member of the family. Their support of Rick and Ana, even when sacrifices had to be made, set an example for other search-team families to follow.

Harley and Dusty, Ana's canine classmates, have also passed on, leaving Ana as the first to be recruited and the last of the founding SDF search dogs to leave us. Ana will be greatly missed by all, but her legacy lives on in a new generation of search dogs.

FROM SEARCH DOGS USA PRESIDENT DAVID KAPLAN:

Over the years, I've had a chance to meet many handlers and observe many teams, but it was Rick and Ana who always caught my eye. There was something about how they worked as a team: their discipline, energy and dedication to the search. The first time I had a chance to see their work up close was at IronDog 2002 in San Diego. When I saw Ana next to her big classmates, Dusty and Harley, I wondered how that little dog could keep up with them. Thirty seconds into the search, Ana and Rick were leading the way, all the way to the very end.

The last time I saw Ana was at the May 2008 event to celebrate the future National Training Center site. How wonderful it was to see her paws and energy touching the ground, as Ana and Rick officially represented our Founding Four: Ana, Dusty, Harley and Wilma's own dog, Murphy. With [Ana's] passing, the ground is blessed with the soul of Ana and of SDF.

"She performed beyond her training and my expectations," Rick said.

In Praise of
Their Partners

"She taught me that with patience, love, faith and a few good ol' squeaky toys or tennis balls, she could become one heck of a 'wonderdog.'"

BELLA

APRIL 12, 1992–MARCH 17, 2007

Profile on pages 38–39

FROM DERESA TELLER:

My dear Bella was my student, but more importantly, she was my teacher. When I came home with this wiggly seven-week-old black-and-white ball of fur, who would have known what an amazing life was ahead of her? Bella was certified in wilderness search at one and a half years old and in cadaver search at age two. She helped locate a woman's body after the Northridge earthquake in Encino, California, in 1994. After Bella was certified in disaster search in 1995, we were off to Oklahoma City's Murrah Federal Building bomb site, where she found the last four victims before the search was called off. We continued working wilderness, cadaver and water cadaver searches; train derailments; building collapses; burned-out buildings; and the aftermath of fires for several years.

In February 2001, Bella was diagnosed with cancer—spindle-cell carcinoma of her right front foot. After eighteen radiation treatments, she re-entered service in July and, two weeks later, located the body of a missing murder victim in a ravine near Simi Valley [California]. One month later, on September 11, we deployed with the Los Angeles Fire Department USAR FEMA team to the World Trade Center. Bella, my shining star, located close to twenty deceased victims.

Besides being a great search dog, Bella enjoyed another life—going to churches, schools, earthquake fairs, scouting events and Hug-a-Tree demonstrations. She was a gentle soul to my daughters and to all children, and she loved to mother every type of tiny animal that came her way, including baby goats, birds, kittens, ducklings and her own puppies, but her favorites were her *chickens*! She herded them around the yard even though chickens don't herd worth a darn, but she didn't care. Some of the chickens became her buddies, and when Bella laid down, they would pick through her fur and then climb onto her back for a rest. She would lie very still so she wouldn't disturb her napping friends.

Bella developed kidney and liver disease during her last year. She had only one or two tough days at the end, and she was surrounded by people who loved her when she went over the Rainbow Bridge on March 17, 2007.

Thank you, dear Bella. I will never forget you. You will always be my Number One. Have fun herding your chickens in the sky, and may you never run out of squeaky toys.

BOOMER

JANUARY 28, 1998–DECEMBER 5, 2009

Profile on pages 136–137

FROM MIKE REHFELD:

My search partner, Boomer Rehfeld, was laid to rest during an official police funeral after his death on December 5, 2009. With his remains in a small box flanked by three tiny dog biscuits, thirty uniformed police officers and members of the Gamber & Community Fire Company gathered for a graveside service to say goodbye. Boomer deserved a public farewell because he had touched so many lives in the community.

During his nine years of service, Boomer discovered twelve drowning victims, worked on several homicide cases, assisted the DC Metropolitan Police Department in the 2001 Chandra Levy

In 2007, Boomer received the Maryland Veterinary Medical Association's first annual Pet Hero Award. Veterinarian Dr. Gary Roop submitted Boomer for the award after reading about his work in the newspaper.

search and assisted in the Pentagon recovery effort after the 9/11 terrorist attacks. Boomer especially enjoyed traveling to his search sites in his "Boomer Mobile," my Ford Explorer SUV.

Boomer's heroism earned him two Maryland State commendations, a unit citation from the Baltimore County Fire Department, a certificate of appreciation from the Washington, DC, Police Department and a certificate of appreciation from the North American Police Working Dog Association.

Boomer's big heart extended well beyond the search world. He served as a therapy dog for Pets on Wheels and made over 200 visits to the elderly in nursing homes and assisted-living facilities. So it was no surprise that when Boomer retired from search work at the age of ten, the Gamber Fire Department held a retirement party in his honor. Over 130 people showed up, and Boomer played the gracious host by visiting every table with his usual smile and tail wag.

After September 11, 2001, Boomer attended a memorial service for the victims' families. "Boomer was the hit of the service," Baltimore County Professional Firefighter's Association chaplain, James Westervelt, said. "When people stood up, Boomer stood. When people sat, Boomer sat down too."

After we buried Boomer, I said that I would never be a dog handler again. Boomer was a special dog; he was my first and my only and my last.

In Praise of Their Partners

"She seemed to be born with great wisdom that led us both."

Heather took this group photo of her dogs on what would be Cassy's last Christmas. Cassy is on the left, with Red in the middle and Alley on the right.

CASSY

DECEMBER 6, 1991–MARCH 16, 2006

Profile on pages 138–139

FROM HEATHER ROCHE:

Cassy was a joy to live with, as she thought she was put on this earth to love everyone! I could take her anywhere and do anything with her. She and I worked well together as a team, and we never needed much verbal communication; she just knew what to do and when.

Cassy had many finds during her long career, and many of them were not in her assigned sector, as she never limited herself to the lines we humans draw on maps. She mastered every aspect of SAR, whether it was wilderness, rubble, live or cadaver. Cassy was always determined and focused on the task at hand, and she could problem-solve like no other dog I've seen or worked with.

I don't know how I managed to train such a good dog, because if you add up my other dogs' SAR strengths and knowledge, it doesn't come even close to Cassy's. She accomplished so much in search and rescue work. *Cassy* taught *me*, and she set the standard for all of my search dogs that followed her.

In Praise of
Their Partners

"Of all of Cowboy's talents, one was most apparent: he understood English. Not just simple words but entire sentences."

COWBOY

OCTOBER 30, 1995–APRIL 23, 2007

Profile on pages 50–51

FROM DAVE RICHARDS:

I got Cowboy from a *real* cowboy who used Border Collies to herd his stock. I knew very little about the breed except that Border Collies are high-energy and smart. I wanted a companion to accompany me on my 20-mile-plus runs through the mountains.

I took Cowboy to puppy kindergarten when he was ten weeks old, and he was eerily smart. We joined Rocky Mountain Rescue Dogs when he was about a year old, and he learned search skills as quickly as he had mastered obedience. Within a year, he was certified in wilderness, tracking and avalanche. During that same period, he won AKC obedience awards, earning his Companion Dog (CD) and Companion Dog Excellent (CDX) titles. A year later, we joined the Utah FEMA Task Force. Cowboy tested to national standards and was certified as a FEMA Type II live-find dog. Later that year, we tested in Sacramento for advanced status, and Cowboy nailed it. Our task force finally had a Type I dog. We were deployed on 9/11 and spent two weeks searching the debris at the World Trade Center.

Cowboy continued with Rocky Mountain Rescue Dogs, going on dozens of searches, many of them high-profile, such as the search for Elizabeth Smart. He searched busy city areas as well as extremely remote areas in the Grand Staircase and in Utah's vast desert, high mountain peaks and deep slot canyons, snow-covered valleys and mountain lakes. He rode in pickup trucks, on ATVs, in helicopters, in dozens of light planes, in commercial airlines and even once in a Lear jet.

I usually had to explain things [to Cowboy] only once, and he mastered each skill in only one training session. I don't think he ever realized he was a dog. He thought he was just a short person with four legs. I never tried to convince him otherwise.

In February 2007, Cowboy was diagnosed with bone cancer in his left front shoulder. The options were to have the leg amputated and gain perhaps another year with him, or to have the symptoms treated and hope for six months. I couldn't bear the thought of Cowboy struggling on three legs, so we chose to enjoy him as long as we could.

After seven transfusions over several weeks, it was obvious that things were not working out for Cowboy, and I had to let him go. He loved watching people, and we spent our last day together at the park, lying on a blanket, watching the world go by one more time. I will never forget him.

Fide canem—trust the dog.

In Praise of Their Partners

DUKE

BORN AUGUST 22, 1997

Profile on pages 54–55

FROM HOWARD ORR:

Duke retired from active search work at eleven years of age; we had been partners for eight years. He served during 9/11 and located at least four victims on that mission; three of them were firefighters in Tower Five. Even though he was trained to find live by giving his bark alert, he also would indicate with his body language the presence of human scent by stopping and freezing at the source.

Duke worked Hurricanes Katrina and Rita, the San Clemente [California] earthquake in 2003 and the La Conchita [California] mudslide in 2005. In one Los Angeles apartment building collapse, he indicated the body of the only person buried in the rubble.

Over the years, Duke has done public-relations work and presentations with me, doing demonstrations for firefighters who were considering disaster search work. He loved the traveling and climbing in and out of those rubble piles.

Duke was never allowed to have treats when he was working so that he would ignore food smells at disaster scenes. Now that he's retired, he can have treats and live the good life with my family.

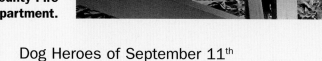

Duke takes a break during an SDF training exercise at Santa Barbara County Fire Department.

Photo Beverly Pavone

In Praise of Their Partners

DUSTY

FEBRUARY 16, 1995–MARCH 13, 2007

Profile on pages 56–57

FROM RANDY GROSS:

It is very difficult, if not impossible, to put into words what Dusty meant to me and what she did for me and so many other people.

When Wilma [Melville] rescued Dusty from a Golden Retriever rescue organization in Southern California, she described Dusty as a "bombastic wild animal" that she had to corral into a corner of her house when she first brought her home. Dusty did not know one command, but she had all of the characteristics to make a great search dog: hunt and prey drive, energy, boldness and determination. She just needed an avenue for release. SDF trainer Pluis Davern was just about to wash her out of the program, but after Pluis gave Dusty a few more days, she said, "Just like that, it clicked!"

I'll never forget the day I met Dusty. It was our first day at Sundowners, the SDF training center. Pluis brought out the three dogs—Dusty, Ana and Harley. As soon as I saw Dusty, I almost felt as if I were seeing my newborn child. She was a beautiful dark golden color, strong and energetic. When Pluis matched me with Dusty, I must have

been glowing. That was the start of a twelve-year relationship that changed my life.

It was very challenging at first. Even though you can feel the bond, you have to develop a respect that isn't easily given away by these search dogs. They have a tremendous amount of energy and drive that you need to learn how to control and direct. In the beginning, there were many times when Dusty would not respond to my commands or didn't want to stay on leash. We trained for twenty to thirty hours a week. I loved training, as each day we got better and better. The way she manipulated the rubble with both power and grace was breathtaking to watch. In one exercise that I will never forget, a victim was buried 20 feet deep in a pile of concrete culverts just below a 6-inch diameter culvert pipe that was sticking straight up. She worked the scent, then jumped up and tightroped the entire perimeter of the pipe while looking down toward the victim. I couldn't believe what I had just seen!

Five years after our first meeting, we were put center stage at the World Trade Center after 9/11. It was there that I realized just how good Dusty

"Dusty was strong, yet soft. She had the ability to be gentle when appropriate, but when it came to work, she was all business and nothing stood in her way."

was. Her performance was beyond what I could have imagined.

The entire time we were on shift at Ground Zero, Dusty wanted to work. She was constantly pulling me toward the pile whether we were on a mission or just changing locations. Dusty was also a source of comfort to other rescue workers, and she offered a way to break the ice when other firefighters, especially from FDNY, would ask about her. Such conversations would open the door for us to talk about the tragic circumstances and let them know that we were there for them.

Our 9/11 deployment changed the SDF and the need for search dogs. Dusty and all of the other SDF dogs put the foundation on the map—a map to saving lives.

Dusty was my partner, coworker and companion. In the twelve years as my partner, we were rarely ever apart. In fact, I think Dusty and I spent more time together than my wife and I of twenty-two years did. My family was very supportive of our work. I integrated her into our family life (as if Dusty gave me a choice!) as much as possible. My kids loved the opportunity to be part of her training, and they loved her almost as much as I did, even though the training, deployments, demonstrations and administrative work took me away from home a lot.

At work, she was part of the fire department. Out of the 700 personnel, not everyone knew me, but they all knew Dusty and loved having her around. They always forgave her when she nudged their arms to be petted and made them spill their coffee, which happened a lot. She was the perfect coworker. She always worked so hard for me.

Dusty brought so much to my life. She gave me unconditional love, no matter what kind of day I was having or no matter how tired she was. I was always the most important person in her life, and we had complete trust in each other. My fondest memory of her is how she was always looking at me or for me. It didn't matter if we were at home, or surrounded by fifty eight-year-old children after a demonstration or meeting celebrities, her eyes were always looking for me.

I will always be grateful to Wilma and Pluis for bringing Dusty and I together. As a team, Dusty and I gained many lifelong friends and met numerous government officials, including governors, senators and President Bush (twice). We worked two of the nation's most tragic disasters (Hurricane Katrina was the second) as well as many local deployments, and we performed hundreds of demonstrations. Dusty made so many people laugh, clap and "ooh and ah" at her demonstrations.

I would also like to thank Rick Lee and Ana and Rob Cima and Harley, the other two dog-handler teams with us in the SDF pilot program. We have developed special friendships and have shared many of the experiences that I've mentioned here.

Dusty was nothing short of remarkable. She touched many lives, and so many kind words were said about us as a team. She was a wayward child who became a poster child. Her legacy will live on in the future generations of disaster search dogs.

Photo: Chris Cantle

Photo: Chris Cantle

Photo: Eliot Crowley

*"She always made
things better with a
nudge of
her nose, a bark
in my ear, or just
coming up to
me and
resting her chin on
my leg."*

Remembering the Rescuers   **255**

In Praise of
Their Partners

JAZZ

JULY 24, 1994–MARCH 24, 2006

Profile on pages 184–185

FROM NANCY BROOKS:

Jazz passed away two weeks after being diagnosed with bone cancer. I think of her often—when I see the sweetness of a new puppy, the gentleness of our Golden Retriever, Sonny, or the drive of my new partner, Chief, when he's trailing human scent.

Jazz and I were partners for eleven years. Her first search was the 9/11 recovery effort at Fresh Kills, and we had many searches and training events after that. We traveled, camped out, hiked, did SAR demos, ate bagels and took naps together.

Jazz loved people. Her favorites were little kids and seniors. And she would sleep with her ball in her mouth, always ready to play or work. If Jazz had her ball, she was "packed" and ready to go to work.

Because of Jazz, I am a better person. She was my student and, more importantly, she was also my teacher.

*"Semper Fido, Jazz.
Our hearts still ache in sadness,
and secret tears still fall.
What it meant to lose you,
no one will ever know."*

—*SAR News*, January 2010

JERRY

MAY 20, 1997–NOVEMBER 26, 2009

Profile on pages 186–187

FROM SUE LAVOIE:

Jerry was diagnosed with congenital megaesophagus at ten weeks of age, and he was not expected to live to see his first birthday. But the amazing Jerry had his own plans. He lived almost twelve and a half fantastic, adventure-filled years. Originally intended to be my husband's search dog, Jerry again had his own ideas. After sitting on my lap on the 2,000-mile trip home from the breeder, he was my dog. We shared so many good times together, and I am happy that I have wonderful memories of those times.

We traveled around the country, from coast to coast, with Jerry. He swam in the Pacific Ocean, the Gulf of Mexico and the Atlantic Ocean. He went to Mount Rushmore, the Crazy Horse Memorial and Metropolis (the home of Superman!). He marched in the Presidential Inaugural Parade and visited the Lincoln Memorial. These things only scratch the surface of the places this dog went and the things he did in his life. Jerry took everything in stride.

Jerry was ready to play and ready to search anytime, anywhere. He had 100 percent trust in me and would do anything I asked of him. It tore my heart out to say goodbye to him on his last day, but even then, he trusted me to make the right decision.

If I were to describe Jerry, I would tell you that he was devoted and trusting, a play fanatic who was also my teacher, my partner and my dear, dear friend.

Jerry wears the medal that he received from the New Jersey Veterinary Medical Association upon his 2009 induction into the organization's Animal Hall of Fame.

In Praise of
Their Partners

KAISER

BORN OCTOBER 9, 1998

Profile on pages 72–73

FROM TONY ZINTSMASTER:

After Kaiser's mission to Ground Zero following the 9/11 disaster, he went on to serve during many more, including Hurricanes Isabel, Ernesto, Dolly, Katrina, Gustav and Ike; tornadoes in Indianapolis and Evansville, Indiana; and the mudslide in Laguna Beach, California.

I thought that Kaiser would have to be retired around the age of six, when the scar tissue from a ripped muscle in his right inner thigh caused a permanent limp that we could not keep repaired surgically. But he showed me that he wanted and needed to work and that the injury did not hurt him (per Kaiser, three veterinarians and two physical therapists!). At age eleven, he is still working. He does mostly local searches, and while his endurance has diminished some, he usually makes up the difference with reliable expertise. He has the respect of his teammates, who still like to watch him work training exercises to see how the air is moving the scent of the victim.

He, of course, protests rather vocally when I take our young dog to train in SAR or Schutzhund and he is left behind. I will work Kaiser as long as he enjoys it, and then we will enjoy his retirement.

Despite all of Kaiser's SAR strengths, he is the most affectionate dog we have owned and trained, and his current assignment is the very important role of my wife Annette's "snuggle buddy."

"Kaiser has been a great dog for me on many levels, and I know I will miss him in the field, where he looks so perfect."

In Praise of
Their Partners

Penny and Lolli at the Fresh Kills site show that nothing is better than good teamwork.

LOLLI

JULY 1, 1994–MARCH 12, 2009

Profile on pages 192–193

FROM PENNY SULLIVAN:

My dear girl, Lolli, lived an incredibly long and productive life, passing away only three months short of her fifteenth birthday. Besides her work at Fresh Kills following the 9/11 attacks, Lolli served our Ramapo Rescue Dog Association on numerous occasions.

Her most noteworthy search occurred when she was ten-plus years old. We were asked by law-enforcement officials to look for a man, suspected of drug involvement, who had disappeared two months earlier in upstate New York. Our unit was instructed to search wooded areas near the subject's last known location. Our team requested that we first search an abandoned "crack house" that had been torched around the time of the man's disappearance and was now boarded up.

The structure was intact, with whole sections on several floors charred and damaged. We worked the entire building, but Lolli repeatedly indicated one specific area piled high with debris, giving her trained paw-touch indication each time I brought her back to that area. The officials dug through the debris and did indeed locate the missing subject's body. The murder was apparently gang related, and eventually a murder suspect was brought to trial and convicted.

Throughout the years, my Lol was the steadfast "rock-dog" of our pack, and "Ms. Mellow" on every search deployment. I miss her terribly.

RIGHT: Lolli does a paw-touch exercise during an American Rescue Dog Association (ARDA) training weekend.

*"He took each day in stride, and we are glad for
every day we had with him," Annette said.*

MAX

APRIL 15, 1995–NOVEMBER 16, 2010

Profile on pages 88–89

FROM ANNETTE ZINTSMASTER:

At fifteen years of age, Max was in failing health, was almost blind and had trouble walking. But his relentless personality was the same as it was at Ground Zero, and he was determined to overcome those physical limitations. Although he had to work a bit to get around, he remained happy and tried to chase the ball or start a game of tug with anyone he could coax into playing with him. His veterinarian told me that if he could have installed a new rear end, Max could have gone for another 200,000 miles!

Max was always a good soldier and enjoyed any work that we gave him during the years following 9/11, but as a retiree, his job was that of "dog alarm." He toddled around the house every morning at 5:30, reminding us to feed him and take him out. He took each day in stride, and we are glad for every day we had with him. We learned so much from him about not feeling sad about our limitations and just moving forward with all that we do have.

FROM TONY ZINTSMASTER:

Annette's boy Max left us on November 16, 2010. Max was Nettie's partner at Ground Zero but, more importantly, he was our friend.

I have often referred to him affectionately as "the most stubborn dog in the world," but this quality served us all well on many searches. On Ground Zero, wilderness searches, human remains searches and article searches, he never quit and was always ready for more. Annette called him "Sassy Pants" because he was always "talking back" to her, but if one word described him, it was *heart*.

Max is working on ahead of us, and we look forward to the day when we see him making us play with him again.

In Praise of
Their Partners

Quest's work at Ground Zero was just one of the many accomplishments of his SAR career.

QUEST

JUNE 29, 1997–MAY 9, 2008

Profile on pages 100–101

FROM PENNY SULLIVAN:

From missing people buried under piles of rubble to drowning victims to lost senior citizens to a lost caribou hunter in far northern Quebec, Quest loved the work and gave his all on every mission. We were among the first teams to arrive at Ground Zero, working the night shift for live victims but sadly finding none.

Perhaps Quest's finest hour came when he was deployed to search for a missing nineteen-year-old who had been partying with his friends on a secluded ridgetop in the country on a Saturday night. The group had scattered when the sheriff's deputies discovered the teens as they were running off into the woods. When one teen was still missing on Monday, we were called in to assist in the search.

Arriving near darkness on Monday afternoon, we worked down to the party site but then encountered sheer rock cliffs. While struggling to find a way down, we suddenly heard persistent barking far below us. It was Quest; he had already reached the search area.

He continued to bark for over three minutes until we reached the base of the cliff. Quest was standing directly over the missing teen, who lay

unconscious on the ground beneath him. In the darkness, the young man had apparently fallen 100 feet down from the cliff's edge. He was placed in a rescue basket and hoisted up the cliff to the waiting ambulance. He remained in a coma for several days but eventually made a full recovery.

Quest continued in search work for both the NJ-TF1 and the Ramapo Rescue Dog Association. I have never known a dog to love the work more. Quest was, without a doubt, one of the finest search dogs I have ever known.

In Praise of
Their Partners

RED

BORN OCTOBER 17, 1999

Profile on pages 158–159

FROM HEATHER ROCHE:

Red was just beginning her SAR career when the events of 9/11 happened. I was proud of her then, and I have continued to respect her, as she has proven her talent, drive and heart over the years on numerous searches. She has worked some of our worst disasters, including the 9/11 terrorist attacks and Hurricane Katrina.

Because Red was only one year younger than Alley, my next-youngest search dog, their careers are parallel and often overlap. When I look at Red now, in her senior years, I can see how she followed in the pawprints of Cassy, my senior search partner, by doing anything I've ever asked of her in a variety of SAR disciplines.

Working dogs like Red love what they do, and they are never content to sit on the sidelines. At ten years of age, she worked a house fire. The scene was still smoking, and she navigated across dangerous and unstable debris and located the body of the missing homeowner. She obviously was not ready to retire. I trust her to tell me when that time comes.

"No matter the difficulty of the task, Red always wanted to please and serve."

In Praise of
Their Partners

RILEY

NOVEMBER 23, 1997–FEBRUARY 26, 2010

Profile on pages 102–105

FROM CHRIS SELFRIDGE:

On February 26, 2010, our very special Riley passed away. He was my friend and search partner, but most importantly, he was our family pet and especially meant a lot to my young son. He lived a good life, enjoyed a great career and taught me many lessons during our time together.

In February 2010, we found a mass in Riley's abdomen. X-rays confirmed my biggest fears, and I had to face the realization that the odds of a recovery were not good. Riley fought the biggest battle of his life, but we lost him two weeks later.

Riley always did everything I asked of him, whether it was directional training in the backyard or jumping into a wheelbarrow in a search scenario. I miss you, Bub.

Author's note: The photo of Riley in a Stokes basket crossing the 70-foot chasm between the Twin Towers has been seen online and in publications worldwide. He became the face of the 9/11 search dog hero and the cover dog for this book.

"He worked hard for me every day, and he will be greatly missed."

In Praise of
Their Partners

"He was like a bull in a china shop—his whole heart was in the search."

SHERMAN

MARCH 15, 1996–SEPTEMBER 9, 2009

Profile on pages 106–107

FROM STEVE SWANEY:

Throughout his lifetime, Sherman always remained true to his nickname—"the Shermanator"—after the famous World War II Sherman Tank. Sherman once tried to run through a plate-glass window—three times—in search of a victim. He was an amazing dog. He had speed and drive and would tackle anything. He tried to use his brute strength to get the job accomplished, even during play. At the fire station, he would play with an extremely heavy fire hose like it was a toy, pulling it as far as 150 feet. "This dog was so strong that when his path was blocked, he just tore apart whatever stood in his way," said Pluis Davern, SDF lead trainer.

Sherman was deployed to Hurricanes Katrina, Rita and Ernesto, and to the Torrey Pines bluff collapse near San Diego. He and I also traveled to Texas to help train a Taiwanese task force that came to America to learn search and rescue.

In 2007, Sherman retired to enjoy his well-deserved golden years with Icon, the search partner I lost to cancer in July 2010. Two years after his retirement, Sherman struggled with various medical conditions, and I had to make the heart-wrenching decision to have my partner of eleven years put to sleep. The "Shermanator" passed away peacefully at the age of thirteen.

In Praise of
Their Partners

From the day that Socks came home with Sue, dog and handler became one.

SOCKS

APRIL 26, 1991–DECEMBER 31, 2002

Profile on pages 206–207

FROM SUE LAVOIE:

I met Socks when I boarded her as a young puppy, and I instantly fell in love with her. I knew she had the potential to be a super working dog. Two years later, she fell into disfavor with her owners because of her misbehavior, and I offered to adopt her. When I went to pick her up, she hopped right into my truck and never looked back! It was as if she knew she was in the right place.

Socks didn't know how to play when she came home with me because she had been corrected by her owners for playing with her toys. It took a lot of work to bring out her play drive, but it was there and was worth the effort. Until the day she died, she played only with a tennis ball.

Socks died from a blood clot in her lung at age eleven. As she lay on the floor in the middle of the night, I held her in my arms and told her it was "OK" to go, and she took her last breath. It was almost as if she couldn't let go until I told her it was alright.

We worked together for eight years, until she retired after the 9/11 disaster. My dear Socks was unimposing, loyal, grateful and always a lady. She was my partner and my dear friend.

"Our friends never saw one of us without the other close at hand. We seemed to have a nonverbal connection; we just understood each other without any words."

In Praise of
Their Partners

ANNA
Profile on pages 34–35

Unrelated to her deploy-
ment, Anna became ill two
months after working the
World Trade Center site.
Handler Sarah Atlas lost
her in 2002. "Anna was a
beautiful dog and very gentle," Sarah said. "I
still mourn her loss."

On October 1, 2002, at the request of US
Rep. Robert E. Andrews (NJ), the American flag
was flown over the Capitol in Washington, DC,
in memory of Anna. The certificate presented
along with the flag reads, "...for the bravery
and courage displayed while serving as a rescue dog at the World Trade Center after the
terrorist attacks on September 11."

BEAR
Profile on pages 36–37

Two years after 9/11, John
Gilkey lost Bear at the age
of eleven. John reflects, "He
was an awesome dog, a
great friend and a wonderful
teacher. There is not a day
that goes by that I don't think about him, and
very often I ask him for guidance with my new
search partner, Bailey. Although I hope there
is never another disaster of that magnitude, if
there is, I hope Bear will be looking down on
me, helping me do my job."

BILLY
Profile on pages 40–41

"Billy is still hanging around,
although he is getting old
and beginning to have some
health issues," said handler
Mike Scott. "Responding to the tragedy at the
World Trade Center on 9/11 was a real mixture
of emotions. There was a tragic loss of life at
a very significant event in our country's history.
On the other hand, we felt honored to be able
to do our small part....While survivors were not
to be found in the days of our searching, we
were able to say that we had shared with New
York the best search dogs in the country."

CHOLO
Profile on pages 48–49

At nine years of age, Cholo
died in 2004 of an appar-
ent aneurysm. In tribute, a
USAR colleague wrote about
the special partnership be-
tween Cholo and handler Joanne Reitz: "Theirs
was a path to making life better through search
and rescue."

JENNER
Profile on pages 68–71

Jenner was diagnosed with
a blood plasma cancer
in 2002 and spent many
months on chemotherapy. Sadly, Ann Wichmann said goodbye to her partner in 2004.
"He went as he lived, with courage and dignity
right to the very last moment."

KEYSER
Profile on pages 210–211

Keyser worked "courageously until the last year of his life," said handler Lisa Lepsch. He passed away on November 17, 2007, at the age of eleven.

MANGUS
Profile on pages 212–213

Mangus passed away on April 10, 2007, at the age of fifteen. "To this day, law-enforcement officers and firefighters still ask for him," handler Kathy Chiodo Holbert said.

LOUIE
Profile on pages 82–83

Sadly, in 2004, Amy Rising lost Louie. He was eleven years old. While she will never replace her hero, another special Golden Retriever will follow in his pawprints, and Louie will be looking down on Amy and her new partner as they begin their search journey together.

NIKKO
Profile on pages 152–153

"He was killed a year later [after working at the Pentagon] in a tragic accident while responding to a search for two young kidnap victims," said handler Sonja K. Nordstrom.

LOUIE
Profile on pages 194–195

Louie passed away in October 2004 from an illness unrelated to the work he did at the landfill. "Louie taught me much more than I taught him, and he still guides me every day," handler Michele Verrall said. "I have a new Boxer now, and I know that Louie is watching over us."

THUNDER
Profile on pages 172–173

Bob Sessions lost Thunder just a few weeks before her sixteenth birthday. In tribute to Thunder's memorable career, PA-TF1 handler Bobbie Snyder wrote, "…I don't know of another dog in the USAR community that has served her country as well or as many times as Thunder without asking anything in return except a Frisbee toss and a pat on the head. Thunder, I loved your true spirit and will miss working with you."

Horse Creek:
The Rescued Honor the Rescuers

The American flag and 9/11 memorial plaque (BELOW) are displayed in a place of honor near the entrance to Horse Creek so that they will be seen by all who visit the animal sanctuary.

Horse Creek Wildlife Sanctuary and Animal Refuge could easily be renamed "animal heaven." Located on 2,000 scenic acres in Hardin County, Tennessee, the sanctuary provides shelter, basic medical care and adoption services for abandoned and abused domestic animals. Horse Creek was established in 1998 by the Sharon Charitable Trust and is dedicated to the welfare of domestic animals and the preservation of wildlife. The American flag that flies above Horse Creek has been dedicated to all those canine heroes, specifically including those in search and rescue, who have dedicated their lives to helping fight the war on terror.

"We believe that there's a little bit of hero in every dog."

—Horse Creek Wildlife Sanctuary and Animal Refuge

After September 11, 2001, the caretakers at Horse Creek Wildlife Sanctuary and Animal Refuge grieved with all of America at the tragedy that unfolded at the World Trade Center, at the Pentagon and in Shanksville, Pennsylvania. They were especially touched by the heroic canines that were profiled in the first edition of this book.

Trustees Ron and Linda Pickard wrote, "Since Horse Creek originated from our love of dogs, we decided to support the National Disaster Search Dog Foundation. A photo of firefighter Randy Gross and Dusty, his special search and rescue partner, is proudly displayed in our office."

In 2007, Horse Creek abandoned their long-standing tradition of naming their rescued canines alphabetically; instead, the caretakers paid tribute to the 9/11 effort by naming each dog that came into the sanctuary after one of the search and rescue dog heroes that served after the September 11 attacks. The following happy endings are among the many recounted in the Horse Creek rescue journals.

SAGE
Mixed breed

Arrived August 8, 2007

Named in tribute to search and rescue Border Collie Sage, who served courageously at the Pentagon following the September 11 terrorist attacks on America.

Sage and her two siblings arrived at Horse Creek from a local animal shelter on August 8, 2007. Happy, healthy puppies, they romped and played for hours and then collapsed into long naps.

What breed are they? Your guess is as good as ours! But they didn't grow to be very large dogs. Sage was full of love, kisses and tail-wagging.

Sage joined the Clem family from Eads, Tennessee. The family had recently lost their beloved dog of fifteen years, and they felt that their hearts were ready to love and care for another dog. They immediately fell for Sage. Who could blame them?

Linda Pickard later wrote about an email that Horse Creek received on October 22, 2007, from search and rescue dog Sage's handler, Diane Whetsel:

My name is Diane Whetsel. I am the trainer/owner/handler of K-9 Sage. I was surfing the Web the other day and saw your SagePage. I was surprised to see that you had named a pup after my little girl. How cool is that?

Sage and I are currently serving in Iraq. We are living in Camp Victory, the US base just outside of Baghdad. Our mission here is to search for our American MIAs. Because you have shown interest in our nation's service dogs, I thought you might like to hear of Sage's latest adventure here in Iraq. Sage also searched in Aruba for Natalee Holloway and then deployed to Mississippi after Hurricane Katrina. I must be one of the most fortunate handlers to have been blessed with such a wonderful fur partner. Thank you for what you do for all of the less fortunate animals, and thank you for your support.

Horse Creek:
The Rescued Honor the Rescuers

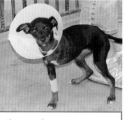

JAZZ

Miniature Pinscher mix

Arrived May 23, 2007

Named in tribute to search and rescue German Shepherd Jazz, who served courageously at the Fresh Kills landfill following the September 11 terrorist attacks on America.

Jazz arrived at Horse Creek from the Hardin County animal shelter on May 23, 2007. She was all alone and begging for attention. She immediately got ours!

We believed that she was a Miniature Pinscher mix and that she would eventually weigh about 10 to 12 pounds, and she did indeed grow to about 12 pounds. Her estimated age of fourteen weeks backdated her birthdate to around Valentine's Day, so we called her our "little Valentine girl." She was playful and loved people, and she was so tiny and bouncy that just watching her made us smile.

Unfortunately, x-rays revealed a dislocated shoulder from a previous injury, and her leg was so tiny and fragile that surgery could not repair it. We gave her every chance, but in the end, the veterinarian had to remove her leg.

The good news is that Jazz couldn't care less; she never missed a beat. She is healed and happy, and her life is better than ever. This sweetheart girl is so cute and tiny that no one could avoid loving her!

Jazz now lives with the McAdams family in Collierville, Tennessee. She shares her home with two other small dogs—one is another Horse Creek rescue named Abigail. Mrs. McAdams fell in love with Jazz because of her handicap and felt that her family's home was the right place for this little girl. She was right: Jazz lives a full, wonderful life with her family.

OSA

Treeing Walker Coonhound

Arrived October 17, 2007

Named in tribute to search and rescue German Shepherd Osa, who served courageously at the World Trade Center following the September 11 terrorist attacks on America.

Osa had obviously been living in the woods for some time when she arrived at Horse Creek; she was very thin, undernourished and heartworm positive. We had her spayed and treated for heartworm, and she recovered well, becoming more loving every day.

Osa now lives in Loretto, Tennessee, with the Neidert family and two other Horse Creek rescue adoptees. Her human father, Jay, is an artist. Thanks to him, a portrait of Osa hangs in the Horse Creek Villa. Osa, her Walker Hound brother, Ancil, and her Australian Cattle Dog-mix sister, Kahlua, have three human siblings who keep them busy. The family's backyard is complete with a giant doghouse that includes a long front porch—a requirement, we are told by the family, for a proper southern hound.

RED

Labrador Retriever/ Basset Hound mix

Arrived June 19, 2007

Named in tribute to search and rescue Labrador Retriever Red, who served courageously at the Pentagon following the September 11 terrorist attacks on America.

Red arrived at Horse Creek with two siblings, Logan and Pacy, all very playful and each one begging to be the center of attention. They all had short legs and long bodies, but Red was different, and she quickly outgrew her siblings by leaps and bounds. Named Red, despite her black coat, she was definitely ready to entertain and be loved by some lucky family.

Now named Savannah Red Bunny Belle, she lives with the Gnuschke family in Germantown, Tennessee. She shares her family with three other dogs: an older Dachshund, a Labrador Retriever and another Lab mix.

Savannah Red is reportedly the "most challenging dog" that the family has ever had; she gets into everything and is highly energetic. They laughingly report her exploits, such as the time she was discovered lounging on top of the kitchen table while chewing on the placemats. She is "curious to a fault," but also the happiest dog they have ever known.

DUKE

Bluetick Coonhound

Arrived November 9, 2007

Named in tribute to search and rescue Labrador Retriever Duke, who served courageously at the World Trade Center following the September 11 terrorist attacks on America.

Pending a miracle, Duke will live out his life at Horse Creek Sanctuary. He arrived here with severe congestion in his chest; he had been shot with a large-caliber shotgun, resulting in a wound that had left infected scar tissue in his lungs. X-rays showed that he had also been shot in the face, leaving his sinus cavities badly scarred. On top of that, he also had heartworm, but he was so severely congested that we had to delay heartworm treatment until he gained enough strength to handle it. It was a miracle that he was still alive.

Duke's tear ducts were so badly damaged that he is unable to produce tears to keep his eyes clear, and we have to put drops in his eyes every day. After what people have done to him, it is amazing that he still trusts us.

Duke is showing his age and doesn't move as fast as he used to. He can't exercise much and he breathes heavily in warm air, but he plays well with other dogs and still enjoys spending time with his girlfriend, Tilly, in the exercise area. Dry, crisp days are his favorite, and his daily rawhides are his passion.

Only a special home would work for Duke. In the meantime, he has a home and family at Horse Creek, and he gets all the love we can give him.

A Teammate Tribute

**by Teresa MacPherson and
Sonja Heritage**
Virginia Task Force 1

Heidi Yamaguchi and a young Fuyu.

Heidi Yamaguchi and her German Shepherd Dog, Fuyu (VA-TF1), were the first certified FEMA canine search team on the East Coast. Heidi's USAR mission, which began in 1986, included her deployment to El Salvador, Panama, the Philippines, Oklahoma City, Nairobi and the Pentagon as well as to numerous other disasters, including hurricanes and tornados in the United States.

Heidi lost Fuyu in 2002. She certified her second dog, Ondo, to the FEMA Type I level. After seventeen years of USAR service, Heidi passed away in 2003. We will always remember the high standards she set for herself, for her dogs and for everyone in the USAR system. She has made our world a better place, and she is sorely missed.

DOGNY: AKC's Salute to Search and Rescue Dogs

by Daphna Straus
Project Manager, DOGNY

As the largest purebred dog registry in the world and a not-for-profit corporation, the American Kennel Club has been serving dogs and the people who love them since 1884. From disaster relief for pets in the Gulf States to supporting military working canines and search and rescue dogs, AKC is devoted to the health, well-being and advancement of dogs nationwide.

AKC is especially committed to educating the public about the dogs who serve our citizens.

© 2002 American Kennel Club

© 2002 American Kennel Club

Two profiles of Mary Ann Paredes's *The Precision of a Dog's Heart* capture many photographs and accounts of the dogs' work at Ground Zero. Among the dog heroes painted on the sculpture are two Golden Retrievers, Bretagne and Riley.

DOGNY:
AKC's Salute to Search and Rescue Dogs

Paul Farinacci's *Wooftop Rescue* captures the awe the artist has for rescue dogs and reveals the heroic nature of the SAR beast.

© 2002 American Kennel Club

Aurora: Angel of Rescue, painted by artist Robert Perless, shines like a rainbow to celebrate the "cooperative relationship between dogs and humans."

© 2002 American Kennel Club

Search and rescue dogs protect and save Americans in small towns and in military units all over the world, but their focused work, intense training and sometimes top-security duties leave little room for public fanfare. That's why the American Kennel Club endorsed *DOGNY™: America's Tribute to Search and Rescue Dogs*. When hijacked planes hit the World Trade Center and the Pentagon, and another crashed near Shanksville, Pennsylvania, dog-and-handler teams rushed in to perform an unspeakable duty. AKC's president and CEO, Dennis B. Sprung, knew it was time to honor these heroes with a public show of thanks and a nationwide effort to support their future missions. He created DOGNY to answer the call of duty on behalf of dog lovers everywhere.

On the first anniversary of 9/11, AKC and its affiliated clubs, friends in the pet-products industry and many other supporting organizations joined forces to display over 100 uniquely painted statues of a search and rescue dog all over the five boroughs of New York City. With names like *Patriot, Let Freedom Ring* and *Stars and Stripes,* the statues guarded police precincts, fire stations and office buildings with a show of pride and dignity that no New Yorker or tourist could resist. Some statues even stood sentry in Fifth Avenue department-store windows while the usual commercial fare was blacked out, in deference to the solemn events of the prior year. The many events and programs supporting DOGNY have included DOGNY Day at famed Yankee Stadium, a Broadway salute to DOGNY in the Theater District's Shubert Alley and a series of collectible items.

DOGNY observed the first anniversary of 9/11 until Thanksgiving of 2002, at which point

The plaque on the wall reads:

CITY OF NEW YORK
F. H. LA GUARDIA
MAYOR

FIRE DEPARTMENT
JOHN J. McELLIGOTT
FIRE COMMISSIONER

DESIGN & CONSTRUCTION
UNDER SUPERVISION OF THE
DEPARTMENT OF PUBLIC WORKS
IRVING V. A. HUIE
COMMISSIONER

1940

Flanked by floral tributes is Mary Fragapane's *Brave New World*, which the artist rendered to capture the "resounding sense of patriotism" that swelled in the United States following the terrorist attacks on 9/11. America truly became a "brave new world."

Remembering the Rescuers   **285**

DOGNY:
AKC's Salute to
Search and Rescue Dogs

One of over 100 sculptures created by DOGNY to honor search and rescue dogs. *All Breeds and Bones* was painted by Beata Szpura.

© 2002 American Kennel Club

the sculptures were brought to Sotheby's for a charity auction that launched a holiday season of unprecedented generosity in the name of canine search and rescue organizations. One hundred percent of funds raised by AKC for DOGNY— including sponsorships, donations and auction sales—has been earmarked in the 501(c)3 AKC Companion Animal Recovery (CAR) Canine Support and Relief Fund for professional and volunteer canine search and rescue organizations throughout the United States. In just the

first three years of DOGNY, AKC raised over $3,000,000 for this noble cause.

While most of the DOGNY statues have gone home with their sponsors, several remain on public display, and others have joined the collections of museums. AKC has continued to keep canine search and rescue in the public eye with DOGNY events throughout the year. In 2004, AKC instituted the DOGNY Heroic Military Working Dog Award, presented to military search dogs and handlers who have distinguished themselves in

Tribute to FEMA K-9 Elvis by Nancy Carey portrays black Labrador Retriever Elvis, one of the dog heroes who served at Ground Zero.

Remembering the Rescuers **287**

DOGNY:
AKC's Salute to
Search and Rescue Dogs

active duty. Each time a team is awarded, a medal of honor and certificate are bestowed upon them in an emotional ceremony. The first two award ceremonies were held aboard the USS *Intrepid*, one of the most successful aircraft carriers in US history. To date, the AKC has honored three dog-and-handler teams.

The first DOGNY Heroic Military Working Dog Award winners were Sgt. Herman Haynes and German Shepherd Dog Frenke, a certified explosives-detection dog. They received their award on May 27, 2004, during the Intrepid Fleet Week Gala and were recognized for their outstanding service in Afghanistan and Iraq. In addition to honoring Sgt. Haynes and Frenke, AKC Chairman of the Board Ronald H. Menaker presented the original DOGNY bronze sculpture for dedication to the people of New York City and for installation

aboard the historic ship as part of the *The Intrepid Remembers 9/11* exhibit.

The next awards ceremony was held on November 11, 2005—Veterans' Day—aboard the *Intrepid*, with the honors going to Specialist Jacob S. Nelson and his German Shepherd Dog Ranny. The 2007 award recipients were S.Sgt. Charles Shuck and yellow Labrador Retriever Gabe, who received their award in a ceremony at Fort Hood, Texas, from AKC representative Dr. Carmen L. Battaglia. Gabe is a specialized search dog (SSD), trained in explosives and weapons detection, and the duo was recognized for their work during a deployment to Iraq.

Whether working at home to recover victims of disasters, accidents or crimes or serving overseas to protect our troops and interests abroad, search and rescue dogs are truly America's unsung heroes. AKC is committed to educating the public about the vital work that American canine search and rescue organizations perform all around the world. To apply for a grant, make a tax-deductible donation or find out more about *DOGNY: America's Tribute to Search and Rescue Dogs*, visit www.dogny.org. One hundred percent of all contributions to DOGNY benefits professional and volunteer canine search and rescue organizations located throughout the United States.

DOGNY Heroic Military Working Dog Award winners receive a medallion and certificate from the AKC.

Photo: Tilly Grassa © American Kennel Club

Photo: Mary Bloom © American Kennel Club

Photo: SPC Amanda Morrissey; US Army

ABOVE: The AKC's Ron Menaker congratulates Sgt. Haynes and Frenke; ABOVE, RIGHT: Ranny and Specialist Nelson receive the 2005 DOGNY Heroic Military Working Dog Award at a Veterans' Day ceremony in New York City; RIGHT: "He's the reason I'm staying in the Army," S.Sgt. Shuck has said of his teammate, Gabe.

National Disaster Search Dog Foundation

When California firefighters Rob Cima, Randy Gross and Rick Lee partnered with Golden Retrievers Harley, Dusty and Ana from the National Disaster Search Dog Foundation (SDF), they knew that the dogs would be an excellent resource for their department. They never imagined that four years afterward, they would be taking their dogs into the worst disaster scene in United States history.

Ana, Dusty and Harley were the SDF's "pilot" dogs—the first three canines fully trained by the foundation for urban disaster search work. The foundation's canine graduates are among the most highly trained in the nation and are relied upon for providing first-responder disaster search services to communities across the nation.

When disaster struck New York City on September 11, 2001, thirteen SDF teams were deployed to the World Trade Center as members of FEMA task forces. All but one of those teams were FEMA advanced certified—not bad for a service organization that was still in its infancy.

The Search Dog Foundation began in 1995 as a seed of hope after the Oklahoma City bombing and was officially founded in 1996. Wilma Melville, a retired physical education teacher, and her black Labrador Retriever, Murphy, a FEMA-certified advanced disaster search dog, were deployed to Oklahoma City to help search for victims at the disaster site. Melville witnessed how few certified disaster-search dogs were available to help locate live victims in the building rubble. Dismayed at that reality, Melville embarked on a personal mission to create a training program that would train more handlers, train them faster and train them more cost-effectively.

Until that time, all disaster search dogs certified in the United States were trained and handled by civilian volunteers at a personal cost of up to $15,000. Training to the advanced certification level took three to five years, with little professional help available to the handler. Dropout and failure rates were high.

Melville had trained Murphy with the help of professional gundog trainer Pluis Davern, owner of Sundowners Kennels in Gilroy, California. "My experience with Pluis taught me that three ingredients were paramount," Melville said, "a good dog, a good handler and professional training for both." With that guiding philosophy, Melville and Davern worked together once again, and the National Disaster Search Dog Foundation was born.

California firefighter Rob Cima shares a moment with his Golden Retriever, Harley, at Ground Zero. Harley was one of the Foundation's three "pilot" dogs.

Sergio Morariu and his Labrador Retriever, Tammy, served at the WTC with CA-TF4.

"We test by having the dogs chase a ball. Then we toss the ball into heavy cover. We want a dog that will go in there and dig it out and want to keep doing that. It must be prey drive versus play drive. The dog must be so driven that he won't stop looking, regardless of where the ball is tossed."

After the foundation has chosen one or more candidates, the dogs are professionally trained at Sundowners. The trained dogs then are paired with pre-selected handlers, and the teams continue to work with SDF until they reach certification and beyond. Most SDF handlers are professional firefighters because they are the first responders to the scene of a disaster.

Before entering formal training, each canine candidate spends two to twelve months with a volunteer foster family who teaches the dog basic obedience and necessary social skills. Advanced training then begins with Davern at Sundowners.

Davern explains that during the training process, the dogs are just doing what comes naturally: working in order to get their reward. "It's got to be a game for the dogs," she said, a phrase often repeated by the handlers who worked during 9/11. "The dog is not thinking he is going to rescue someone. He's thinking, 'Somebody out there has a toy for me!'"

Davern teaches her canine students advanced obedience and the entire set of disaster search skills needed for urban search work: verbal and nonverbal direction control (hand signals); balancing on ladders and on shifting, uneven surfaces; searching through complex rubble piles; and alerting the handler (with a sustained bark alert) when a survivor is located. "We really stress the bark alert," Davern said. "We must have a solid bark alert before starting advanced training."

SDF selects its search-dog candidates from animal shelters and breed-rescue groups, from service-dog organizations and, occasionally, from breeder donations. The best prospects come from the sporting breeds, primarily Labrador Retrievers and Golden Retrievers, high-energy dogs who are bold and confident and display a high, almost obsessive, prey drive, traits not always suitable for the average family pet.

"We're becoming much more specific in the dogs we select," Davern said. "It has to be a perfect dog to work with every handler. We have some Goldens and a few Border Collies, but most are Labs. You don't have to explain things to Labs; they just do it. Border Collies are more sensitive and will empathize with their handlers' feelings and respond to negative energy.

The dogs also are trained in scent work specifically to ignore cadaver scent and any odor other than that of a live person. "FEMA-certified dogs are trained to know the difference between live human scent and all others," Davern said. "They do not alert on dead human tissue or on human clothing, food or anything other than a live human." Advanced training takes approximately six months.

The trained dogs are then paired with firefighter handlers who have themselves completed an intensive SDF training course, which uses experienced search dogs as training tools. The new dog-and-handler teams practice their skills together at Sundowners for five more days before heading home to begin a most important bonding period. With ongoing training already part of a firefighter's regimen, a dog is easily incorporated into his or her lifestyle.

The foundation then provides continuing on-site training in the home and workplace to monitor the team's progress and polish its teamwork; this training consists of five days each month for six months. The goal is basic, and later advanced, FEMA certification. It takes about twelve to eighteen months for the team to reach advanced certification. Teams continue to practice on a daily basis, and each team meets with other teams in its group twice weekly throughout the working life of the dog. This ongoing commitment to training ensures that the FEMA standard of excellence is maintained.

Answering the call on September 11, the thirteen SDF disaster search teams were sterling examples of Melville's original vision. "The foundation dogs performed beautifully in the biggest test of their lives in New York," she said. "As a result of their performance at Ground Zero, the foundation was catapulted into the national limelight."

In late 2010, the Search Dog Foundation had seventy-four trained teams active in California, Florida, Nebraska, New York, Oklahoma, Texas and Utah, all ready to serve their communities and country. Melville's mission at SDF, however, is far from complete. "We still need more certified dog/handler teams on-site so that loved ones stand a better chance of being found alive."

Three of the thirteen SDF handlers who worked at the World Trade Center were not interviewed for this book due to personal or other reasons. Rob Cima and Golden Retriever Harley were deployed with CA-TF7 in the first wave of handlers to deploy; Harley was one of the aforementioned three SDF "pilot" dogs. Sergio Morariu and his black Labrador Retriever, Tammy, went out two weeks later with CA-TF4. Sergio and Tammy helped search a few rooftops before Sergio was called to work backfill for the FDNY. Seth Peacock and PupDog were deployed in the first wave with CA-TF1 from Los Angeles. PupDog is the only personal dog to have been "grandfathered" into the foundation's training program.

Handler Seth Peacock and PupDog served at the WTC with CA-TF1.

The SDF National Training Center will provide unlimited access to permanent rubble piles, setups for deep victim searches, collapsed structures, mudslides and large-area search sites.

SDF Today

by Wilma Melville

The National Disaster Search Dog Foundation is a survivor among nonprofits. We have grown from a tiny, volunteer-driven group to a strong, vital agency with seventy-one canine disaster-search teams in seven states. We have a dedicated Board of Directors, an army of volunteers and a variety of stable, sustainable income streams.

We are now embarking on our greatest challenge to date: the building of a National Training Center for the United States. It will be a place where rescued dogs will become rescuers, and all of America's search teams will have a chance to train at a state-of-art facility that is like nothing else in the nation. Currently, handlers must search continually for rubble piles that fall short of their needs. The center will bring all of SDF's components—canine evaluation and training, search-team training and advancement and SDF administration—under one roof. SDF will continue to be the nation's leader in canine disaster search, and the National Training Center will be the destination for *all* search teams dedicated to achieving the highest deployment readiness.

THE PLEDGE

THE NATIONAL DISASTER SEARCHDOG FOUNDATION™
www.searchdogfoundation.org

Disaster Training Zone

Wilderness Canyon Search & Rescue Training

Disaster Dome

Canine Pavilion

Handlers Lodge

Covered Training Area

Canine Training Areas

SDF Offices
Caretaker's Residence

Welcome Center

Canine Memorial

Search Team Showground

Entrance Gate

Search Dog Foundation
National Training Center
"We have not forgotten"

An American First:
The SDF National Training Center

GOAL

To strengthen our country's emergency response network by teaming rescued dogs with firefighters to find people buried in the wreckage of disasters.

LOCATION

125 acres in Santa Paula, California.

CHALLENGE

In order to prepare for disaster deployment, search teams need to train on rubble piles that simulate what they will encounter during actual disasters. Such sites are difficult to find—or keep! For example, a mound of boulders used one week might be ground up and turned into a road the next.

SOLUTION AND PURPOSE

To address this obstacle to effective emergency response training, the National Training Center will provide all of America's search teams with unlimited access to permanent rubble piles, setups for

Photo: Courtesy Search Dog Foundation

Lily-Belle navigates the "wobbly monster" while Julie Padelford-Jansen looks on.

deep victim searches, collapsed structures, mudslides and large-area search sites.

Additionally, the center will offer kennels for the housing and care of up to forty dogs; canine training areas for agility, direction control and obedience; classrooms; a veterinary clinic; housing for visiting handlers and trainers; and SDF administrative offices.

In December 2010, there were 258 FEMA-certified Canine Disaster Search Teams in the United States. A total of 336 teams—or 12 teams for each of America's FEMA task forces—are needed, along with additional teams for state and regional task forces. The new National Training Center will help close that gap to help ensure that no one is left behind when disaster strikes.

Photo: Jan Lopez

Glacier surveys the rubble.

SDF IronDog:
Search Excellence Unleashed

In keeping with SDF's mission to produce the most highly trained search dogs in the country through its recruitment and training program, the foundation developed in 2003 its annual IronDog event, which started as a five-day intensive training exercise that replicated a real-life disaster deployment and included a competition. The IronDog site was a complex series of search sites—immense rubble piles of concrete and debris, pitch-black warehouses, crumbling buildings and shaky lumber piles. Annually, about forty teams participated in IronDog, each team anxious to perform at the top of its game.

Upon arrival, the teams were divided into deployment groups under the command of search-team managers from various task forces. For the duration of the event, the handlers and dogs slept in tents, ate military rations and were awakened before dawn to spend the day searching for "victims" buried in the search sites.

Daily assignments sent each team into search mode to locate victims hidden amid tempting (and sometimes tasty) distractions such as live rabbits, bags of food, cadaver scent, human voices and sudden loud noises. The challenge for the dogs was to ignore all distractions and go straight for the target—a live human, buried or

LEFT: Marsi and handler Jason Geary, ready for action. RIGHT: Krissy works the wobbly.

Photo: Abbey Hull

Photo: Tony Panzica

Photo: Sharon Hanzelka

Photo: Tony Panzica

otherwise hidden from view. The handlers used hand signals, obedience commands and GPS signals to direct their dogs, with a focus on safety and control. Some of the exercises were extremely difficult, requiring the dogs to follow exacting and complex commands. In one breathtaking exercise, the dog and handler were strapped in a harness dangling from a helicopter; this is a need-to-know maneuver, as a team must be ready to descend from an aircraft or a mountaintop to launch a full-scale search.

Other events included a timed obstacle course, a send-out-and-retrieve relay, a direction-control exercise, the "bull's-eye recall and stop" and the "long crawl." Awards were given to the teams with the highest cumulative scores earned throughout the course of the event.

In 2007, the IronDog event was upgraded to a one-day deployment training exercise restricted to sixteen FEMA-certified teams, which allows the most experienced teams to focus on the actual deployment aspect of a disaster by working a full twelve-hour shift. Orchestrated with the help of local police and sheriff's departments, the Coast Guard and other government agencies, the teams deploy under search-team managers and an incident commander who oversees the rescue operation. In 2009, the teams were deployed to a destroyer at sea; they were transported in Coast Guard rafts, hoisted by harness up to the deck and tasked to search the many complex levels of the ship. The teams faced the same demands of IronDog but in a totally foreign and more challenging scenario.

While the complexity of the search scenario may change each year, the teams still perform with the same skill and determination that characterize the SDF search and rescue teams. SDF handler Deresa Teller of the Los Angeles City Fire Department, with her search partner, Ranger, lauds the IronDog event: "I consider it a personal barometer of how well my canine partner and I are able to complete each assignment and how much our hard work and training throughout the year have paid off."

"The recurring benefit of IronDog is that it raises the bar for handlers and their dogs, challenges them, demands their very best. We watch the teams rise to the occasion. They make me very proud," says Pluis Davern, SDF lead trainer.

"You have to see, hear and smell the IronDog to fully understand what an amazing experience it is. The word 'training' does not fully capture what happens here..."

—Ben Hendrix, DVM, observer, IronDog 2005

Major: Growing Up in the SDF Family

by Nona Kilgore Bauer with co-breeder Jason Myers

Major was one of the author's nine field-trial-bred, highly energetic Labrador puppies whelped in November 2008. By the time Major was five weeks old, he and his littermates had mastered shredding their chew toys and chewing holes in their training table. They waged puppy wars inside their training tunnel and battled constantly for the title of "biggest and baddest pup." Major courageously defended his puppy honor, and win, lose or draw, he remained a bold and confident pup.

When Major was twelve weeks old, I drove him to the airport in St. Louis so he could travel to California and begin his new life as a search and rescue trainee. SDF canine recruiter Karen Klingberg strapped him into his too-big orange "Search Dog in Training" vest, which captivated everyone at Gate 15. As we walked through the terminal, Major must have been so excited by the prospect of his new career that he stopped briefly, lost his dignity and pooped! We knew instantly he had a brilliant future as a hero dog.

In California, Major went to live with SDF volunteers Jeff and Jill Wenig, who socialized him and laid the groundwork for formal disaster search training. "We knew he was special when he came to us," Jeff said. "If you told him something once or twice, he understood it and retained

it. We were together 24/7, and he was clearly and actively trying to learn and to please." Major's first adventure was a trip to the Thousand Oaks Mall. "He loved strutting his stuff with his search vest on," Jill said. "He got very excited when it was time to put it on and go into town."

The Wenigs live on a 10-acre ranch and have several horses, so Major was introduced to various outdoor activities and other four-legged creatures. Jeff's contractor work also exposed Major to busy places and noisy heavy equipment. "I looked for new situations to try him on," he said. Jeff sometimes put Major over his shoulders and carried him up the ladder to the rooftops he

LEFT: Major trains on a ladder. BELOW: Major with his SAR partner, firefighter Russell Tao. FACING PAGE: Major with his SDF puppy-raiser, Jeff Wenig.

worked on. He also would hide Major's toy in a concrete rubble pile at a nearby construction site. "I was looking for that focus, that drive and the work ethic so necessary in a search dog."

After five months with Jeff, Major had progressed to doing basic searches, hand signals and full whistle recalls, and he was ready for formal training at SDF's Sundowners Training Center in Gilroy, California. By eighteen months of age, Major was job-ready; in 2010, he was partnered with firefighter Russell Tao of California's Orange County Fire and Rescue. It was official—Major was the real deal and was anxious to go to work.

Jeff reflected on the time that he and Major were together and Major's important place in the Wenig family. "During your time together, the dog becomes an extension of you, a true partner," he said, "but Major was also a pet and part of our family. It's always hard to say goodbye. But if he saves even one life, it's worth all the work of raising him and all the tears when we let him go."

A dog who liked a challenge, Icon met the rigors of disaster search head-on, putting his all into whatever skill he was learning or whatever mission he was working.

BowTie Protégé Icon: Disaster Search Dog

Icon, a yellow Labrador Retriever, was born in Rochester, New York, in September 2004. Bred to be a guide dog for the blind, he started training at eight weeks of age with volunteer puppy-raiser Shannon Bradford. Growing up, Icon enjoyed a happy and busy puppyhood, napping in Shannon's office, riding city buses, wrestling with other puppies and swimming in Lake Ontario.

He sailed through basic and advanced obedience classes and distraction training, and he loved new experiences such as riding escalators and climbing open staircases. Icon loved to work, but despite all the fun stuff, he began to lose interest in regular training. He needed bigger challenges. When the guide-dog association with whom Icon was working closed its doors unexpectedly, ending Icon's future as a guide dog, Shannon realized that life as a pet would not be suitable for his high-powered personality.

Working with a local search and rescue group, Shannon researched other canine organizations and discovered SDF. She spoke with their canine manager and then met with SDF lead trainer Pluis Davern. When Davern met Icon and tested him, she immediately said, "We'll take him!" It was a great opportunity for Icon, but a huge sadness for Shannon, who would have to say goodbye to him.

Icon went to SDF's Sundowners Training Kennel in Gilroy, California, and then spent several

weeks with the SDF-volunteer DeMartini family until a training spot became available. During his stay with the DeMartinis, Icon played with the children in their pool and on the waterslide, and the kids hid in the family's avocado orchard so that Icon could "find" them. When Icon went to Sundowners in May 2006, he was already geared up for search and rescue work.

Icon's first task at Sundowners was learning to bark for his toy, after which he was rewarded with a game of tug-of-war. "He was an absolute monster at tugging!" trainer Kate Davern said. In SAR terms, being a "monster tugger" is a great thing, and this trait matched the rest of Icon's "monster" personality and energy.

Icon with his SAR partner, Steve Swaney, and Steve's retired search dog, Sherman.

During his specialized disaster training program, Icon learned to climb over unstable and uneven surfaces, distinguish a live victim from other scents (including other animals) and signal with a bark alert when he found a "victim" (a person who hides so that the dog can find him in a training scenario). After several months of training, Icon was ready to be paired with a firefighter. Enter SDF firefighter-handler Steve Swaney, whose first K-9 partner, Sherman, was ready to retire. Sherman and Icon met, and they "agreed" that Icon should go home with Steve.

Steve and Icon graduated the following March, and Eric DeMartini and Icon's former puppy-raiser, Shannon, were part of their graduation ceremony. Together, they walked Icon up onto the stage and proudly handed him off to Steve. Shannon remembers, "When I heard Steve's voice as he praised Icon, my last doubts about his new search life melted away. In that instant, I knew that he was in the best possible hands and that I could finally let him go."

Steve and Icon earned FEMA certification in February 2008 and were deployed seven months later to work in the aftermath of Hurricane Gustav in southeastern Louisiana. Two weeks later, Steve and Icon were working in Galveston, Texas, searching for survivors after Hurricane Ike, the most devastating storm in Texas history.

Sadly, Icon died unexpectedly during the night of July 3, 2010. After a game of tug with Steve, Icon retired to his crate for the night. The next morning, Steve discovered that Icon had passed away overnight.

Icon's veterinarian performed an autopsy and found several cancerous tumors on his lungs and heart. Icon had never displayed any symptoms of illness and had sailed through his annual health checks. The vet concluded that his heart had failed due to the extent and stress of the disease.

During his short life and career, Icon put his soul into the search to make sure that no survivors were left behind. He left a lasting impression on the SDF's disaster search program.

THE BOWTIE CONNECTION

BowTie, Inc., was awarded honorary sponsorship of Icon based on the funds raised for SDF through the success of the first edition of *Dog Heroes of September 11th*. Icon—with his outgoing personality and natural love of the camera (just look at that smile)—was a perfect choice to be paired with a pet-book publisher.

Helping Paws in Haiti

When the magnitude 7.0 earthquake hit Haiti on January 12, 2010, destroying most of Port-au-Prince and many surrounding communities, the Haitian government reached out to the Office of US Foreign Disaster Assistance, which is charged with deploying FEMA task forces to overseas disasters.

As part of the American response effort, seven canine disaster search teams trained by the Search Dog Foundation were deployed with US FEMA task forces. Six teams were part of the seventy-two-member California Task Force 2: Los Angeles County Fire Captain Ron Horetski and Labrador Retriever Pearl of the Los Angeles County Urban Search and Rescue Task Force; Los Angeles County engineer Jasmine Segura and Labrador Retriever Cadillac; SDF handler Ron Weckbacher and Border Collie Dawson; Los Angeles County firefighter-paramedic Gary Durian and Golden Retriever Baxter; Los Angeles County engineer Jason Vasquez and German Shepherd Maverick; and Los Angeles County Fire Captain Bill Monahan and Border Collie Hunter. These six teams assembled in Pacoima, California, and then traveled about 80 miles to March Air Force Base to await boarding a C-17 military cargo plane that would take them to Haiti. The seventh SDF team of Florida firefighter Julie Padelford-Jansen and German Shepherd Dakota deployed as part of Florida Task Force 2.

Airlifted on January 14 into the Haitian disaster zone, the task-force teams arrived at 6:30 a.m. and were dispatched to the American Embassy, where they set up their tent-city base of operations on the embassy grounds. Six teams were assigned to two squads to establish alternate work shifts. Pearl, Dawson and Baxter and their handlers joined the Red Squad, with Cadillac, Maverick and Hunter and their handlers working with the Blue Squad. Dakota and Julie were assigned to work with international teams, searching for survivors in the marketplace.

One hour after arriving in Haiti, Ron and Pearl worked their first shift with Jason and Maverick, assigned to search the Arrivé Hotel and the condominium complex that had collapsed behind the hotel. Pearl searched the front of the destroyed buildings while Maverick was sent to search the back, but after several hours of searching, neither dog indicated the presence of survivors.

SDF teams in Haiti (LEFT TO RIGHT): Jasmine and Cadillac, Bill and Hunter, Jason and Maverick, Ron and Pearl, Gary and Baxter and Ron and Dawson.

"We walked the streets, searching building after building," Ron said. "Finally, we approached a row of stores three storeys high. Pearl is a smaller Lab and can get into some pretty tight spaces. I sent her in, and she went 40 to 50 feet inside. She had to crawl over two dead bodies and through pools of bodily fluids to search but came out with no indication of survivors. She had never been exposed to those conditions or that much death, and I was so proud that she never hesitated as she worked."

Pearl's ability to enter those small voids is also a major concern for Ron. "She is just 60 pounds, and I'm 6-foot-6," he said. "If she gets stuck or into trouble, I can't get in there to help or pull her out. Yes, I worry about my dog, but I just have to trust her to do her job."

Working in designated shift periods, the six teams were assigned to canvas large areas of the city. Every structure had collapsed, and streets were difficult to navigate, crowded with vehicles and pedestrians and littered with downed wires and dead bodies. Wild chickens and goats roamed everywhere, and stray dogs scavenged in packs among the corpses. The added possibility of a dog attack made walking the streets more dangerous.

"The local people were burning the bodies in the street," Jasmine said. "The odor of death was overwhelming."

Cadillac and the Blue Squad searched their first building—a collapsed house with deep voids—during the night shift but gave no indication of survivors. "The dog works an area or a pile on his own," Jasmine said. "The dog is trained to range away from the handler, so you don't manage the dog; he knows what to do. You send him into a hole, not knowing where he is or where he will end up. Not seeing your dog is a scary feeling. Yes,

Photo: Courtesy California Task Force 2

he is your tool, but he is also your family and best friend. Cadillac is my second son!"

"We leapfrogged from one building to the next," she continued. "We searched a four-storey building that was collapsed at one end. The rooftop was about 40 feet up, and we had to climb up about 16 feet with the dogs and then lift them up onto the rooftop. Again, they searched the area but showed no interest."

Jasmine and Cadillac search the rubble.

Jasmine and Cadillac share a moment. The bond between SAR dog and handler goes much deeper than simply working together.

Photo: Karyn Newbill

Bill and Hunter set out on foot to patrol an area near the Presidential Palace and search the rubble of a collapsed four-storey building. After crisscrossing one area, Hunter detected survivors' scent and gave his bark alerts to pinpoint their location. Three young girls were trapped beneath several feet of broken concrete. Bill called to the girls that help had arrived, and the rescue crews began digging to extricate them from the wreckage. Bill attached water bottles to a long stick and passed them down to the girls. One of the girls whispered a grateful "thank you." Each rescue effort took several hours, with canine handlers working with the rescue teams to remove layers of concrete and other debris.

Nearby, Julie and Dakota were called to help confirm the location of two more victims; both were pulled out alive.

Jasmine said that the Haitians would sometimes approach them to say that they heard voices coming from the rubble. "On our third day in, a woman told our rescue team that the locals had heard a voice in the wreckage of a day-care center,"

she said. Jasmine's rescue team set up a listening device called a Delsar and was able to detect a tapping sound. Cadillac was sent into one of the voids to verify the possibility of survivors. He began sniffing intently, and with his body language showed lots of interest in the area. CNN journalist Anderson Cooper arrived with his crew to follow the dogs' work and report live from the scene. "We de-layered for about four hours," Jasmine said. "We sent Cadillac in again, then Maverick and Hunter, but this time none showed any interest. We stayed on the pile for another four hours, but after a full eight hours of working on the pile, the task force finally determined that no one was alive. We did one final sweep with all three dogs for a final confirmation, then to call it off."

Ron and Pearl, with Baxter and Dawson and their handlers, spent another night searching for possible survivors beneath the rubble of a bank building. Finding no one alive, they returned to their base of operations at 4:30 a.m. on Sunday. After every mission, the dogs were examined for cuts or injuries, put through a decontamination process, fed and put in their crates to rest. "We are our dogs' doctors," Ron said. "It's our job to make sure they don't get sick or hurt."

On the fourth day, task-force rescue workers discovered a woman trapped in the rubble of a hotel. Jasmine and Cadillac, Bill and Hunter and Jason and Maverick arrived to assist in her rescue. As with other searches, the Haitians gathered in the streets to watch the operation and show their appreciation for the search teams and their task force. As soon as the woman was pulled from the wreckage, the crowd started chanting "USA! USA! USA!" Jasmine said that this was a huge morale boost for the search teams.

Jasmine, Bill, Jason and their dogs moved on to a collapsed three-storey building nearby to assist in the rescue of two women trapped beneath the rubble. Two sisters, nineteen and twenty years old, were discovered when they called out to the rescuers. Rescue teams spent six hours digging to remove concrete and debris and free the girls. They were safely extricated, unharmed, and were able to walk away.

Cadillac, Maverick and Hunter were then sent to search an adjacent apartment building where the rooftop had collapsed. When Cadillac sniffed and showed some interest in the area, the rescue team dug to open up a hole that was large enough to crawl through. Jasmine, Bill and Jason took their dogs into a small space, and Cadillac searched again. This time, he became more animated, smelling one area very intently. The team began to dig and soon discovered a woman buried about 40 feet below, pinned to her mattress by the concrete blocks of her bedroom ceiling. Trapped there for four days, she was weak, ill and dehydrated. After the rescue team enlarged the cavity, Jasmine was able to get close enough to see the woman waving and hear her say "thank you" in English. The handlers and rescue teams dug for several hours, often using hand tools to remove the concrete. They succeeded in removing enough debris to cut out the mattress she was lying on and slide her to safety. As with other victims that were rescued, her fate remained unknown, as there were no Haitian ambulances or emergency personnel to transport people to a hospital or other place of safety.

During the next work shift, Ron and Pearl, Gary and Baxter and Ron and Dawson helped to extricate a fifty-year-old woman from a collapsed building. Although she was dehydrated, she was not seriously injured.

Captain Bill Monahan reported back to SDF to update them on the dogs' search effort. "The dogs are working great, and all are eating and drinking well…. We're working to make it fun for them so they'll stay motivated. It's a giant team effort—from the canines to the logistics team to communications—everyone is working at full capacity, using everything we have been trained to do to find survivors. It's an honor to be here."

As with most disasters, after the first five or six days, the possibility of finding survivors is unfortunately unlikely. The SDF search teams continued to patrol the streets for the rest of their deployment, looking for buildings where survivors might be found. The dogs were kept in air-conditioned vehicles, provided by the government, in case they were needed to help locate victims. The handlers responded to requests from their task force to confirm possible finds and provide general support in relief operations for the city's population.

At 6 p.m. PST., on January 28, the six SDF teams from California, along with the rest of California Task Force 2, returned home from Haiti, and Julie and Dakota returned to Florida, after a sixteen-day deployment. They were welcomed by family, friends and fellow firefighters.

SDF founder, Wilma Melville, spoke of the rescue effort: "Twelve lives have been saved by the combined effort of dogs and humans. Our rescued dogs have become rescuers. Our handlers are true American heroes. And the nation is better for it. Disaster response will be stronger because the teams were there. Because they said 'Yes' to years of training and sacrifice. 'Yes' to the call to action."

ASPCA's Dog of the Year: SDF's Pearl

Ron and Pearl put their skills and training to work as they search the rubble following the Haiti earthquake.

"Black Pearl" was a typical rebellious runaway, roaming the streets of the city, looking for love and entertainment. Owned by a well-meaning young man who worked long hours, Pearl was left unattended in the yard all day. Energetic and creative, she mastered the art of fence-jumping to look for adventure in her neighborhood. She was a frequent guest at the Plumas County Animal Shelter, compliments of the animal control officer who took her into custody. Pearl's owner paid several handsome bail-out fees before he decided he could no longer afford her expensive travel habits, and he surrendered her to the shelter.

Pearl's "bouncing off the walls" yet friendly disposition, and the shiny black coat for which she was named, caught the eye of canine behaviorist Jack Cumbra, a volunteer with High Sierra Animal Rescue in Portola, California, during his rounds at the shelter. So Pearl was "remanded" to High Sierra for evaluation as a possible search dog and a new beginning. Her high energy and eagerness to please impressed rescue volunteer Penny Woodruff, also a member of the SDF's recruitment team, and she alerted SDF that they had a potential candidate.

"Within five minutes I knew we had a winner," said Karen Klingberg, SDF's canine recruiter. Pearl could not sit still; she ran after her toy over and over again, even barreling into thorny bushes without hesitation. "She would disappear over the dune into the thicket, and I couldn't even see her," Karen said, "and a few minutes later, she would pop out with the toy in her mouth, ready to do it again." So Pearl drove off with Karen to the SDF Sundowners training center in Gilroy to begin formal training for disaster search.

In July 2008, after a year of intense training at SDF, Pearl was assigned to Captain Ron Horetski of the Los Angeles County Fire Department. The

Photo: Courtesy Search Dog Foundation

Photo: Kelly Morrison

Photo: Laura Pollick

Photo: Courtesy Search Dog Foundation

ABOVE: Ron and Pearl enjoy their appearance at a book signing for *A New Job for Pearl*.

two achieved FEMA certification in May 2009 and were deployed two months later to their first mission, a building collapse in La Puente, California.

In January 2010, Pearl was once again running the streets, this time in Haiti, searching for victims of the earthquake. Deployed with six other SDF canine teams with Los Angeles County Task Force 2, she and Ron worked for sixteen days and helped rescue multiple survivors.

Later in 2010, two California grade-school teachers, Allyn Lee and Connie Forslind, decided to share the story of Pearl's new life at SDF and her mission with Ron after the Haiti earthquake. In their book, *A New Job for Pearl*, with illustrations by their students, they describe how a homeless dog became a hero. Their goal is to earn $10,000 in proceeds to donate to SDF for the care and training of a new search dog.

Understanding the Search and Rescue Canine

Search and rescue dogs work in close contact with their trainers and handlers as they learn to navigate a variety of obstacles.

To fully understand what the disaster search dogs or the HRD (human remains detection) dogs are trained to do and how they are able to perform such extraordinary deeds, you must first understand the basics of canine mentality and behavior. Search dogs of all disciplines must first be high-prey-drive dogs who are endowed with a strong work ethic—a desire to work that is part of their genetic make-up, part of their very souls. Their desire to "do something" supersedes all else. Search-dog trainers harness that desire by reinforcing it with something fun and positive, usually a toy. The "work" has to be fun for the dog, a game in which he gets a reward for performing a certain task. Finally, the dog performs his job to please the person he loves most: the handler at the other end of his leash.

The SAR dog is trained in two search disciplines: live find, in which the rescue of a live victim is the ultimate goal; and cadaver, in which the dog is trained to identify human remains and the goal is recovery of those remains. Some SAR dogs are cross-trained for both live find and cadaver. (During the 9/11 crisis, many live-find dogs gave subtle indications on cadaver.)

Cadaver dogs are specially trained to find human decomposition scent and alert their handlers to its location. They are used most often in the search and recovery of dead bodies and human remains. These canine specialists are trained to alert only on human scent, ignoring any other decomposing material, such as animal remains. They can detect the odor of dead bodies not yet decomposed as well as bodies that have been buried for several decades. They also will indicate on soil that has been contaminated with human fluids or decomposing human flesh. Cadaver dogs often are used in conjunction with live-find dogs to locate deceased victims as well as survivors of natural and man-made disasters. Their job is equally vital to the families of victims.

Alert is the term used to describe the method or signal used by the dog to tell the handler that he has located the victim or object of the search. The live-find dog alerts his handler with a *focused bark* for a minimum of thirty seconds. In a *passive alert*, the dog may sit or down at the location of the find; this alert is sometimes preferred because it will not disturb any evidence in the area. A dog trained to give an *aggressive alert* will dig at the location of his find. In a *refind,* the dog returns to the handler, barks and then returns to the location of the victim. The sequence is repeated until the handler reaches the person.

The SAR dog can be certified according to the environment in which he is trained to work. *Urban* or *disaster* dogs are trained to work on difficult, dangerous and unstable surfaces or terrain. *Wilderness* or *large-area* search dogs are used most often in remote or rural areas where the status of the missing or lost person is unknown. *Forensic* or *evidence* search refers to finding human evidence, which includes bodies or body parts, body tissue or fluids and any other human remains. *Water* and *avalanche* dogs are trained to find humans, dead or alive, in those specific

Future World Trade Center hero Kaiser learns the ropes of search and rescue as a puppy under the guidance of his handler, Tony Zintsmaster.

environments. All of these dogs utilize airborne scent to locate their subject. *Trailing* dogs, which find lost people by following the scent deposited along their path, are also used extensively in wilderness and urban settings.

Certification of a search and rescue dog also depends upon the organization of the handler's affiliation. The FEMA standards for the urban search and rescue (USAR) dog are the most demanding, and teams must pass a rigorous canine evaluation as well as written and verbal handler tests in order to qualify at the basic (Type II) and advanced (Type I) levels. The FEMA mission statement is specific for live find, the philosophy being that time is vital to the survival of a live victim. Therefore, the dog must be trained to ignore cadaver scent and pursue only people who are still alive.

The National Association of Search and Rescue (NASAR) is an umbrella organization for all categories of search dogs that offers its own certification standards. In certain states, SAR teams must pass state certification tests before they can be deployed in an official capacity.

Law-enforcement officers frequently maintain specialty dogs that are trained in narcotics and bomb detection as well as search and rescue. Only in recent years has the value of the canine nose been recognized as a powerful tool for assistance in today's volatile society.

Argus of NJ-TF1 is rewarded for making a live find during a training session. Dogs can be trained to perform unbelievable tasks for the simple pleasure of playing with a favorite toy.

Argus is at it again, negotiating some obstacles and rough terrain during his training session.

The handlers, just like the K-9s, must be schooled in SAR. Photo courtesy of the Nebraska Task Force.

Not to be outdone by his teammate, Nutmeg also "alerts" on a live find.

The Search Tool with a Tail: The Air-Scenting Dog

by Bob Sessions
Pennsylvania Task Force 1

In recent years, air-scenting canines have been gaining increased recognition in the SAR community. Rescuers have realized that dogs can be trained to use their natural instincts to find trapped or lost people quickly and effectively.

Dogs have been used for many years to conduct wilderness and open-country searches in the United States and Europe. In the wild, undomesticated canines use their air-scenting instincts to find food, locate females in heat or even avoid predators. Humans have recognized these basic scenting abilities and have trained air-scenting canines into valuable tools for locating people in emergency situations. But while movies and the media have brought the abilities of Bloodhounds in tracking down escaped criminals to the general public, the air-scenting canine is not as widely understood.

Simply stated, instead of tracking scent along the ground as Bloodhounds do, air-scenting dogs pick up scent that is transported by movement.

Also, Bloodhounds are limited to tracking a specific person's scent from a known starting point or the last point at which the person was seen. Air-scenting dogs don't need a specific starting point; they can start from anywhere in the search area and can make a find without knowing a specific person's scent.

In addition to performing wilderness searches for a lost child or an Alzheimer's patient who has wandered away, air-scenting dogs can locate survivors and deceased victims in collapsed buildings during disaster scenarios, an application demonstrated in Oklahoma City and during the September 11 terrorist attacks. These dogs can make survivors out of skiers buried in an avalanche with timely finds followed by quick extrications. They can find drowning victims or subjects of homicide or suicide searches. Although the probability of making a find while using air-scenting dogs is relatively high, this probability does vary based on the prevailing conditions.

As scent is carried downwind from the subject in an open area, it spreads out into a cone shape that is narrow at the source and widens with the distance from the source. The dog uses this scent cone to find the source of the scent.

How is an air-scenting dog able to detect the presence of a lost, hidden or completely confined subject? It all begins in the nose. Humans have approximately 5 million sensory cells in our noses dedicated to detecting scent. In contrast, canines have an estimated 125 to 200 million sensory cells to carry out that same function.

When air-scenting dogs zero in on a human scent, they're really detecting dead skin cells. The average human body sheds approximately 40,000 dead skin cells a minute as a normal biological function. These skin cells are covered with bacteria, even on a person stepping out of the shower. The bacteria eat and digest the skin cells, giving off a gas that we call body odor. This body odor, combined with other scents given off by the human, is what the air-scenting dog targets.

A grouping of skin cells is called a *raft*. A flake of dandruff is a recognizable raft. Larger rafts typically fall to the ground, and these larger rafts are what the Bloodhound tracks. The smaller rafts, or individual cells, are light enough to be carried by the slightest movement of air. These rafts can travel great distances in open areas or pass through small cracks, porous materials or crevices. They can even be carried through water to emerge on the surface. During movement, rafts continue to give off the gas generated by the bacteria.

The air-scenting canine is trained to find the source of this scent: the person. Teaching a dog to find the source of human scent is accomplished through an imprinting and rewarding process. After a successful find, the handler must immediately reward the dog for a job well done. This reward might be food, enthusiastic praise

and petting or, such as with my dog, several tosses of a small pocket Frisbee. The immediate reward is a very important part of the process that keeps the canine eager to search.

The majority of dog/handler teams used for local searches and with FEMA task forces are volunteers, and search dogs and their handlers are an integral part of the search and rescue team. Properly trained dogs can cut down on search time and help limit the rescuers' exposure to danger. In addition, they are reliable and hard-working and can be a comfort to team members working long missions. In many ways, this search tool is a rescuer's best friend.

Bob Sessions is a more than twenty-year veteran of search and rescue. He has been involved with the USAR program since its inception in 1989.

Pentagon hero Alley truly is the epitome of the "search tool with a tail."

The USAR canine team is one of the key components of a FEMA task force's response to a catastrophe.

FEMA-certified Bretagne catches up on some much-needed rest during down time at Ground Zero.

The FEMA-Certified Dog

They climb rickety ladders and scale mounds of broken concrete and debris. They balance on wobbly teeter-totters and crawl into dark, tight spaces. Strapped into special lifting harnesses, they dangle calmly as their handlers scale steep rock walls.

Prospective search and rescue dogs are challenged with these and many other difficult tasks before they can be certified as urban search and rescue (USAR) dogs. The goal is certification by Federal Emergency Management Agency (FEMA), considered the ultimate credential in disaster search work.

The USAR canine team is a vital ingredient in the FEMA task force. FEMA is the nation's premier resource for rescue and assistance. Utilizing the best in people and technology, FEMA has designed a task-force program to provide immediate emergency assistance to local agencies across the country when a catastrophe occurs.

"Best in People" most aptly describes the FEMA canine handler. Year after year, these dedicated handlers, volunteers all, devote themselves and their dogs to the world of search and rescue. Canine search teams train at least twice a week, year-round, in all types of weather with their task-force teammates at home-based training sites and out-of-state training seminars. They purchase their own survival gear and pay their own expenses, which can amount to several thousand dollars each year on training and travel. Such dramatic demands on their personal lives and the enormous commitment in time and money further illustrate the sacrifice and dedication of the FEMA USAR K-9 handlers. The constraints necessarily limit the number of volunteers who are willing to tackle, indeed embrace, the challenge of urban search and rescue. "We're not in this for the glory but instead to help people when they need it the most," said Lynne Engelbert of California Task Force 3.

Because the challenge of searching structural collapses differs greatly from the natural settings of wilderness, water or mountain search, FEMA developed the highly specialized USAR program in 1990. FEMA's twenty-eight USAR task forces are strategically located across the country, ready to respond at a moment's notice. Each task force is composed of four sections: Rescue, Medical, Technical and Search, the latter of which includes four teams called K-9 Search Specialists. Each task force is sponsored by a local agency, typically a fire department. Within that structure, about 160 FEMA-certified USAR canine teams nationwide stand "mission-ready" at all times, training consistently year-round to maintain their skills in the event that they are deployed. Tests are held monthly around the country with new teams reaching certification.

In an early demonstration, technical search specialists using seismic listening devices and search cameras took two hours to find a victim. The dogs were able to locate the same victim in approximately five minutes.

FEMA certification requires intense, consistent and dedicated training, as demonstrated by Border Collie search dog Blitz.

After a task force is deployed to a disaster scene, one of the first "tools" called upon is the canine search team. Disaster search canines are healthy, athletic, high-drive dogs that must be nonaggressive and able to cope with the stress, noise and confusion of a typical rescue scene. More than purely canine super-sleuths, FEMA search dogs are also super-workhorses, driven by a work ethic that is programmed in their genes.

Working without collars, leashes or harnesses, these amazing canine sniffers can cover large areas with great speed and agility, often searching otherwise impossible-to-reach places. Blessed with an estimated 200 million scent receptors, the dogs can locate with high accuracy live victims buried in vast amounts of earth, snow and complicated rubble.

Developing such specialized skills can take up to two years of consistent, dedicated training. The dogs must master technical obedience skills and then learn to navigate complex and unstable surfaces, high elevations and small, dark spaces—jungles of concrete, debris and heavy vegetation—and charge through it all without qualm or question. The dogs must be completely focused on the task at hand, oblivious to the chaos that attends a typical disaster scene.

FEMA canines are classified as Type II (basic) or Type I (advanced). To achieve Type II certification, the dog must prove that he is non-aggressive; must be able to work off leash; must be able to negotiate ladders, teeter-totters and elevated planks; and must be willing to crawl through small dark tunnels. The handler must be able to direct the dog with hand signals through a "baseball-diamond" course in a maximum of three minutes. The dog must indicate two live "victims" by barking for a minimum of thirty seconds (sustained bark) and must be able to search rubble piles and alert on victims while out of his handler's sight.

In another early demonstration, firefighters took approximately two hours to find a victim hidden in the rubble. The dogs were able to locate the same victim in about five minutes.

FEMA Type I teams also must prove that the dog can locate and alert on six victims buried in three separate rubble piles that have been contaminated with food, clothing and animal distractions. Each site tests a different ability of the team: one site has full access for the dog and handler; one allows the handlers perimeter access only; and one limits the handler to a specific area until the canine alerts, proving that the dog can search and alert on his own. Testing is done by qualified evaluators from a national roster of FEMA evaluators.

In addition to mastering the canine skills, the handler must pass verbal and written tests regarding search and rescue strategies and briefing and debriefing skills. Teams must be recertified every two years to maintain their FEMA status.

The events of September 11, 2001, presented the ultimate challenge to the training and abilities of the K-9 teams who were deployed to the various search and recovery sites. All of them responded with characteristic courage and enthusiasm, never faltering in their resolve to find even a single survivor in what became known as "the pile at Ground Zero" as well as in the wreckage at the Pentagon.

Dusty (ABOVE, LEFT), a Pentagon hero, keeps up pace with his FEMA training in case he and his handler, Mary Berry, get the call to deploy. K-9 heroes Dusty (ABOVE, CENTER) and Ivey (ABOVE) show off their fearlessness and agility.

K2 Canines:
the
IED Detection Solution

*The capability they
[Military Working Dogs]
bring to the fight cannot be
replicated by man or machine.
By all measures of performance,
their yield outperforms any
assist we have in our inventory.
Our Army (and military)
would be remiss if we failed to
invest more in this incredibly
valuable resource.*
—Gen. David H. Petraeus,
February 9, 2008,
from the United States War Dog
Association website

This IED program is about more than winning a blue ribbon in competition. This job is about doing the best you can with the dog and the Marine, because that will save lives. I feel like fate has put me here, that after thirty years of dog training, now I can do something with it that will save someone's life. This is an opportunity to give something back, and I thank God every day that I am here.
—Bobby George, K2 trainer and team leader, pictured with K2 demo dog Tex, a half-brother to the author's field champion FC-AFC Chances R Mein Schatzie. Bobby trained Schatzie to her titles before joining K2.

I found out it wasn't just training dogs. It was training them for a higher purpose.
—Glen Curtis, K2 trainer

If I can be a part of this and help save lives of young men who are fighting for our country, that's what it's all about for me.
—Gary Cook, K2 trainer and team leader

These young Marines are like sponges and want to learn everything. Their military background prepares them mentally for this. They don't handle the dogs with emotion or get mad when the dogs do something wrong. All they can think of is what they can do to make it right. And you can believe that from that moment on, [the Marines] will never make that mistake again.
—Erin Kendrigan, K2 trainer

The dog doesn't care what his reward is; he just needs recognition that he did his job for you. All the Labs I've worked with have been excellent dogs, and every one got certified.
—Glen Curtis

Photo: Susan Kjellsen

We take our time to figure out the personalities of the dog and the Marine to match them up perfectly. When our first group graduated, it was like peanut butter and jelly. When that marriage comes together, it's like a breath of fresh air, and I cannot believe I did that!
—**Bruce Koonce, K2 trainer and team leader**

Photo: Susan Kjellsen

During every class, one or two Marines will ask what happens to their dogs at the end of their career and if they can get the dogs. Later, the head of our program will brief them on the adoption process. When he asks how many want to adopt their dogs, every hand goes up.
—**Erin Kendrigan**

We owe it to our war dogs and their handlers that serve us all to continue to educate the public about their courageous exploits.
—**United States War Dog Association**

Canines have been used for centuries as auxiliaries in warfare. Recognized in many cultures for their acute senses, speed, docility and affection for man, they were, and continue to be, of great value for military purposes. During the Middle Ages, the early Greeks and Romans used enormous hound-type dogs, many outfitted with spiked collars and heavy armor, to attack the enemy and defend caravans of soldiers. The North American Indians utilized dogs for draft work. During the Spanish–Moroccan War, dogs were camouflaged in dressings to appear as people and trained to run along the front lines to draw enemy fire, thus revealing target gun positions.

By the early part of the twentieth century, most European countries used canines in their military. Trained primarily as sentry and attack dogs, scout and messenger dogs and sled and pack dogs, their training and utilization gradually evolved along with other weaponry. As methods of warfare changed through the ages, so too did the role of the dogs of war.

Dogs have served honorably in the US military since World War I, although they were utilized only minimally during that conflict. After the attack on Pearl Harbor in 1941 and the subsequent escalation of the US war effort, the dog-breeding community mobilized and was instrumental in launching the Dogs for Defense program in 1942.

However, civilian inexperience with training dogs to military requirements and the military's position on the experimental use of canines in various theaters of war delayed the development of successful training programs. Despite those issues, by 1945 over 10,000 war dogs had been

What we're doing with detection work is learning a more refined art of using the dog's nose to find something, which correlates directly to how they actually find birds. We want to develop what the dog naturally wants to do, and mold that natural state into what we want. It's not just A-B-C-type training.

—**Mike Osteen, K2 senior trainer**

The dog sniffs an odor and gets a reward. It sounds so simple, but there are so many theories about the best way to do that.

—**Bobby George**

When we go to California with the Marines after they graduate, we are there to observe them. It's their show. We just introduce this new product into their system and advise the whole battalion what the dogs can do and how important they are. We tell them they just acquired a new tool to use to their advantage to fight this war of IEDs. Once they see what the dogs are capable of, they are all very receptive.

—**Glen Curtis**

This is by far the most rewarding thing I have ever done. To watch these Marines and see the look in their eyes, that they need you and feel like you're doing something really big for them, is awesome.

—Bruce Koonce

Photo: Mark Williams

When the Marines show up, there are always a couple of skeptics who question what the dogs can do...until they see the dog run full speed ahead, then sit on command and turn around; they become believers. One young Marine said to me, "That's crazy awesome!"

—Bobby George

trained for all branches of the military, guarding, protecting and serving with courage, loyalty and honor.

Dogs continued to serve the armed forces with distinction in the Korean War, the Vietnam War and the Persian Gulf War. Vietnam veteran and former Air Force dog handler Larry Chilcoat remembers patrolling his Vietnam camp perimeter with his sentry dog, German Shepherd Geisha, in 1969. In an article titled "Honoring a Soldier's Best Friend" by Mike Baird, Chilcoat says that after more than forty years, "...I still carry a photo of Geisha in my wallet; she changed my life. [She] was my lifeblood in a jungle nightmare, and we both relied on each other day and night to survive. She heard things I didn't and let me know. I knew she would die to protect me."

According to the United States War Dog Association, "It has been estimated that these courageous canine heroes saved over 10,000 lives during the conflict in Vietnam."

As America's response to the 2001 terrorist attacks increased our military fighting presence overseas, the need also increased for canines to assist in that war effort. The canine as a bomb detector has become the latest tool in the US war on terror and has been invaluable in the Middle East, including in mine-infested countries such as Afghanistan, "the most mined area on Planet Earth" according to the Hahn's 50th AP K-9 website by Tom Newton.

Enter the Labrador Retriever. In recent years, advanced studies at the Auburn University College of Veterinary Medicine's Canine Detection

The dog is looking for an odor instead of a bumper, and we're just exploiting his natural desire to retrieve. The only thing that changes is the final response.

—Glen Curtis

Photo: Mark Williams

The Marines tell us they would rather walk with their dogs than with all of the other sophisticated equipment out there. One handler had been in Afghanistan last summer and spoke about his dog in reverential terms. His dog slept with him and would get up in the middle of the night and check the entire perimeter and all of the outposts.

—Bobby George

Photo: Susan Kjellsen

We have the best trainers in the country at K2, and what we are doing here and have accomplished with these dogs is in itself amazing.

—Bobby George

Photo: Susan Kjellsen

They are really proud of their dogs. It's like, "Don't say anything bad about my wife...and don't say anthing bad about my dog!"

—Gary Cook

When the Marines show up at K2 every day to work with the dogs, they're on time and ready to work, and they don't care how late they work. It can be raining or hot, and they're out there working their butts off. By the time they graduate, they almost have tears in their eyes to leave their dogs for a few days before they get them again in California to deploy. They are leaving their best friends.

—Glen Curtis

Photo: Mark Williams

I am very passionate about these dogs, and I know it's going to be a sad goodbye when they leave, but it's what I have to do. If I train these dogs with compassion and that "connection," they're going to be that much better when I hand them over to a Marine. Then they can stand next to that dog like it's their own.

—Amy Cook, K2 trainer

Research Institute developed a new approach to improvised explosives detection. And the versatile Labrador, with its estimated 125 to 200 million sensory cells and an "I-can-do-it" attitude driven by the breed's insatiable desire to retrieve, was declared the ideal candidate for the role of Improvised Explosive Device (IED) Detection Specialist.

That conclusion led the Marine Corps to select the Labrador Retriever to assist its military forces in Afghanistan. In 2009, the Corps contracted with K2 Solutions in Southern Pines, North Carolina, to train new Labrador recruits.

President and founder of K2 Solutions, Lane Kjellsen, believes that the Marines' selection of the Labrador Retriever is, in fact, testament to the total Lab. "This is a combination of decathlon skills that takes the breed to a whole new level. It is really the evolution of the field-trial Lab and a tribute to the last fifty years of Labrador competition."

At the K2 training camp, potential candidates are evaluated, and those selected spend four to six months in canine boot camp to learn the basic skills of IED detection, perform search tasks and achieve Marine Corps-approved certification. Each dog is paired with a Marine handler after certification, and the K2 trainers then teach the dogs and their new partners to work together as teams and to trust each other unconditionally, with each dog bonding tightly to the Marine at the other end of the leash, and each Marine understanding that his or her Labrador partner may someday save his or her life. S.Sgt. Gregory S. Massey, Military Police Task Force, said in an article titled "'Dog Teams' Take On Climate of Iraq," "When they do find something,

Photo: Mark Williams

Once the dogs are assigned to the Marines, we as trainers don't touch the dogs. When [the Marines] show up each day, [the dogs] are their dogs. They take them out of the kennel, feed and water them, groom and exercise them and do health checks. And during their down time between training sessions, they're stroking their dogs and smooching with them. They know they can pet their dogs, but they also understand that when it's show time, it's all business and you do not pet your dog. And the dog also has that off-and-on switch about when it's time to go to work.

—Bruce Koonce

Photo: Mark Williams

Photo: Mark Williams

The Marine handlers are also their dog's doctors. The certification process includes medical training to handle on-site combat injuries and emergencies.

The dogs coming in are good. They come with all different types of person- alities; some are so smart, some have huge hearts.

—Bobby George

The Marines come in, and some don't have a clue about dogs and have just a few weeks to learn. Then you mold them into trainers and form a bond between them and the dogs to go to the other side of the world to save lives. It's amazing how quickly they just come together. I think it's the desire of the Marine, wanting to learn so badly, because he knows this is his guardian angel and he has to connect with this dog.

—Bruce Koonce

MORE ON MWDs

To find the websites and articles quoted in this chapter, please visit the following:

Corpus Christi Caller Times (www.caller.com): "Honoring a Soldier's Best Friend" by Mike Baird

Defense Video & Imagery Distribution System (www.dvidshub.net): "'Dog Teams' Take On Climate of Iraq"

Hahn's 50th AP K-9 Web site by Tom Newton (http://community-2.webtv.net/Hahn-50thAP-k9)

United States Department of Defense (www.defense.gov): "Military Working Dogs Protect Forces, Bases During Terror War" by Donna Miles, American Forces Press Service

United States War Dog Association (www.uswardogs.org)

it may be just one bomb to save one Marine, but that is enough. They save lives."

While the dogs live in a kennel environment during training and later at their assigned US military bases, during deployments they live with their Marine handlers twenty-four hours a day, seven days a week, sharing food rations and sleeping quarters in their bunks—much to the delight of the dogs, who by far prefer their Marine handlers as bed partners. That emotional bond continues with these life-or-death best friends for the duration of their deployments.

In a combat environment, where the dogs perform lifesaving missions in the field, they are still trained daily during their "down time" to maintain their search and detection skills. They also provide emotional support for their handlers and their handlers' Marine buddies, who face death and danger every day. Thanks to their naturally affectionate nature, the Labradors act as interim therapy dogs, providing comfort and relaxation to help relieve the stress of life in combat zones. As for the dogs, their work is also play, since finding an IED is just a means to getting their reward. They don't get combat pay, and they ask only for an "Atta boy!" You can bet that the Marines are more than generous with that praise.

Dogs have a heart—something that makes them an invaluable asset to our fighting forces.

—Army Col. David Rolfe

A two-sentence email sent to Lane Kjellsen said it best: "The dogs save lives. We need more dogs." What better job could there be for the irrepressible Lab than lifesaver…and Marine best friend.

It's pretty amazing when you have trained this dog for six months and after a couple of weeks, the dog won't come to you but prefers to stay with its Marine. That guy's ego just shoots up 100 percent. Then you know you've done your job.

—Bruce Koonce

Photo: Mark Williams

I pair the dog with the Marine; the next day, they are already best friends. It's amazing...if the dog's foot hurts, the Marine will pick the dog up and carry him on his shoulders to the kennel rather than make the dog walk. The Marines know that, when they go over there, when they're out on a mission, it will be just them and their dogs.

—Gary Cook

MWD...Military Working Dog

by Sandra Allen (from K9Pride.net)

Dedicated to the brave military dogs and their human partners, heroes all.
Because of you, terrorism will never win. To all who have fallen, you are missed.

MWD...Military Working Dog
Three little words to describe an elite soldier,
An American K-9 soldier.

MWD...three little words
To describe the exuberant, joyful streak toward a target,
The courage under fire,
The pure power in motion,
The gentleness when all is well,
The puppy dance when a mission is over.

Military Working Dog...three little words
To describe a soldier who ignores injury when the voice he loves calls to him to go,
Not to find safety,
But to find danger,
So that those he claims as his own can live free,
Because that's what it means to be an American soldier.

And if he should become one of the fallen,
Or if his partner makes the ultimate sacrifice,
They will mourn deeply for each other because a part of their heart has died too.
But there is a bigger part of each one that has come alive on their journeys together,
Because they mirror the greatness in each other.
And that can only be celebrated.

Military Working Dog...
Three little words.

K2 Military Working Dogs

Portraits by Mark Williams

Sergeant Zazzy

Sergeant Socks

Staff Sergeant Rush

Corporal Mia

Corporal Maggie

Certified United States Marine Corps
Improvised Explosive Device Detector Dog

K2 060 Libby

Sergeant Libby

Certified United States Marine Corps
Improvised Explosive Device Detector Dog

K2 123 Kate

Corporal Kate

Certified United States Marine Corps
Improvised Explosive Device Detector Dog

K2 114 Kane

Corporal Kane

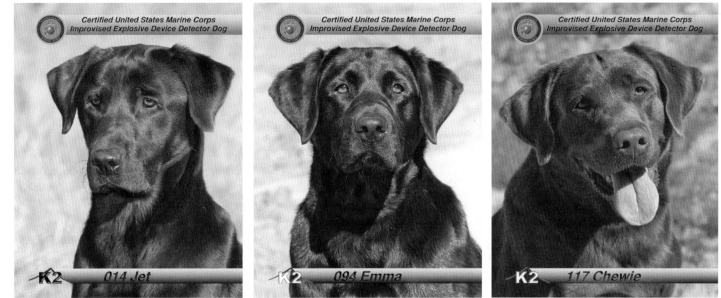

Certified United States Marine Corps
Improvised Explosive Device Detector Dog

K2 014 Jet

Corporal Jet

Certified United States Marine Corps
Improvised Explosive Device Detector Dog

K2 094 Emma

Corporal Emma

Certified United States Marine Corps
Improvised Explosive Device Detector Dog

K2 117 Chewie

Chewie (did not deploy due to illness)

These Are the Dogs of War

by Susan Kjellsen
from *Retriever News,* April 2010

Daisy, Bingo, Petey, Tex, Rocky, Boomer, Rupert, Sugar, Holly, Merlin, Page, Emma, Bullet, Gretchen, Kate…these are the dogs of war. These are the dogs that are saving the lives of our Marines. These are all Labrador Retrievers.

Labrador Retrievers have been the most popular breed of dog in the United States, and perhaps even the world, for the past eighteen years—and with good reason. These dogs are friendly, loyal, smart and eager to both please and play. They are retrieving machines that, with the proper training, will reliably bring back anything from balls and bumpers to upland game and waterfowl. They will do this all day long, unceasingly and with joy, until they drop. Just ask anyone with a Lab and a tennis ball! Added to all of this is a dog with a nose that can sniff out just about anything.

These attributes of instinct, loyalty and drive have not gone unnoticed by the US military. In the ongoing Global War on Terrorism, military strategists are continually looking for an edge in keeping our troops safe while enhancing their effectiveness. When confronted by improvised explosive devices (IEDs), the most lethal weapons in use by our enemies, these strategists began to consider the innate traits of Labs as a possible way to mitigate the threat.

The use of dogs in combat goes back to World War I, but the use of Labs in combat is new. German and Dutch Shepherds along with Belgian Malinois have served long and honorably in combat

situations and are still valuable assets. But as the battlefield has changed, so have the requirements to protect our fighting men and women. Based on the positive results of the use of Labs in detection work by Auburn University's Canine Detection Research Institute, the US Marine Corps made the decision to develop a full-scale effort to train these dogs in the latest explosive detection techniques and place them with combat troops.

In the late summer of 2009, K2 Solutions, Inc., a federal contracting company located in Southern Pines, North Carolina, was chosen to go forward with this effort. Their first task was to find quality Labs with very specific qualifications. The dogs had to be between twelve and forty-three months old, have clear hips and eyes, be collar conditioned and, perhaps most importantly, be trained to handle to a pile at least 100 yards distant. K2's owner, Lane Kjellsen, a retriever field trial judge and former "trialer" himself, turned to the field trial/hunt test community to find the dogs. In an almost heroic effort, the K2 team combed not only this country but also Canada to find the best dogs available. In the end, more than 170 Labs came into K2 for evaluation, and 135 were purchased and put into training.

During the same time, K2 began to recruit nationally known retriever trainers to become a part of this exciting effort. Trainers from throughout the country signed on to pilot the program, bringing with them years of combined knowledge and experience in the retriever world. K2 brought law enforcement and military working dog specialists on board as well, and these two groups of trainers came together to teach the dogs their new job of finding IEDs.

Throughout the summer and fall of 2009, the trainers put the dogs through their paces, teaching them to find hidden explosives. The trainers carefully worked the dogs in diverse conditions, in the cold, the heat, and the rain and in a wide variety of environments to condition them and prepare them for whatever they might face in the theater of war.

When the dogs were trained and ready, the Marine Corps tested each one on a series of tasks specific to the battlefield. Once the dogs passed this rigorous evaluation, each was certified as ready to learn to work with a novice Marine handler.

The Marines came to town in successive groups. While many of these young men had had dogs in their lives, some had never even owned a dog before. It is safe to say that none of them had ever owned a dog like the Labs they were paired with now. They were in awe of their Labs' natural ability and advanced training and even apprehensive about the task that lay ahead of them. But as the dogs and handlers were matched up, it soon became evident that it was love at first sight—for both the dogs and the Marines.

The K2 trainers spent time in the classroom and in the field, teaching subjects ranging from simple first aid to advanced handling techniques. Practical exercises filled each day, with the dogs and men learning how to work together. Soon that initial bond turned into something deeper, an understanding that they were teammates who would have to rely upon each other in combat.

Photo: Shutterstock/Lee Price

At the end of training, the new teams were ready to head out for more advanced preparation and eventually for deployment to Iraq and Afghanistan. At one graduation ceremony, while speaking of the dogs, trainer Bobby George summed them up in a voice thick with tears, ***"When I came here, I thought I might be giving each Marine a guardian angel to take with him into war. After this training, I know I am."***

This effort is ongoing. As the dogs rotate out of combat, they come back to K2 for rest, relaxation and time to just be a dog. As soon as they are ready, the K2 trainers take over again, sharpening the dogs' skills with an emphasis on discipline and handling. It's then time to introduce the dogs to a whole new class of Marine handlers, and the process begins again.

Healing Our
Canine Heroes

Within nine hours of the attacks on September 11, the Suffolk County Society for the Prevention of Cruelty to Animals (SCSPCA) arrived at the World Trade Center to provide veterinary care for disaster search canines. Under the direction of Humane Officer Chief Roy Gross, the SCSPCA staff set up a fully equipped MASH station three blocks from Ground Zero. One of only three such units in the United States, this 40-foot state-of-the-art mobile veterinary hospital is equipped with an operating room, x-ray unit, medical laboratory and wash stations.

Over two hundred veterinarians and several hundred vet technicians volunteered their services, some for two or three days, others for weeks at a time, with two and three vets working twelve- to fifteen-hour shifts around the clock. Dr. John Charos spent two months at Ground Zero, working twelve and often sixteen hours every day. "We got very little sleep for the first few weeks," he said. "The first week was the hardest on the canine teams because they were still searching for survivors. The dogs actually fared better than the handlers; they

[the dogs] just wanted to keep on working."

Chief Gross recalled the chaos of those first few weeks: "When the animals first came in from the pile, they were covered with so much debris that they could not even smell what they were looking for. We gave them hot-water baths, sometimes doing as many as fifteen dogs at a time. We hooked up the wash stations to fire hydrants and used special hoses to feed the water into big tanks to be heated.

"We washed the dogs' feet in buckets; some of their paws were cut up and burned. Many of the dogs were dehydrated from heat stress, and we gave them IV fluids before and after working on the pile. We had rows of IV bags hanging, just like in a war zone.

"I'll never forget one dog that came to the unit. His back legs were collapsing and we had to give him IVs to rehydrate him. As exhausted as he was, he was still pulling his handler back to the pile to work again."

Comprising volunteer professionals, the Veterinary Medical Assistance Teams (VMATs) provided yet another vital arm of medical care and treatment

A VMAT medical station at the Jacob Javits Center in Midtown Manhattan. The Javits Center served as the base of operations for many of the handlers and their dogs.

Photo: Michael Rieger/FEMA News

A Red Cross volunteer examines a SAR dog at the VMAT tent near Ground Zero.

LEFT and RIGHT: Pentagon heroes Gus and Jake go through decontamination after their shifts searching at the site.

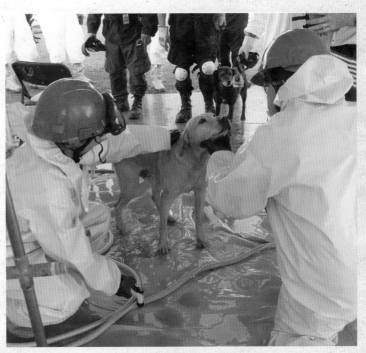

Rescue workers administer fluids intravenously to hydrate one of the search dogs at Ground Zero.

Photo: Andrea Booher/FEMA News

four VMAT teams, structured like FEMA task forces, includes veterinarians, vet techs, pharmacists, firefighters, hazmat techs, support personnel and mental-health professionals. VMAT set up medical stations at the West Street command post and another at the Jacob Javits Center to provide twenty-four-hour care and counseling to the FEMA task forces stationed there. VMAT veterinarians also operated a six-wheel utility vehicle called a Gator that drove around the perimeter of the worksite twenty-four hours a day to assist any dog that needed rest or medical care.

The canine teams reported to the MASH or VMAT stations after each work shift for decontamination. "Decon" started with the feet first—the dogs' paws were thoroughly cleaned with surgical disinfectant—followed by a warm-water shampoo bath to remove contaminants and debris. The dogs' eyes were flushed and their nasal passages irrigated to remove inhaled dust particles, and each dog received a complete physical exam.

Thankfully, most of the injuries were minor: cut and bloodied foot pads, burned paws from the smoldering debris, congestion and respiratory problems from inhaled dust. One dog was sent to a veterinary clinic in New York for treatment, but remarkably no dog died as a result of working at Ground Zero.

Jodi Witte, a veterinary technician from Hilton Head, South Carolina, was deployed to New York the day after the attacks and spent fifteen days working at the VMAT stations. "The dogs were amazing," Witte said. "They just wanted to get back on the pile and keep on working. We treated cases of stress diarrhea and some bladder infections due to stress. There were times we had to say, 'This dog needs to rest.'"

for the canine teams. Since 1994, VMATs have supported the veterinary community in times of national and regional disasters. A branch of the federal government at the time of September 11, VMAT teams were deployed to the World Trade Center by the US Department of Health and Human Services. Sponsored by the American Veterinary Medical Association (AVMA) and funded by the American Veterinary Medical Foundation (AVMF), each of the

342   Dog Heroes of September 11th

"We had about 12,000 pairs of booties donated, but few dogs ever wore them." The SCSPCA shipped most of the booties to Iraq and Afghanistan.

The VMAT teams aided the SAR dogs and handlers until October 31. The SCSPCA maintained their operation for two months, serving the NYPD K-9s who continued searching for victim remains.

On March 22, 2002, the SCSPCA held an awards ceremony to honor the dedicated firefighters, police officers, EMTs, animal-rescue workers and other personnel who volunteered at the World Trade Center. Dr. Charos and over 200 veterinarians, vet techs and police K-9s from the NYPD and Suffolk County PD received service awards for their contributions to the recovery effort during 9/11.

The role of the medical crews, animal-rescue workers, city professionals and other helpers who cared for the search canines cannot be underestimated. The handlers were lavish in their praise for the veterinary care that their dogs received around the clock. Those services were vital to the physical and mental health of not only the dogs but also their handlers, who were able to continue their mission knowing that their partners' welfare was in the best possible hands.

Large tents set up outside the SCSPCA mobile unit were stocked with medical supplies, water, dog food and dog treats, towels and other canine paraphernalia, all donated by well-wishers who were anxious to help the search teams in some way.

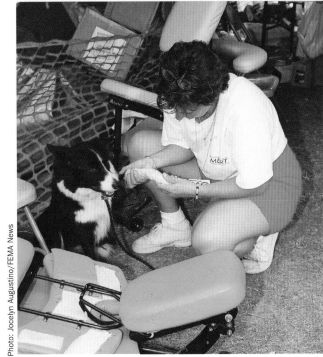

Photo: Jocelyn Augustino/FEMA News

ABOVE: The free K-9 store at the Jacob Javits Center with dog treats, dog toys, booties and more for the dog heroes. LEFT: A SAR dog receives a well-deserved massage from a volunteer at one of the many stations set up for the benefit of the K-9s and their handlers.

Health Care for MWDs: Holland Hospital

They are trained to guard and protect, to search for land mines, drugs and IEDs. These four-legged warriors and bomb detectors can save a dozen lives with one good sniff. And like any soldier or Marine working in a combat zone, sometimes they get injured in the line of duty.

In years past, health care for military working dogs (MWDs) was provided at a 15,000-square-foot veterinary hospital at Lackland Air Force Base in San Antonio, Texas (also the world's largest MWD training center). As the military canine corps grew, along with advancements in medical technology, so too did the need for a new veterinary facility. After seven years of planning, today our canine warriors are treated at Lackland's state-of-the-art 38,000-square-foot veterinary hospital, part of the Department of Defense Military Working Dog Veterinary Service.

Named the Holland Military Working Dog Hospital after Army Lt. Col. Daniel E. Holland, a veterinarian killed in Iraq in 2006, the hospital officially opened on October 21, 2008. Lieutenant Colonel Holland was the first Army veterinarian to be killed in action since the Vietnam War.

Holland's approximately forty-member medical staff provides routine medical care and treatment for the approximately 900 MWDs that serve under the Department of Defense MWD program. Dogs that work for the Transportation Security Administration, US Customs Service and other government agencies also receive routine and emergency medical care at Holland. Care typically includes semi-annual check-ups, dental care and treatment for minor medical conditions as well as life-threatening emergencies. Combat-injured MWDs that cannot be treated on-site or at overseas veterinary facilities may be returned to Holland to be treated, rehabilitated and, whenever possible, redeployed.

Holland director, veterinary surgeon Col. Robert Vogelsang, refers to the $15-million facility as the "Walter Reed of the veterinary world" in an October 2008 article titled "'Walter Reed' for Combat Dogs Opens at Texas Base" by Michelle Roberts (www.stripes.com). Equipped with high-tech ICU and surgical units, digital radiography, a CT scanner and a C-arm fluoroscope, the hospital can treat canine patients with the same advanced technology used on injured military personnel. Each month, the surgery center performs about seventy surgeries and thirty dental procedures. Approximately sixty dogs are treated daily for minor to major medical problems. The radiology section provides medical consultation via satellite for wounded MWDs overseas. Military-animal behavior specialist Dr. Walter F. Burghardt monitors the canines' mental health. "I treat behavior problems that cause distress in dogs or get in the way of them doing their jobs," he explained in a March 2010 *People* magazine article by Alicia Dennis titled "Healing the Dogs Who Serve."

Rehabilitation at Holland is also state of the art. In a fully equipped rehab unit, recovering dogs get hands-on physical therapy, work out with exercise balls and pace themselves on an underwater treadmill. As trained canine professionals, the dogs enjoy the rehab process as "just another day of work." Successfully rehabbed dogs can return to work with their handlers or partner with new ones to go back to their military posts and, ultimately, save more lives.

Those dogs that do not recover after treatment or are retired due to age or health issues can be adopted by their former handlers or, if an injured handler is unable to return to military service, the dog may be retired to live with his or her handler. Others may be placed in an adoption program for retired MWDs and adopted by families that are screened and approved by military authorities.

MWD German Shepherd Fritz was one such lucky dog. A retired explosives-detection expert, Fritz had been used as a demo dog for military canines in training. He was adopted at age twelve by Larry and Jennifer Cox of Duncannon, Pennsylvania, in October 2009. "Somebody's son came back because of a dog," Jennifer said in "Healing the Dogs Who Serve." She described Fritz as "almost" perfect and went on to tell of a time when the UPS delivery truck arrived and Fritz jumped into the truck to sniff all of the packages and make sure that they were safe.

Fritz passed away after only three months with his new family, and two months later Larry and Jenn adopted Ringo, an eleven-year-old Belgian Malinois who was retired due to hip dysplasia. Trained as a bomb-detection and patrol dog, Ringo first served on a presidential detail and then was deployed to Kuwait, the United Arab Emirates and Iraq. While in Iraq, Ringo's camp experienced heavy bombings very close to his kennel; soon afterward, his response to voice commands diminished. Although he passed subsequent hearing tests, he may have developed problems with certain frequencies.

"Ringo slept a lot when he first came to us," Jenn said. "I think he slept to escape this upside-down world he was in. We just gave him his space until he was ready to bond again. Now when he falls asleep, he snores like a man, almost like a totally relaxed 'I'm safe now' sleep. He has become my shadow and follows at my heels wherever I go."

Sadly, Larry and Jenn lost Ringo to an irreversible spinal condition after only three months. "We had his ashes placed in two urns," Jenn said. "We are keeping one with us, and the other will go to Patrick Air Force Base so he can rest with his fellow soldiers. We miss him so very much."

Col. Vogelsang said in "Healing the Dogs Who Serve" that the military wants its working dogs to live out their years "chasing squirrels and getting loved." In a 2008 CBS news article titled "Mending Military's Injured 'Canine Heroes,'" he said, "They are out there doing their thing every day, just because they want to please us. They really are the quiet warriors."

Ringo and his last handler, John Petcoff, sit in former dictator Saddam Hussein's chair in the Water Palace, Baghdad, Iraq.

Finding One Another:
Courage Beyond Measure

Tails of Hope Foundation (www.tailsofhope foundation.org) spearheaded Finding One Another: The 10th Anniversary Tribute to the Canine Search & Rescue Community of 9/11 (www.findingoneanother.org) to educate the public and raise funds to support the search and rescue field, including the canines, their first-responder human partners and the veterinarians and VMATs who treat them by contributing to the establishment of standards of

Tails of Hope Foundation child ambassador Molly poses with Catana, Ramapo Rescue Dog Association, at a Macy's Shop for a Cause event that benefited the foundation's Finding One Another tribute.

Photo: © 2010 Michelle Schaller

practice, care and research needed to safeguard all those engaged in SAR work. Most SAR teams are volunteers who incur tremendous personal operating expenses while serving.

Funds generated by Finding One Another (FOA) will provide financial assistance to
- underwrite veterinary expenses for those SAR canines in need;
- increase the number of specially trained SAR-focused veterinarians;
- expand targeted research benefitting working dogs and their human partners;
- develop and implement programs to educate the public about the work and ongoing needs of the SAR community while elevating the human/animal bond and fostering a dialogue toward a more peaceful future.

The yearlong commemoration—from September 2010 through the tenth anniversary of 9/11 on September 11, 2011—of the work done by the canine SAR community included educational programs at schools and colleges, an exhibit of photography and artifacts depicting the SAR community's work at the 9/11 sites and elsewhere, and co-sponsorship of the University of Pennsylvania School of Veterinary Medicine's 2011 International Working Dog Conference. Going forward, FOA continues to focus attention on and support to the working-dog and SAR canine community—

the heroes who put themselves at risk for the benefit of others, most without pay or acclaim.

FOA is compiling a historic registry of those in the SAR and working-dog community, including the dog/handler teams, veterinarians and VMATs who served at the 9/11 sites. Those who served are encouraged to register at www.findingoneanother.org and to sign up for an oral history project to be conducted by the National September 11 Memorial & Museum.

A "legacy charm" featuring a German Shepherd Dog was created to honor all working dogs and is available on the FOA website and at events; with additional breeds to be added to the line.

Finding One Another's Advisory Committee includes veterinary and medical experts, search and rescue volunteers, acclaimed artists, educators, businesspeople, trauma professionals and not-for-profit professionals, many of whom served at the 9/11 sites and all of whom are dedicated to honoring the canine/human partnership.

ABOUT THE PENN VET WORKING DOG CENTER
Established in 2007, the Penn Vet Working Dog Center (www.pennvetwdc.org) at the University of Pennsylvania School of Veterinary Medicine under the direction of FOA co-chair Dr. Cynthia Otto addresses critical issues through collaborative research, shared knowledge and application of the newest scientific information and veterinary expertise. The mission of the center is to serve as a consortium to bring together programs that employ dogs to detect threats to local, regional and national security. Goals include collecting and analyzing genetic, behavioral and physical data; integrating the latest scientific information to optimize the success and well-being of detection dogs

Artwork © Tails of Hope Foundation, Inc.

and developing a detection-dog selection, breeding and training program that will implement, test and disseminate the knowledge gained.

TAILS OF HOPE FOUNDATION
Tails of Hope Foundation is a New York-based 501(c)3 charitable organization dedicated to advancing the fields of veterinary and human medicine through a comparative approach focusing on eradicating cancer and other life-threatening diseases that affect companion animals and people. The organization brings together veterinary and medical experts, artists, educators, businesspeople, trauma professionals, and nonprofit organizations and the public. Tails of Hope Foundation carries out its mission through financial assistance, educational and therapeutic programs, sponsorship of seminars, and dissemination of knowledge. Additionally the organization supports special projects, such as Finding One Another and Pediatrics and Pets: Coping with Cancer Together.

Photo: © 2010 Nancy Katz, www.zazacreative.com

Front and back of the legacy charm, created in honor and support of working dogs and the people behind them.

FRONT ROW: Ramapo Rescue Dog members Sean Dunn with Sheba and Nancy Brooks with Chief. BACK ROW (LEFT TO RIGHT): Aubrey A. Strickland and Alana Marie Urda, co-founders of Amalgamate Dance Company, with FOA's Barbara Ela, Linda Blick, Dr. Rachel St.-Vincent, and John Cimino.

Saluting Our Photographers

September 11, 2001, was the most photographed event in the history of the world. Thousands of photographers, professional and amateur, produced heart-wrenching, amazing images of the most tragic day in American history. The publisher of this book and the author are indebted to many of these individuals whom we cannot identify by name. We extend our gratitude to all of the photographers featured in this book as well as to all of the handlers who shared their own photographs of their dog heroes.

The publisher would like to acknowledge photographers from the Federal Emergency Management Agency (FEMA), the US Navy, the Federal Bureau of Investigation (FBI), the Associated Press (AP), Reuters, the American Kennel Club (AKC), the National Disaster Search Dog Foundation (SDF), Nebraska Task Force 1 (NE-TF1), California Task Force 2 (CA-TF2), the New Jersey Veterinary Medicine Association, K2 Solutions, and Tails of Hope Foundation.

Additionally, we acknowledge the following photographers for their contributions to this volume: Jocelyn Augustino, Mary Bloom, Andrea Booher, Brian Buff, Chris Cantle, Tom Clark, Close Encounters of the Furry Kind, Eliot Crowley, David Engelbert, Alan Freed, Frontpage, Glen Gardner, Tilly Grassa, Sharon Hanzelka, Abbey Hull, Jim Inglis, Bill Jonas, Michael Justice, Nancy Katz, US Navy Journalist First Class Preston Keres, Susan Kjellsen, Jan Lopez, Wade H. Massie, Caitlin Mirra, Mishella, Kelly Morrison, SPC Amanda Morrissey US Army, Karyn Newbill, Andrew Olscher, Tony Panzica, Beverly Pavone, Photos by Dart, Laura Pollick, Lee Price, Michael Rieger, SFC Thomas R. Roberts, Lori Sash-Gail, Michelle Schaller, Patty Shaffer, Alice Su, Mpozi Tolbert (*Indianapolis Star*), Vacclav, Tom Walters, Katherine Welles and Mark Williams.

Glossary

Air-scenting canine
A dog that follows airborne human scent

AKC
American Kennel Club, founded in 1884 to oversee the registration and showing of pure-bred dogs, the largest pure-bred dog registry in the world

AKC CHF
American Kennel Club Canine Health Foundation, a non-profit organization dedicated to the well being of dogs and the largest non-profit funder of exclusively canine research in the world

Alert
The means or signal used by the dog to tell the handler he has located the victim or object of the search

ARDA
American Rescue Dog Association

Avalanche dog
A dog trained to find people buried under a snow avalanche

Bark alert
One of the methods a dog uses to signal he has found the victim or object of the search

Bark and hold
An alert method where the dog stays at the location of the find and continues to bark for a minimum of thirty seconds to alert his handler

Bark barrel
A device used to teach a search dog how to use the bark alert

BOO
Base of operation, where the canine handlers sleep and eat

Cadaver dog
A search dog trained to find dead bodies and human remains

Certification
The process of testing a dog's skills for search and rescue

Cross-trained
A dog that is trained for both live-find and cadaver search

CSS
Canine Search Specialist

Decon
Decontamination, the cleaning process handlers and canines go through to remove hazardous materials following a work shift

Disaster dog
A dog trained to search for live victims in an urban disaster setting

DOGNY
A public art project commissioned by the American Kennel Club post-September 11 to honor search and rescue dogs and to raise money to support future endeavors

EMT
Emergency medical technician

FAC
Family Assistance Center

FEMA
Federal Emergency Management Agency

Forward BOO
The canine handler's base of operation close to the worksite

Fresh Kills
The landfill on Staten Island, NY where the World Trade Center debris was taken

Gator
A utility vehicle made by the John Deere Company used in various types of work

Ground Zero
The disaster site at the World Trade Center

HazMat, Hazmat
Hazardous materials

HRD
Human-remains detection

IED
Improvised explosive device

Jacob Javits Center
The NYC convention center where the canine handlers stayed during the WTC search and recovery effort

K-9
A colloquial term for canine, used primarily for search and rescue, police and military dogs

Live find
Locating a victim who is still living; the main goal of FEMA

MASH
Mobile Army Surgical Hospital

MWD
Military working dog

NESAR
Northeast Search and Rescue

Port Authority of New York and New Jersey
Bi-state agency that manages most of the regional transportation system (i.e., airports, seaports, bridges and tunnels) within the NY–NJ Port District

Rafts
Dead skin cells containing bacteria that emit human scent

SAR
Search and rescue, a general term referring to all types of search canines

Scent discrimination
A canine's ability to distinguish between different types of scents or odors

Scent cone
Human scent dispersed in an area that widens from the source, which the search dog uses to locate the source

SCSPCA
Suffolk County Society for the Prevention of Cruelty to Animals

SDF
National Disaster Search Dog Foundation

SEMO
State Emergency Management Office

Staging area
A designated place near the worksite where handlers wait for work orders

Stokes basket
A basket device on cables that carries equipment over deep voids

Task force
A group of FEMA specialists, mostly volunteers, who respond to catastrophes and other large-scale emergency situations

Task
Assigned job

TF
Task force. Task force abbreviation can be used to identify specific task forces according to their locale, e.g., CA-TF1 (California Task Force 1), CO-TF1 (Colorado Task Force 1), etc.

USAR
Urban Search and Rescue, the FEMA task force

VMAT
Veterinary Medical Assistance Team

Wilderness dog
A dog trained to work in large remote or rural areas, usually off lead

WTC
World Trade Center

Index